The Making of a Marriage

The Making of a Marriage

A JANET THOMA BOOK

THOMAS NELSON PUBLISHERS
Nashville

Published in Nashville, Tennessee, by Thomas Nelson, Inc.,
and distributed in Canada by Word Canada.

Library of Congress Cataloging-in-Publication Data

The Making of a marriage.
p.   cm.
Includes bibliographical references.
ISBN 0-8407-6896-6
1. Marriage.   2. Man-woman relationships.   3. Marriage—
Religious aspects—Christianity.   4. Man-woman
relationships—Religious aspects—Christianity.
HQ734.M256   1993
306.81—dc20   93-9620
                                                                CIP

Printed in the United States of America.
1   2   3   4   5   6   —   98   97   96   95   94   93

Contents

Contents

Introduction

What does it take to make a marriage?

If you are just starting over the threshold, the many choices that lay before you as a couple can be overwhelming—even if you've been married before. How will you keep the flames of intimacy burning as you venture down the road of life together? How will you ever understand one another when he acts so strangely, when you can't seem to understand the way she thinks? And what about the everyday choices, like how the two of you will manage your money?

You may be more seasoned in your marital experience. Perhaps children have entered the picture and you are wondering if you will ever have time alone again. Or your parents are getting older. Who will be the primary caretakers and how is that going to affect your relationship?

Together, those of us contributing to *The Making of a Marriage* have several hundred years of counseling and ministry experience. And though we haven't lived quite that long, all of us—from Dave and Claudia Arp to Zig Ziglar—have had a chance, in our own marriages and in our years of counseling, to learn and even practice some time-honored principles which helped us through those early stages of love and into the later passages of life.

Dr. Charles Stanley, author of *How to Keep Your Kids on Your Team* and longtime senior pastor of First Baptist Church in Atlanta, has been married for more than thirty-five years. Ruth Bell Graham, wife of evangelist Billy Graham and author of *Legacy of a Packrat,* speaks with experience on marriage and family, having five children, eighteen grandchildren, and even a great-grand-child. Dr. Frank Minirth, co-author of *Passages of Marriage* and co-founder of the Minirth-Meier Clinics, has been married to his wife, Mary Alice, more than twenty-six years. Together they are the parents of four girls. Linda Dillow, author of *How to Really Love Your Man,* has been married more than twenty years and is the mother of two daughters.

We and the other authors have chosen chapters from our books published by Thomas Nelson Publishers to help you explore the issues of loving one another and living together, such as, intimacy and communication, forgiveness, the differences in men and women, the art of sexual intimacy, how your parents affect your ability to trust, relationships with in-laws, handling crises, the roles involved in raising children, and having fun. At the back of the book, you will find a bibliography that lists our other books that are in print, which may be of additional help in your personal or marital journey.

Savor your time reading these chapters alone or together. Use this book in your prayer group or couples' Bible study. Turn to it as a resource when you are dealing with a specific issue in your relationship. But whatever you do, enjoy yourself.

The Making of a Marriage is our gift to you, a lifetime of insights to help you keep saying "I do."

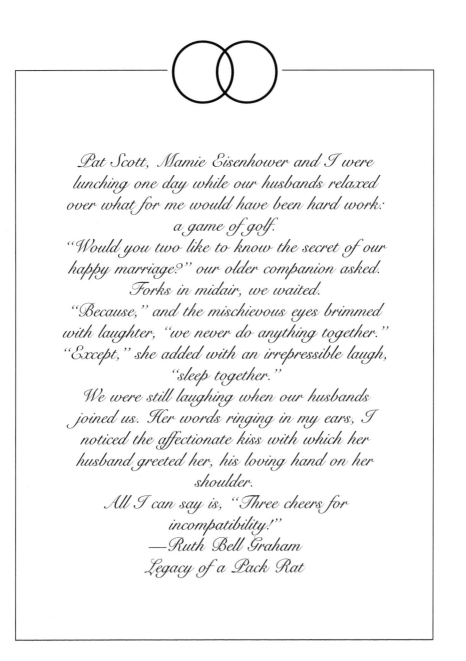

Pat Scott, Mamie Eisenhower and I were
lunching one day while our husbands relaxed
over what for me would have been hard work:
a game of golf.
"Would you two like to know the secret of our
happy marriage?" our older companion asked.
Forks in midair, we waited.
"Because," and the mischievous eyes brimmed
with laughter, "we never do anything together."
"Except," she added with an irrepressible laugh,
"sleep together."
We were still laughing when our husbands
joined us. Her words ringing in my ears, I
noticed the affectionate kiss with which her
husband greeted her, his loving hand on her
shoulder.
All I can say is, "Three cheers for
incompatibility!"
—Ruth Bell Graham
Legacy of a Pack Rat

PART ONE

*Men and Women
Viva la difference!*

Chapter

1

How Shall We Live Together?
Mutualization and Gender Differences

From my book As for Me and My House, *we now speak of the life patterns of the marrying partners—their schedules, priorities, opinions, tastes. Mutualization is the seeking after the one pattern which will harmonize the two patterns that the husband and wife have brought together. Partners will always play on separate instruments, because they are separate individuals. They will always have a different line of notes to play. It's foolish to believe their lives should be exact copies of one another. Nevertheless, unless they learn to play a duet in the same key, to the same rhythm—unless their lives finally achieve mutuality—a slow process of disengagement will wedge them apart, first secretly, psychologically, and then openly and miserably.*

—*Walter Wangerin, Jr.*
As for Me and My House

"How Shall We Live Together? Mutualization and Gender Differences" adapted from *As for Me and My House*, Walter Wangerin, Jr. (1990).

What work can bring the young couple to mutuality? First to know, and then to nourish, the genuine "oneness" of their marriage.

Know the Oneness

Let's make a careful distinction here. When newlyweds blush and say, "We are one," they may, in fact, mean any of four separate definitions, but only the fourth permits a complete mutualization.

"One" may mean: "We are exactly alike." Some couples strain to duplicate each other, and then suffer the persistent differences or else repress them. They force an unrealistic similarity upon their tastes, their opinions, their priorities, their customary habits. They may do so with the best of intentions; but this "oneness" is no more real than was Adam and Eve's when they covered their differences with clothes. It is a seeming similarity only —a looking alike—which makes the marriage a pretense and will finally tire the partners with pretending. For God created each one unique. To make two beings carbon copies of each other is to deny that uniqueness, the handiwork of God. Neither person could flourish, then, and grow into the special creature God had planned him or her to be, and the marriage itself would stall. It could not enter new realms.

"One" may mean no more than this: one of the partners has taken control of the marriage, and that one will dominates the other. The second will has become silent or submissive or extinct. But this isn't one*ness;* this is one alone. Indeed, there is no disharmony in such a marriage: no arguing, no clashes, no division of opinions, just an evident and absolute order. But neither is there harmony of any kind. The drum has overwhelmed the flute. Then, though one person may flourish and grow, two do not, for the second is always shaped by the character and personhood of the first. And therefore the marriage *as a marriage* does not develop either. The marriage has become the servant of one of the partners.

Neither of these definitions of "oneness" is mutuality. The first is only simulation, the second subordination, and someone is lost for the sake of good order. Mutuality takes two whole humans. The third definition is no better, because it merely plays with words.

"One" may mean: "We have a fifty-fifty marriage, half and half." But mutuality is accomplished by two *whole* persons; and if each partner truly intends to be but the fraction of a relationship (thinking *My whole makes up a half of us*) he or she will soon discover that these halves do not fit perfectly together. The mathematics can work only if each subtracts something of himself or herself, shears it off, and lays it aside forever. There will come, then, a moment of shock when one spouse realizes, "You don't want the *whole* of me? Not the whole of me, but only a part of me, makes up the whole of us?"

So which parts are to be cut off? Who decides? This turns marriage into a procrustean bed, where those too big are cut to fit. And often the partner of the stronger willfulness consciously or unconsciously swings the knife, for someone finally must decide *how* the two should fit together; so we are, in practice, back with the second definition after all. This third definition sounds better than it is: "Fifty-fifty means that we take turns at deciding things." I will believe that so long as no one feels that the "turns" are cheating him out of his own presumed rights and privileges; thus, good feelings can continue. But sin destroys such sharing. And I repeat: mutuality must acknowledge the wholeness of both partners.

The fourth definition, then. This asks that you think in a new way. Up till now we have assumed that there are only two beings in a marriage, the husband and the wife. In fact, there are three complete beings in a marriage—you, your spouse, and *the Relationship* between you, which both of you serve, which benefits each of you, but which is not exactly like either one of you. This Relationship is itself very much like a living being—like a baby born from you both. It has its own character. It enters existence infantile, when you speak vows to one another. It comes cuddly and lovely, but very weak and in need of care and nourishment. As time goes on, as this baby-Relationship grows up, it becomes stronger and stronger until it serves and protects you in return. This "being," this living thing, this Relationship which needs you both (the whole of each of you), but which is *not you* (it is not the two of you added together, because it is distinct from either one of you)—that is your "oneness." Serving *it,* you both enact a harmony. You are co-laborers committed to the care of a single (third!) life between you. You are each a whole, unique, free creature of God. Yet you are one.

This Relationship . . . that is your "oneness."

Now, then: when you look upon your marriage, you are not just looking upon one another (possibly feeling at odds with one another), but upon this third being which requires the complete attention, all of the wisdom and skills, and the holy prayers and faith of you both.

Nourish the Oneness

This is the real work of mutuality. This brings your various lifestyles into harmony (without canceling either one, without a forced similitude): that you have realized a common purpose together; that you are both committed to the nurturing, not of oneself and not of one's partner, but of this third being, the Relationship; and that together you seek the wisest ways to do so—and you do them.

Serving this Relationship, neither partner has to feel that change was imposed upon you; rather, each of you offers your various talents and the best of yourselves to the Relationship. This becomes a willing offering, never fearing that your spouse is "getting more than he deserves." Why? Because both of you benefit in the Relationship's good health. Now neither of you must submit humiliatingly to the other; rather, each *chooses* to serve the third being, the Relationship.

Listen: when a baby cries in the middle of the night, do the parents bicker and neglect their baby's needs? Not if they love it.

Or do they blame one another because the baby *is* a baby, help-less, in need of human care? Of course not. Instead, they willingly adjust their lives in order to nurse the infant; they adjust without accusations because the baby's needs are no one's fault, and their dear one is more important to them than their own desires. Each trusts the love that the partner also has for this child. They adjust their lives, feeling in no way oppressed by such necessity.

Likewise, when the marriage Relationship (like a baby!) here at its beginning cries out for attention, even at unexpected and inconvenient times, the husband and the wife can sit down to-gether as co-laborers, partners (not as antagonists), and willingly each adjust their lives in order to nurse this Relationship to matu-rity and to strength. If they work together for the sake of this third being, they can adjust without complaint: no one is whining; no one is grasping; no one is losing something unreasonably, or be-ing oppressed. Both apply their separate skills, and each respects the judgment and the offering of the other.

There is a world of difference between: "You must include me in planning our future, because you hurt me when you neglect me; you destroy me, my sense of worth," and: "The Relationship needs our planning, but I can help you in that, because I know some of its needs: I've got a thought or two about its future." There is a world of difference between: "You wasted my money! How am I going to buy food? When do I get a dress?" and: "I've been looking at the budget. How can we increase the percentage for groceries?" The issues are no longer personal. As *both* see it that way (not as accusations, but as problems to be solved), both may apply their creative minds to the common questions. You will not pitch ready-made solutions at one another (which sound very much like commands) but will pose questions for the con-sideration of both.

In this way a husband will use his wisdom and ability when he best can solve a problem—but never command just because he is a man. Likewise, a wife will use her experience and talents when they best enable her. Each of them can willingly allow the other some charge of this mutual, beloved being, the Relation-ship.

In this way spouses do not need to become *like* each other, mimicking one another's opinions, tastes, and habits. Their differences shall have become too important to lose, their various skills too respected to ignore. On the other hand, their schedules will, naturally, meld together; their priorities will become mutual not by the imposition of one on the other, but because the single priority of the baby-marriage has been accepted by both. As they work toward a more harmonious integration of their lifestyles, they will fight less (since they focus less upon one another) and they will confer more (since they focus more on the being which requires both of them).

And when one defaults in his or her new duties to the marriage, the spouse need not take that personally either. Again, there is a world of difference between: "He failed me," and: "He failed the marriage." If he fails *me,* I might be so hurt that I can't speak to him. Or I will shout, shutting down all wisdom, both his and mine. Anger gets in the way. The true issue—and the Relationship—shall be forgotten in the midst of feelings. But if he fails the *marriage,* I can still speak to my co-laborer, without the distortion of wounded feelings, about the baby who wants our whole and cool attention—and he can listen to me after all, since I do still respect his abilities and am asking him to use them for the benefit of the thing we both love: the Relationship.

Finally, as a baby rewards its parents with healthy laughter and burblings and many tokens of love, so shall the Relationship, thus nourished, reward its marital guardians—with stability, trustworthiness, warmth, and security. So a little mutuality encourages more and more mutuality. As the marriage blesses you with a harmonious sound, you'll play your instrument better and better, for the sake of the sweet sound alone, and you will marvel that your spouse could play so well.

The third piece of the work of accommodation comes from gender differences, the natural dissimilarity between man and woman that becomes clearly apparent only after the marriage begins.

WHAT HAPPENED TO THE MAN (THE WOMAN) I MARRIED?

In our present culture (though this is changing) men are bred to have an "instrumental" character, while women develop an "expressive" character. (Not all men are "instrumental" nor all women "expressive." This is a general classification and not a rule. But the sexes fall commonly enough into these categories that we may handle the difference here according to gender.) These tendencies are radically different from one another, but during the period of courtship the difference is hidden. After marriage that difference pops up as a rude surprise. First it must be understood and then it can be managed by the early marriage work.

The "instrumental" character is a pragmatic person. He focuses upon a future goal and needs to believe in the practical value of that goal. He justifies a present activity by what it shall accomplish in the future. He can be very patient doing precious, little things—so long as they shall ultimately prove productive. He likes the words *progress* and *useful*. His values are utilitarian. "What good is this?" means "What good can this *produce?*"

The "expressive" character, on the other hand, is a more artistic person. She focuses on the feelings and the activities of the present—for their own sakes. She needs no future goal; it is enough to take pleasure in the moment. She is content and patient doing precious, little things because the doing has its own value. To be "in touch with one's feelings" and to say so is living in itself; she asks no more, nor even understands the necessity of progress, production, or utility; these demands feel deadly cold to her, and distracting. "What good is this?" means to her merely "What *is* this thing, anyway? Help me know and feel it." Her values are relational. She doesn't know the word *useful*, but loves the word *you*.

He lives in the calculating mind. She dwells satisfied within the heart.

He would grow vegetables—and grow them efficiently—for

food. She grows roses for their beauty, whether anyone sees them or not, and can weep at the color red.

He studies in order to gain employment. She reads to live the story.

He rests in order to be prepared for tasks the following day. She loves her bed; sleep is good, simply because sleep is good.

He (and now we come to our point) courts to get married; but once he's married, the purpose of courtship is accomplished and he moves on to other, more productive, things. She, on the other hand, courts and kisses for kissing's sake; and once she's married expects simply that the kissing will continue between them forever.

Before the marriage, these two characters look exactly the same: both are glad to spend time holding hands. Both find value in quiet moments together. Both seem content, seem pleased, seem fulfilled *merely to be together.* And he speaks such "sweet nothings" in her ear. Yes, he likes roses. And she weeps to have found one man in a thousand who is patient, gentle, kind, and loving, who doesn't want to use her.

They look alike; but they are not alike. This instrumental man has made a worthy instrument of courtship. He can do all he does because it is, after all, useful: it shall produce his goal of marriage. The marriage of the future justifies these cuddling activities in the present. They are not sweet "nothings" after all, but whisperings calculated to persuade her to the altar. Please don't think evil of this poor fellow. Again, this is not a conscious deception. In fact, he likely presumes that she is like himself and, like him, intends to continue these foolishnesses only so long as they have practical consequence; after that he expects them both to progress past nonsense to the real business of living.

Then comes marriage, and the goal of "being together, doing nothing" is fulfilled for the instrumental personality—and doing nothing, thereafter, is a senseless thing to do.

Then the wife is chagrined to find that he has forgotten flowers and dispensed with touching for touching alone. (Why must he always touch her, now, with sex in mind? Why must there always be an ulterior motive for every gentle gesture, ruining the goodness of that gesture?) Now she feels used, indeed, and very mistrustful of the man who has two faces. Sex begins to feel like a job, a duty, since he seems to care only for the climax (his purpose) and not all the valuable foreplay (her purpose). Was he lying to her all through the courtship? Or what has changed the gentle man she'd learned to love?

Well, no, he wasn't lying. And nothing's changed *him;* it's just that the circumstances have changed. The goal that made him patient has been met.

For his own part, he is also chagrined by his wife. Why has she so suddenly become emotional? Why does she cry so easily, now, and withdraw from his touch as though he were brutish or dirty? What's wrong, that she keeps wanting to go back to the past and do all the old things over and over again? Didn't she ever mature beyond her adolescence? Is she stuck in some earlier stage? Did I marry a child? Let's get *on* with the marriage. And no —I do not understand the importance of flowers; I'd rather buy a lube job for her car; it costs less and means more. Lord, I never knew she was so hypersensitive. Doesn't she like me—or appreciate all I do for her?

But the woman hasn't changed either. Simply, she had expected marriage not to revise their relationship, but to preserve what she had valued in it before.

What, then, is required but the work of understanding? I repeat again (and again) that our natural differences are good and ought finally to be celebrated. As one body must have both a calculating mind and a feeling heart, so one marriage is blessed with mind *and* heart; these are not antagonistic elements, but complements one of the other. It would be a cold couple who could not glory in a purple sunset. Do not belittle the cry in her throat, thou pragmatic man; participate in it! It would be a stagnating couple who could not risk new ventures nor plan against the future. Do not dismiss him as hard-hearted, thou sensitive woman; benefit from it! Let each one teach the other; but let each attitude temper the other's. The thing which you do not know by nature is not, therefore, valueless. Be willing to learn it. And the thing which you do naturally know, but which your spouse does not, is not the only good in the world, proving him a nincompoop for ignorance. Take patient time to reveal it to him. Be glad that your marriage has two eyes instead of one, and let both of you see through both of them. With two eyes wide open, the marriage can see depth. It gains perspective.

Our natural differences are good and ought finally to be celebrated.

Most important: don't judge your spouse as evil. He did not deceive you. She is not now loathing you. It took marrying to reveal these varying characteristics, the "instrumental" and the "expressive"; marrying did this thing, not some devious action of your partner. But marriage is the perfect arena in which to join your differences, for marriage gives you time and the lasting willingness both to realize that the other's tendencies are, after all, good, and then to take that goodness for yourself.

Oh—and here is how I know that men may be "expressive" while women may be "instrumental": Thanne took a long time to understand the value of poetry. And I was the one who wondered why she grew so businesslike two days after our wedding, going to work, forgetting me. Mine is the womanlike soul; hers the manlike.

Learning to Be a Woman —Learning to Be a Man

In order to develop the one-ness that is so essential to a healthy marriage, we must first explore the astounding differences between men and women. Sure, there are the obvious ones we learned when we were kids—boys and girls look different! But God's creative plan for a man and a woman covers a whole realm of differences, and in this chapter from That Man! *we take a look at those important aspects of our uniqueness as men and as women. Those differences encompass biology, hormones, sexuality, anatomy, and neurology—from the way we're built to the way we think. It's no surprise that it's so difficult for a man and a woman to understand each other, considering all the dynamics involved. But there's hope! And we hope that you'll gain enough understanding*

"Learning to Be a Man—Learning to Be a Woman" adapted from "Understanding the Differences" in *That Man!* William and Nancie Carmichael and Dr. Timothy Boyd (1988).

from this chapter to be able to celebrate those glorious differences.
—*Bill and Nancie Carmichael*
Dr. Timothy Boyd
That Man!

No one can deny that anatomically a man's body is quite different from a woman's. Some of the differences are obvious; some are not. The growing trend in our society, however, has been to de-emphasize the biological differences between the sexes. In the name of equality, women are viewed as being able to perform the same tasks as men. Women now march along with men in the service ranks of our nation, and women are doing jobs that were once designated "men only."

In a recent court case in Oregon, a teenage girl and her parents brought suit against a school district because the girl was not permitted to wrestle on her high school team. The girl and her parents won the case. Some ask, "Why would a girl or her parents even want the girl to be on an all-boys wrestling team?" but others applaud the victory, viewing it as a blow against discrimination.

As a rationale for male domination, women have often been described as the weaker sex. After all, men are stronger than women and, therefore, better suited to take control. We intend to challenge the notion that men are *simply* stronger than women. It is not a simple matter. As we explore the intricacies of the biological differences between the sexes, we will see that men and women are *different* (not simply stronger or weaker). In some ways men are stronger than women, and in other ways women are stronger than men. Women can't run as fast or lift as much weight as men, but women's longevity is well established. As we understand more about the differences, it will become apparent that men and women really need each other. We can celebrate the differences once we understand them. Then we will be able to more rationally discuss how we will live, and we will be able to function more flexibly.

A missionary to Africa related a story about an American visitor to Zimbabwe. After observing the African women traveling a few paces behind their husbands as they walked down the jungle path, the visitor asked one of the women, "Why do you let him walk in front of you that way?" The surprised African woman replied, "But who would kill the snakes?"

As we begin to appreciate our biological heritage, some of the differences in the ways that men and women behave will become more understandable. And we can better deal with what we understand.

BIOLOGICAL DIFFERENCES

Let's look at how a fetus develops so that we understand how fragile our sexual identity really is. Every cell in our body contains forty-six chromosomes, each of them packed with genes in a mixture that's different for everyone. Out of the forty-six, two determine sex. They are called X and Y. Men have one of each, an X and a Y. The Y chromosome determines maleness. Women do not have a Y; they have two X's instead.

Every egg contains twenty-three chromosomes, one of which is an X. Every sperm also contains twenty-three chromosomes; but some contain an X, and others contain a Y. If an X-sperm fertilizes the egg, the embryo will have two X chromosomes, and the baby will be a female. If a Y does the job, an XY combination will produce a male baby.

In the first month or so after fertilization, the cells of the embryo divide and redivide until the fetus has a head and a body with arms and legs, but it is neither male nor female. About six weeks after conception, the fetus's sex is established. If nothing happens, the embryo's gonads will become ovaries. But if a Y chromosome is present and prodded into action, the fetus will develop testes.

Only in the last ten years have scientists discovered that a scrap of material called the H-Y antigen, which clings to the outside of male cells, must spur the Y chromosome into causing the embryo to develop testes.

But even then the baby's sex is not certain. Something else must take place. The hypothalamus, a part of the brain that governs such impulses as anger, hunger, and sex drive, must release a substance that tells the testes that it's time to start producing sex hormones.

Once in action, the testes put out a large amount of testosterone, the male hormone, and smaller amounts of estrogen and progesterone, the female hormones. This hormonal blend facilitates the further development of the sex organs.[1]

The point of this brief biology lesson is that from the beginning a man's sexuality is touch and go. Even a male fetus will become a healthy female if for some reason the gonads do not secrete sufficient testosterone while the fetus is in the womb.

A man's life also seems to be more fragile than a woman's. Dr. John Money and Dr. Stephen Wachtel, scientists who have studied fetal development, have determined that during the prenatal period there are 130 males for every 100 females. At birth, however, there are only 105 males for every 100 females. The gap lessens each successive year, until women outnumber men. Men die, on the average, eight years earlier than women. And of the fifteen leading causes of death, more men than women die from fourteen of them. Women are actually immune to some of the diseases that afflict men.[2]

Dr. Joan Ullyot, from the San Francisco Institute of Health Research, said, "Shipwrecked women survive better than shipwrecked men. It has something to do with better insulation or better natural ability to metabolize fat."[3] Dr. Estelle Ramey, an endocrinologist at Georgetown Medical School, stated that female astronauts could take "a lot more tumbling and disorientation than males without showing signs of shock."[4]

Given the early vulnerability of men, it seems likely that there is a corresponding insecurity. This could help to explain men's insistence that they are not weak, because we usually try to cover up our insecurities.

HORMONAL DIFFERENCES

There are some important differences between hormone production in the male and female bodies. The role of hormones in general, and sexual hormones in particular, is only now beginning to be fully appreciated. Scientists are finding more hormones (180 since 1970), and new information is accumulating so fast that textbooks can't keep up. "Everything is kept in perfect balance by hormones," says Dr. Bert O'Malley, chair of Cell Biology at Baylor College of Medicine, "not only for normal maintenance and survival but in response to anything that comes along —physical insult, mental stress, physical exertion, a thought process."[5]

One woman in our survey wondered, "Why do men always seem to put competition into so many situations?" Testosterone is a major factor.

Testosterone does several things in a man's body. It increases the tendency toward aggression and physical activity, and it spurs the sex drive and the ability to act on it. Have you ever wondered why little boys seem to delight in rough-and-tumble play and are fascinated with guns?

Tim tried to change this biological tendency but found out, as we all do, that sometimes our natural make-up is difficult to change. "My wife, Anita, and I consciously decided early in our parenting that we did not want our children to play with guns, so we never had any around the house and closely monitored other influences," Tim remembered. "This was certainly no problem for Sarah, who never seemed the least bit interested in guns. Much to our chagrin, however, Cameron, a loving and gentle child, had an ingenious determination to make a gun out of any material he could get his hands on."

We can conclude that sexual hormones do indeed affect the way we live and how we die. "Men were designed for short, nasty, brutal lives," said Dr. Ramey. "Women are designed for long, miserable ones."[6]

As a result of this built-in biological clock, men seem to develop a fatalistic view of life, which might explain why men are more prone than women to midlife crisis. They attempt to "grab all the gusto" before the candles they are burning at both ends go out.

SEXUAL DIFFERENCES

Aside from the obvious biological differences in the sexual organs of men and women, sexual differences take on profound cultural overlays. It's probably no secret to you that men and women often approach sex differently. Men, consistent with their performance orientation, focus on the physical aspects of sex, thus successful orgasm becomes the goal. Women are much more interested in the full expression of closeness and communication.

In studies, psychiatrist Marc Hollender discovered that some women trade sex (consciously or unconsciously) for being touched, held, and stroked. Their aim is not sex—it is to be close to another person.[7]

One woman in our study wrote, "I'd like to understand why my husband can't be satisfied with just some cuddling in between times of actual intercourse."

Helen Block Lewis, in *Psychic War in Men and Women,* stated that, "A man's failure to have an erection or to maintain it prevents intercourse; no such burden of responsibility for intercourse is carried by women. A woman has only to be there and willing to permit penetration. A man must be aroused—a state which is not necessarily under his conscious control. The act of intercourse is thus 'easier' for women, and her orgasm plays no role in her fertilization." This leads to feelings of fear for men that they will not be able to perform.[8]

Walter Trobisch, in *The Misunderstood Man,* expressed the idea that men do not feel "at one" with themselves sexually. His belief is that a man has a "peculiar and complicated relationship" with his penis. He wrote: "In contrast to the woman who feels at one with her sexual organs—they are a part of her—the man stands opposite his, as if it were another person, a stranger. The woman *is* her organ. The man *has* his."[9]

In the sexual relationship, men must continue to prove their manhood to women, but women, even if they are frigid, can have intercourse, become pregnant, and give birth. Women perform by merely *being,* without *doing,* while men must do something to be fulfilled. Sexual differences between men and women obviously contribute to our unique perspectives on life, and other anatomical differences increase this gap.

ANATOMICAL DIFFERENCES

Female sprinters cannot beat male sprinters. The reason? A male's larger bones are arranged differently. His shoulders are broader; his pelvis is more narrow. When he walks or runs, no motion is wasted. The female, by contrast, was designed for childbearing. Her larger pelvis causes her hips to sway as she moves, an attractive feature to men perhaps, but nonetheless a waste of motion for a sprinter.[10] What often happens is that this biological trait takes on a cultural overlay. Men often view the sway of a woman's hips as a deliberate attempt to be seductive. The "female" walk then becomes exaggerated, due to the response that it brings.

Have you ever wondered why men are usually better climbers, even on ladders? The reason is that the angle at which a woman's thigh is joined to her knee makes climbing more awkward.[11] Next time your husband laughs at your hesitancy to "scale the heights," let him know that there is a biological reason.

Although it doesn't seem fair, men can also lose weight more easily than women. A male's body contains a higher proportion of muscle to fat (muscle comprises about 41 percent of his body versus 35 percent of a woman's body), and muscle burns up five more calories per pound than fat does, just to maintain itself. In other words, the male metabolic rate is higher than the female's.[12]

One woman was frustrated when she and her husband decided to go on a diet together. His weight loss was more rapid than hers, on identical menus, so he accused her of fudging. If she had known about the physiological differences, she'd have had a quick answer to his accusation.

Basic differences in the ways that men and women use energy directly affect our behavior. A man's blood contains 20 percent more red corpuscles than a woman's. These cells contain hemoglobin, the substance that delivers oxygen to the body's billions of cells, and this oxygen works to release energy in fats and carbohydrates stored in the body. The more corpuscles the blood contains, the more oxygen the body gets and the more energy it has. That's why men typically have more start-up energy than women.[13]

On the other hand, it has also been discovered that women have greater endurance than men. Women's capacity for exercise drops 2 percent for each ten years of age, but the male capacity drops 10 percent for the same time period.[14]

Take two long-distance runners, for example. The male runner uses up his reserves of glycogen (the form in which carbohydrates are stored in the muscles) in about two hours if he's going at 80 percent of his capacity. At this point, he hits the wall, as runners say. By contrast, when a woman hits the wall, she can more easily keep going for a while because her body switches to its fat reserves. Pound for pound, fat yields twice as much energy as glycogen. And thanks to her sex hormones, the female's muscles easily use fat.[15]

This difference in the use of energy explains why a man is often fatigued after his work day and collapses in the lounger in front of the television, while his wife is still producing. The men hit the end of their reserves (just like the runner who hits the wall) while the women have reserves to draw on.

Biological, anatomical, and, finally, neurological differences between men and women contribute to our lack of understanding of one another.

NEUROLOGICAL DIFFERENCES

One woman in our survey admitted, "I don't understand a man's thinking process. Obviously they don't think the same way women do, and I often wonder what their thinking process entails." This woman was searching to understand the basic difference between the male and female brains, a difference which influences the way men and women think.

The fetus has what scientists call a "bipotential and undifferentiated" brain, which means it can go either way (male or female) depending on the influence of sex hormones. The brain is divided into left and right hemispheres. The left hemisphere (the verbal brain) controls language and reading skills. We use it when we "balance our checkbook, read a newspaper, sing a song, play bridge, write a letter. . . ."[16] The right hemisphere (intuitive brain) is the center of our spatial abilities. We use it when we "consult a road map, thread our way through a maze, work a jigsaw puzzle, design a house, plan a garden. . . ."[17]

Sexual differences in the way the brain is organized suggest different ways of thinking and learning. The male brain is specialized. A man uses one side for solving spatial problems, the other side for defining a word or verbalizing a problem. The female brain is not so specialized for some functions such as defining words. In other words, a woman's right-brain and left-brain abilities are duplicated to some extent in each hemisphere, so her right and left hemispheres work together to solve problems.[18]

Have you ever noticed that women can better sense the difference between what people say (the strict meaning of the words they use) and what they mean? Because a woman can zero in on a problem using both hemispheres of her brain, she is able to pick up the nuances of a person's true feelings and can perceive subtleties that go right past a man. Men do not understand this intuitive ability and tend to distrust it. In fact, when a woman picks up on a subtle criticism and confronts the man, often the man may respond that she is being oversensitive. This does not allow us to predict an individual's mental capacity based on sex, but it does explain why it is commonly recognized that women are more perceptive about people than men are. And that is one quality that makes a woman's input in a business decision especially valuable.

The differences [in our physical make-up] spring from the creative will of the Master Designer.

Another interesting aspect of the left/right brain hemispheres is that men and women approach problem solving differently. Men approach a problem in an analytical way—they separate themselves from it and deal with it abstractly. Women do not distance themselves from the problem; instead, they personalize it and maintain a personal identification. One woman, describing this difference, said, "I think differently than they do. I work on several thoughts at once; they think and only want to hear about one thing at a time."

There are many other physical differences between men and women, but we do not intend to belabor the point. Suffice it to say that our physical make-up is foundational to the way we act, and the differences spring from the creative will of the Master Designer, who has equipped us to fulfill unique roles. We can echo King David: "We are *fearfully and wonderfully made.*"[19]

Chapter

3

Beyond Fig Leaves and Cooties: Loving a Woman

So many of the problems that often erupt in a marriage can be traced to the husband's "father-wound"—that is, the lack he feels from not having the kind of strong human fathering that God intended. Despite the best of intentions, too many fathers fail to teach their boys how to deal with their own maleness. This chapter from Father and Son *is offered as a help to husbands who may have missed out on the security of a father's training on how to handle those wonderful, mysterious creatures: women.*

—Gordon Dalbey
Father and Son

There are four things that are too mysterious for me to understand:
an eagle flying in the sky,
a snake moving on a rock,

"Beyond Fig Leaves and Cooties: Loving a Woman" has been adapted from *Father and Son,* Gordon Dalbey (1992).

23

a ship finding its way over the sea,
and a man and a woman falling in love.
(Prov. 30:18–19)

A hundred and fifty men sat waiting for me to teach on "Loving a Woman," and since I had taught on "Fathers and Sons" the previous session, I took a quick poll.

"How many of you men," I asked, "had a father who, when you were around twelve or maybe a teenager, took you aside and said anything like, 'Son, I notice you're checking out the girls these days, and that's fine, but I want to talk with you some about what's going on in your body and spirit as you do that'?"

Of the hundred and fifty, two men raised their hands—about the same proportion I find everywhere I teach, around the country. A third lifted his arm slightly and said aloud, "I don't know if this counts, but once my dad . . ."

"It counts!" I interrupted, looking around the sea of men's faces, their brows knit and heads shaking slowly. "If anything happened even to make you wonder, that's more than the rest."

"That's a sad commentary!" exclaimed Dr. James Dobson when I shared this during a "Focus on the Family" radio interview.[1] Indeed, it's disastrous. Anyone reading Malachi 4:5–6 could predict that men so alienated from their fathers would bear "a curse over the land" as they relate sexually to women.

In any other enterprise worthy of masculine energy—for example, starting a new job—a man would expect, if not demand, training and guidance from older men who had been on the job themselves for some time. Yet in relating to the woman—an enterprise comprising the very life mysteries of creation itself, upon which the future welfare of the species depends, requiring more of his true self than any other life investment of time and energy —a man is sent out utterly empty-handed.

Something spiritual happens when boy meets girl. Any boy young enough not to have eaten the world's "new grain" knows that. If I reach out my hand and touch my desk, I feel my desk. That's something physical. But a man can see a woman from across a room and, without ever touching her, feel something powerful stir inside him. That powerful "something" has not been transmitted physically, but by some means beyond the power of men to engender or control. Thus, the father writing to his son in Proverbs confesses that sexual attraction is simply "too mysterious" for him to understand.

That's scary—no matter how pleasant the initial feeling. Indeed, the good feeling comes in a package labeled, "Warning: Contents cannot be mastered by human powers."

A man can't always turn it off. A high schooler gets excited during algebra class when nearby Janey crosses her legs and the bell rings; embarrassed, he sits at his desk buying time fumbling with his notebook as his classmates rush by him for the door. A middle-aged executive, married with children, has a fleeting fantasy about another woman, feels shame, and puts it out of his mind; that night, the woman appears in his dreams.

Nor can a man always make it happen. Often when a couple decide to get pregnant, the most readily excitable man can experience anxiety—and nothing else—as his wife holds her ovulation timing kit and stopwatch and says, "Now!" Another man may struggle with chronic impotence, from which no amount of muscles, money, or technology can save him.

For the young man whose body is beginning to stir with sexual feelings, the world of attraction to "girls" is an awesome forest, filled with terrors even as it beckons delight. Around the ninth grade it suddenly seems as if girls are everywhere; skirts, blouse buttons, legs, and lipstick cry out to be seized.

In the grip of such power and mystery, any man in touch with reality would humbly take his shoes off. But we who have eaten the "new grain" arrogantly clomp ahead in hobnail boots. And so the world hails the bold womanizer striding into the holy of holies, like Elvis in the movies—who in reality died alone of a drug overdose, divorced from his wife and lost in sexual perversion.

A people who have forgotten the Father God as Author of authentic femininity and masculinity harbor deep fears and seek saving power to confirm sexual identity. Like the ancient pagans, they can only worship the one who conjures the most powerful spirit of lust, genuflecting before the television and showering the Sex Queen and Hunk with adoration and money.

Lust compels us into physical gratification in order to short-circuit the mystery, "saving" us from the humbling unknown and thereby, from trusting relationship with the Father God and His confirmation of sexual identity.

Not long ago, I was driving out Sunset Boulevard in Los Angeles for an appointment, and as the road crested before Hollywood, I was startled to see stretched high above me against the sky a giant billboard picturing twin women, tanned and blond, in bikinis. Presiding over the Los Angeles basin, the sign bore no words. Presumably, any man who had eaten enough of the media "new grain" to be "in the know," would recognize the women.

I did not. But I did recognize at once the age-old spirit of lust which they projected—like the lust goddess Aphrodite, hailed as spiritual patroness of Corinth with a giant naked statue high on the mountaintop overlooking that Greek harbor. "In Corinth, let the sailor beware,"[2] warned ancient wisdom—transmuted today, "In America, let men leap in wherever it feels good."

When such thundering voices call from the forest, a young man cries out for a secure voice of wisdom. He seeks an older man who has lived in the forest and can tell him, "That stream over there looks good, but it's poison; wait 'til further down the trail for the good stream. Over that way is a fantastic view, but it's a rough climb up—watch your step, and don't get too close to the cliff edge. The cave is good for protection once in awhile, but stay near the opening, since it drops off further inside."

Too often today, however, the older men themselves are lost in the forest, having never surrendered their sexuality to Jesus—who is Lord of the forest—and allowed Him to bring them to the Father God for His guidance. They are guzzling the poisonous stream of pornography, falling from the cliff vistas into adultery and fornication, lost in the caves of alienation and fantasy.

And so alone, the boys stumble ahead into the dark woods.

"I can remember in the back of the school bus when I was a freshman in high school," one forty-year-old clergyman told me. "Some older kid—at least seventeen!—was telling us how he'd had sex with a girl in the back of his car one night. There must've been a dozen of us guys packed around him, like fervent disciples listening to this denim-jacket guru.

"Frankly, I felt kind of repulsed by what he was saying. It didn't sound that good to me, actually—kind of dark and sneaky and dangerous, like stealing something. I was definitely disappointed, and confused. I felt ashamed for wanting sex. If that's what sex is like, I thought to myself, I hope it's a long time before I have to do it."

Most men today can tell of going out in the woods years ago as young teens with other boys to look at pornographic "men's magazines"—a graphic example of being lost in the forest without an older mentor.

Contrast these crude stories of darkness, shame, and fear with the loving intention of the Father God—who sees that it is "not good for the man to live alone" (see Gen. 2:18–25), and takes the initiative to meet His son's need. Significantly, the Father first brings the animals to the man, perhaps to surface his deepest needs by meeting his most accessible ones first.

We can imagine God's saying, "I know you've been lonely, Adam, so look what I've got just for you. Here's a couple of dogs to befriend you, some rabbits to hunt with the dog, horses to ride, fish in the waters—you'll have a great time fishing!—some birds to sing in the morning, and all the other animals to keep you company. Enjoy!"

So Adam ran with his dogs, rode his horses, chased his rabbits, caught his fish, sang with the birds, day after day after day—until we can imagine one day God's coming upon Adam downcast in the Garden. "What's the matter, son? How come you still seem lonely? Didn't you like the dog and horse and . . ."

"Yes, Father," Adam interrupts. "I . . . appreciate the animals. All of them. I really do. They do things for me, and they do okay by themselves. It's just that, well, they don't . . . really need me all that much. I . . . don't want to sound ungrateful, Father, but is that . . . all you've got?"

So the man named all the birds and all the animals, but not one of them was a suitable companion to help him.

"Just . . . what else did you have in mind, son?" God asks, suppressing a father's knowing, loving smile.

"Well, I like the way they all have eyes and noses and legs, kind of like mine. But have you got anything that's more . . . like me, Father?"

"How do you mean?"

"I'm . . . not exactly sure. All I know is something's still . . . missing somehow. Maybe if it walked and made sounds more like me? It's really . . . hard, Father. The animals all go off by themselves to sleep at night, and I just lie there awake, feeling . . . kind of empty."

"Can you describe what you're wanting then, at night?"

"It's strange—I thought it would go away when the animals came, but it's even worse now. It feels like . . . something inside of me that's not there. I just don't . . . have a name for it. Father, I need You. I know it sounds crazy, but I need . . . something like me, but different from me."

Then the Lord God made the man fall into a deep sleep. . . .

Because the man is now ready. Until he has experienced all other creatures and found them lacking, he cannot appreciate the depth of relationship which the woman beckons, even out of his own body and soul.

But for the best, the price is highest. Hence, the "deep sleep," the general anesthesia. A local novocaine, a light nap, would suffice to get another animal; for a pig or a fish, God could take a part of the man's ear or tooth. But for a truly "suitable companion to help him" fulfill his calling as a man, something essential to the whole man must be extracted. Hence, a major operation is coming, a deep cut required.

Relating to the woman faithfully exposes deep wounds in a man.

For so the Surgeon would heal.

And while he was sleeping, He took out one of the man's ribs and closed up the flesh. He formed a woman out of the rib, and brought her to him.

How many men, when dating a woman, are oblivious to the bond being formed between them? "I couldn't believe it," as one man exclaimed to me in genuine awe some months after his wedding, when he and his wife began talking about having children. "I happened to mention we'd need to think of names for a child, and right away she pulls out boy and girl names she said she'd picked out for our children after our second date—almost a year before I asked her to marry me!"

"Adam? . . . Adam! Wake up, Adam!"

"Huh? Wha . . . what happened?"

"I've taken a part of you and made it into another, one you may now reach after to draw back to yourself. Don't try to understand it; just come over here. You thought the dog and the fish and the horse were something? Take a look at what I have for you now, son!"

Then the man said, "Wow! Oh, Father! Yes, yes . . . Oh, my Father! *At last, here is one of my own kind—bone taken from my bone, and flesh from my flesh. 'Woman' is her name, because she was taken out of man."*

Wholly submitted to the Father, trusting His power and love, Adam is not overwhelmed by the spiritual mystery of sexual attraction. The Father covers his inadequacy, protects him from fear, and thereby, releases him to joy. "Therefore a man leaves his father and his mother and cleaves to his wife, and they become one flesh" (Gen. 2:24 RSV).

Hallelujah! Through unbroken relationship with the Father, a man can be set free from boyhood parental wounds and rejoice in his marriage.

Furthermore, the story concludes with a promise for the son thus in unbroken relationship with his Father: "The man and his wife were both naked, and they felt no shame" (Gen. 2:25 NIV). That is, they could be vulnerable and wholly exposed to each other—sharing their deepest needs, hopes, fears, brokenness— and still feel fully loved and accepted, without shame.

But the man decided to sin along with the woman, and thus break relationship with the Father. And the bright Garden became a dark forest.

Sadly, at least 98 percent of men in our society today have learned about their sexuality shamefully—as in the back of the school bus and in pornographic materials—instead of through caring relationship with godly fathers. Virtually every man among us today therefore grows up fearful of his sexuality and thus unable to approach the woman without shame.

Through unbroken relationship with the Father, a man can be set free from boyhood parental wounds and rejoice in his marriage.

Why? Because relationship with the father has been broken— even as Adam sinned before his/our Father God, and thereafter felt shame when naked before the woman.

Indeed, turning from the Father breaks not only relationship with Him, but with the woman as well—because the man can no longer see her as the Father's daughter and thus, a sister worthy of love and respect. She is no longer trustworthy. She is unsafe.

The biblical story says that the man cannot reveal himself to the woman when relationship with the Father has been broken. When powers of brokenness have been unleashed, the man's identity must be covered, his masculinity protected. Without the Father to cover him, he must cover himself. Hence, the fig leaves —and a host of other shields we fabricate in order to maintain "safe" distance from the woman.

I was initiated to perhaps the most graphic of these deceptions as a third-grader, on the school playground at recess one day, when a boy several years older approached me holding a strange piece of folded paper in his fingers. Split in four segments each covering one finger, the paper opened like a bird's beak as he pulled me aside and stuck it under my face. "Look at what I've got!" he exclaimed, his fingers pinching and opening the segments.

"What's that?" I asked innocently.

"See this?" he said, squeezing the segments in two pairs and opening them in one direction. "It's clean, right?"

I looked into the open beak of paper—and nodded, puzzled.

"Now watch me," he said. Dropping his hand secretively to his side, he walked over to where several girls were jumping rope. Greeting them, he reached over to one with the paper piece, pecked her shoulder with it, and ran back to me.

"Look at this!" he exclaimed, opening the beak jaws again, this time in the other direction. To my amazement, tiny black dots now filled the inside.

"What's all that?"

"They're cooties!" he declared. "Girls have 'em. All over."

Astounded, I looked back at the rope jumpers. "Really?"

"Sure!" he said, turning to run off. "Just remember not to get too close to girls, or you'll get 'em too!"

Disturbed by this new knowledge, I stood there thinking—and suddenly wanted to ask him, "What about my sister and my mother?" But he was already across the playground, evangelizing other classmates of mine to this gospel of saving power for frightened boys.

Soon, however, I had discovered such cultural reinforcements as Little Lulu's comic book friend Tubby in his "No Girls Allowed" treehouse. Indeed, by the fourth grade, I had learned to make and "use" my own "cootie catcher."

Even though living with a mother and two sisters offered ample evidence for me that "cooties" do not exist, nevertheless I remained strangely seized by the whole exercise—and became quite proficient at drawing large, ugly bugs on the proper segments of paper.

Why?

Because to move close to the girl is for the boy to enter "the forest"—that is, to engage spiritual powers far beyond his ability to discern or negotiate. Untutored, he feels inadequate, and therefore, afraid.

The cootie premise—that a boy *should* not approach girls because they carry contagious bugs—saves him from having to face not only his inadequacy, but the fearful spiritual reality which proclaims it.

Without the father to accept, initiate, and guide him in this essential process of male growth, a boy not only withdraws from himself and his true feelings, but also sacrifices the female's integrity—for the "cootie premise" wounds the feminine soul in little girls by rejecting them as inferior.

Boys who lack godly fathers to guide them in the forest grow up feeling inadequate and afraid before the woman. They therefore perpetuate this puerile charade later. In some Spanish-speaking cultures, a woman is referred to as "enfermada"—literally, "sick"—during her monthly period. Some Middle-Eastern men demand "chador" cloaks cover the woman's body totally, and thus feel safe from the mysterious power she evokes. Men in some African tribes cut off a woman's clitoris to deprive her of sexual satisfaction, ensuring her fidelity.

Closer to home, as a teenager I recall hearing many derogatory jokes among men about "women drivers." On turning sixteen and getting my driver's license, I naively assumed my auto insurance premium would be much cheaper than any woman's. Imagine my shock at discovering I would have to pay almost twice as much, because young men cause auto accidents twice as often as women!

Any man who cannot remember fear in the presence of a woman is, by definition, too old. A helpful memory tool is Elvis's 1958 hit, "All Shook Up."[3] It tells the story of a young man who gets tongue-tied around his girlfriend and begins to shake and have heart palpatations. He thinks the answer is the hobnail boot approach—he'll "have" her.

The unspiritual man can only perceive the awesome power generated in the woman's presence as coming from her. Hence, he fears and resents her for holding such literally body-shaking power over him. He reasons, "She has what I need, but won't just hand it over; how am I going to get it from her?"

The man who lacks a father to confirm his manhood doubts anyone so insecure as himself will ever "get it" from the woman. He may lash out violently and seize her in rape.

A more socially adept man realizes he has only two choices: He can either charge ahead with sports car, sexy clothes, and other accoutrements to seduce the woman and "score," or he can run from her like a coward.

The awesome power which seizes a man in the woman's presence, meanwhile, does not come from her, but rather, from the realm of the spirit. Neither he nor she generates it. Fear in the woman's presence, therefore, is not overcome or "cured" by seizing control—an impossible fantasy for mere human beings—but only by surrendering to the Father who rules that realm.

All too often, men run from this power by committing adultery, chasing another woman, or entertaining such fantasies— and thus short-circuit the intimacy which beckons the power and fear. In order to run but not appear cowardly—to establish a "safe" distance from the woman and even appear righteous for doing so, a man often simply criticizes her.

When moving close to the woman a man may, for example, suddenly begin thinking that she is "too quiet" or "too loud," her legs are "not that good after all," she put "too much/not enough" salt in the dinner, has "weird friends," etc.

Such barbs hurt, causing the woman to get angry and withdraw. Then, the man feels safe—justified in his critical opinions, and not responsible for the distance now between them.

Nancy, who at thirty had been married to Mark for five years, called me early one evening in tears. At her regular physical exam, she said, the doctor had found a lump in her breast and ordered a biopsy. When she told Mark, he hesitated, then burst out, "Well, you always were too fat, anyhow!"

I had played basketball and prayed with Mark several times, and found him to be a decent man. Why in the world, I wondered, would he lash out at Nancy so viciously?

"My educated guess as a man," I told her, "is that Mark's afraid of getting close, and doesn't want to tell you that directly. If you want to get through this, you're probably going to have to push him to speak the full truth. I know you're deeply hurt, and I wouldn't blame you for keeping your distance. But of course, that would play right into his game. If you want, I'll pray that you'll have the courage to talk to him and push through this."

Through her sobs, Nancy hesitated, thanked me, and said simply, "Okay." I prayed, then said I'd continue to pray later, and we hung up.

The next morning she called back, her voice calm and confident. "You were right," she said. "I went back to Mark and said, 'What are you afraid of, that you'd rather push me away than deal with?' He kept balking and saying 'Nothing!' But I kept insisting until finally, he said, 'Okay, I'll tell you. I'm afraid you'll have cancer and die, and I'll be left alone.'"

Instead of surrendering to the Father, Mark—who had been raised by his mother after his parents' divorce—had surrendered to the fear, and bailed out on the woman. Lacking an earthly father as a boy, he did not trust the Father God to be with him in uncertainty, much less to use it as an occasion to draw him into deeper relationship with Himself and with Nancy.

As it turned out, Nancy's body was healthy. But the man's wound to her feminine soul took some time to heal. "It's okay to be afraid," she told him. "I'm afraid too. Just don't run away from me when I need you to stand by me and pray for me."

Whenever a man runs from the truth, others pay for it—usually, those closest to him. But when he trusts that his Father is with him—when he trusts in Jesus, who says, "I am the way, the truth, and the life; no one goes to the Father except by me" (John 14:6)—he walks as a man of God, who bears the truth that sets others free (see John 8:32).

In a remarkably apt country-western song, "You're Talkin' to the Wrong Man,"[4] a teenage son turns to his dad for help after his girlfriend seems to invite affection, and then rebuffs him. But the father can't help. He admits that he still doesn't understand the boy's mother.

Rather than list several points of wisdom, the father essentially tells his confused son, "I understand where you are; in fact, I am where you are. I cannot take your pain and confusion away, but I will not leave you alone in it." And that, for the son, is enough. For it mirrors the incarnate Christ, who demonstrates on the Cross that to be one with the father enables the son to walk in victory through the darkest forest, unto death itself.

Certainly, this father and son are both "talkin' to the wrong man" as long as they talk only to each other and not to the Father God who created both them and the "forest" of sexual attraction that awes them. Without Jesus, men can easily bond together as frightened boys to protect themselves against women, rather than bond with the Father as bold men to love His daughters.

Even as he approaches her, therefore, the man in broken relationship with his father must shield himself from the woman, for the spiritual power generated by their closeness threatens to overwhelm him. Cut off from the father, he is alone in the forest with his inadequacies. He lacks grounding in the masculine through his father's call, and thus, he lacks basic trust in himself as a man. Therefore, to give himself to the woman is to lose himself in her—even as he lost himself in his mother when his dad abandoned him.

The man desires the woman physically, needs her emotionally as "a suitable companion to help him," and misses her as a spiritual complement—but he dares not draw close to her. Only his physical desire seems objective enough for him to control, so he forfeits emotional, spiritual intimacy with the woman, supplanting and thus confusing it with sexual acts.

This pervasive fear of the woman in men is therefore not necessarily rooted in any will in the woman to destroy the man, but more likely, in his own sense of sexual shame and inadequacy from broken relationship with Dad.

The biblical faith, meanwhile, proclaims that the woman is fashioned out of the man. In his sexual desire, the man's body feels the longing to rejoin, to reunite with the missing part of himself that the woman literally embodies—and therein, to become wholly human and completely himself again at last. If, indeed, the Father has come in Jesus to restore relationship with His sons—broken by Adam's sin at the Fall—then as a man surrenders his sexual impulses to Jesus, he allows the Father to reopen the gates to genuine intimacy with the woman, even the missing part of himself.

A simple prayer might be, "Father, I give up—not to my sexual impulses, but to You. Take over my heart and body, Lord Jesus, and give me the strength to cooperate with Your righteous purposes in me."

The boy whose father talks to him openly and compassionately about the mystery of sexuality, however, need not protect himself behind harmful practices that enforce distance from the female. Indeed, such a father can affirm the wonder and mystery of his son's sexual energies, even as he holds the son accountable for expressing them in a godly way.

The father of a sixteen-year-old told me he came home from work late one evening, and his wife greeted him with, "Steve just got back from a date with Sally Smith, and you'd better go talk to him about what he did to her!" Fuming, she turned to leave. "He's in his room."

Startled, the man was left standing alone in the living room. He had heard his son talk disparagingly about Sally Smith, and was as surprised to learn about such a date as to be greeted thusly by his wife.

Sighing uneasily, he went to his son's bedroom, knocked and waited. After no answer, he entered—and found the boy in bed, covers pulled to his head.

Clearing his throat, he approached the bed. "Steve?"

"Huh?"

"Your mom tells me you went out with Sally Smith tonight."

"Yeah."

"She said you . . . did something to Sally—is that right?"

"No—I didn't do that much."

"Your mom seemed pretty upset. What did you do to Sally?"

Steve sat up. "Aw, Mom always gets upset about everything you tell her—it's no big deal."

Uncertain, the father hesitated. "Did you . . . kiss her?"

"Yeah, I kissed her."

"Did you . . . feel her up?"

"Yeah, some."

"Anything else?"

"Just a little. I mean, we didn't . . . go all the way or anything."

Oh, Lord! the father thought. *What do I do now?* After some thought, he said, "It felt good, didn't it?"—surprising even himself.

"Huh? Uh, yeah. Yeah, it did."

The man paused. "Son . . . I know you've talked about Sally before, how she's always chasing after you and you wish she'd go away. You don't like her much, do you?"

"No."

"Was she coming after you again?"

"Yeah."

"So you took advantage of her then, didn't you?"

Hesitating, Steve nodded.

"Do you really want to be a person who goes through life taking advantage of people?"

"No," said Steve.

After talking it over, the father invited the son to pray and ask God's forgiveness for taking advantage of Sally. Then, he told his son to call Sally and ask her forgiveness.

"Do you think I handled that situation okay?" the father asked.

"Definitely," I said, amazed.

Indeed, the father had respected his son, affirmed his sexual energies, and still held him accountable. Sexual contact with a woman does feel good, and no honest man, whether sixteen or sixty, can be convinced otherwise.

Indeed, if sinful acts themselves felt so terrible, we would never have needed Jesus to save us from them; we'd avoid them by ourselves. A father must stand with his son in the truth closest to the son's experience if he is to lead the son to any deeper truth.

In acknowledging matter-of-factly, "It felt good, didn't it?" the father taught the son to distinguish real guilt from learned shame. That is, when he as a man thereby said, "Your feelings are understandable," the son did not need to defend himself. In that security of being accepted by the father, the son could begin to recognize his sin, and take it to the Father God for cleansing.

If the father had stormed into the son's room, condemned his behavior, and punished him severely, he would have broken relationship with the son, who thereafter would surely have shared nothing more about his sexuality. He would have taken off by himself into the "forest" to save face—and ultimately, become dangerously lost.

The Father God convicts of sin in order to transform and heal the sinner; the Enemy, in order to condemn and destroy him. The father must at times declare his son guilty of wrongdoing, but must never condemn his son to the shame of "wrongbeing."[5]

Without such fatherly guidance, men grow up substituting physical sexual expression for emotional/spiritual intimacy with the woman.

The biblical faith, therefore, points to a wholly different basis for intimacy with the woman. Significantly, the Father God who cuts His son Adam to draw forth the woman is the only one who knows where the grooves have been made in the man, and therefore, is the only one who can fit the two pieces together properly. The man and the woman, that is, are designed to unite only under the authority of the Father God.

Failure to respect this reality bears quite practical consequences, in spite of the seductive humanistic view that "sex is okay outside of marriage as long as the two love each other." For example, most men who marry today, including Christian men who became believers later in life and those divorced, have had sexual relations with other women previously. The world, which can recognize only human powers, holds that all bonds cease when the partners decide to break them.

Thus, if the humanly endowed powers of the State comprise all contracts in the relationship, then a court-certified divorce sets the man and woman "free," both emotionally as well as physically, to pursue new partners as if the previous one never existed. But any man who has had intercourse with a woman knows that forgetting her is not that easy. Dreams and fantasies persist long after he has stopped seeing her. For indeed, human governments can break only those bonds which human governments make. Only God can break bonds made in the spiritual realm.

And a bond is formed in the spirit through sexual intercourse.

As Paul declared in dismay when the early Church had apparently forgotten this truth, "Or perhaps you don't know that the man who joins his body to a prostitute becomes physically one with her? The scripture says quite plainly, 'The two will become one body' " (1 Cor. 6:16).

As Eve was taken from Adam, only God can separate two who have become one body.

John Sandford explains it well:

> God has so built us in our spirits that whatever woman a man enters, their spirits are united to each other from that moment on. Each person's spirit seeks, from the moment of union, to find, fulfill, nurture, and cherish the one who entered into that union with him/her. . . .
>
> [O]nce a wrong union has been entered, our spirit still remembers that union and seeks to fulfill the other. If there have been many immoral unions with many partners, our spirit becomes like an overloaded transformer, trying to send its current in too many directions. Having been delivered by confession, absolution, and prayer for separation, counselees have often cried out, "I have never felt so free. I didn't realize how scattered I felt. I feel together again." Of course! Their spirits were no longer having to search heaven and earth to find and fulfill dozens of forgotten partners![6]

Therefore, when I minister to a Christian man who wants to be fully cleansed and ready for a new union under the Father God's blessing and authority, I lead him in a prayer such as this: Father, I confess the sin of fornication with (names of women), and I ask Your forgiveness. In the name of Jesus, I now renounce all bonds of the flesh with (women's names, including ex-wife), and take the sword of the Spirit and cut all remaining spiritual ties between us. I ask for Your blood, Jesus, to cover and cleanse me from all attraction and wounds there, and I release those women to You for Your purposes in their lives apart from me. And I put myself in Your hands, Jesus, to bond me to my wife alone.

Other emotional and spiritual healing may be required to sever fully some past sexual relationships, but this prayer facilitates that process by cutting the major spiritual taproot which has nurtured those relationships and the ongoing fantasies.

Clearly, the man who respects this mystery and its power can offer such wisdom to his son.

Les, thirty-four and a believer, was divorced for eight years and living several hundred miles from his ex-wife and fourteen-year-old son. During a visit, Les encouraged the boy in his many activities—friends, schoolwork, baseball, horseback riding, camping—and noticed him glancing often at girls.

"Before I left," Les said, "I sat down with him and told him I noticed he was looking at the girls, and that was good. I encouraged him to date around when he felt ready. But I told him not to have sex, that if he did at his age, all his energies would go into the girl, and all the good activities he now enjoys so much would take a back seat to her. I told him that when he grows up he will become secure enough in himself that he can get married, and his sexual attraction to the woman won't push him off balance like now. He seemed to understand that, and thanked me for saying it."

Thus, bonding to the woman requires first breaking from the mother, bonding to the father/company of men, and then bonding to the Father God.

At forty, Ted had been divorced for several years and during that time had become a Christian. When he began dating again, he experienced so much anxiety over "how far to go" with a date that he resolved not even to kiss a woman. When he came to see me, he had just met Grace, who seemed especially well-suited for him.

As we talked, Ted demonstrated a good relationship with the Father God and was in regular prayer fellowship with other men, so I encouraged him simply to ask for His Father's word as he walked Grace up to her apartment door next time.

"I asked the Lord if I could kiss her," he reported after their second date, "and I sensed a hug was okay."

After the next date, Ted reported much good sharing between them—and another hug.

The following week, Ted was smiling broadly. "When I asked the Father if I could kiss her, I didn't feel any check like the times before, just kind of open and happy. I waited a minute, asked again, and felt the same—so I kissed her! It was great!"

Some months later, when the two realized God was knitting them together for marriage, and they had talked openly about boundaries on their sexual expression, Ted told me he mentioned those first dates and his prayers at the doorstep. Grace laughed good-naturedly and told him, "You weren't the only one praying! By that third date, I was beginning to pray, 'Come on, Father—make him kiss me!' "

Both Ted and Grace had had sexual relations with other partners previously, but had been celibate for years since becoming Christians. I led them in prayers to cut all past bonds of the flesh. Still, fears and confusions arose soon after their marriage, which drove them to their knees.

"We naively assumed we'd just pick up sexually where we left off with the other partners years before," Ted said, shaking his head and smiling. "But it wasn't long before we were wearing knee-holes in the carpet by our bed, confessing together that we'd bought into the world's approach to sex, and had never been taught differently by our parents. We begged the Father to clean that out of us and teach us what making love really is—and we discovered the Father had a closeness to give us that we'd never before experienced."

In my own marriage, I have learned to go to the Father God readily when differences arise. Once, for example, we had discussed, debated, and argued a point to no agreement or resolution. In frustration I huffed, "Okay, then, I'm going to the Father!"

I took Mary's hand and we knelt. "Father," I prayed, "I've told Mary my opinion on this and she's told me hers; we've gone over and over this and neither of us wants to give up to the other. So we both give up to You. Speak to us, show us how You see all this."

I waited, and sensed the Father's saying simply, "Listen to her."

"But, Father," I protested, "I really feel like I'm right this time!"

"I didn't say you were wrong," I sensed the reply; "I said 'Listen to her.' "

Puzzled, but at my wit's end, I sighed, turned to Mary, and told her what the Lord had said. "Maybe I've been so anxious to make my point that I haven't really listened to you. Would you tell me once more how you feel about all this, and I'll try my best to listen?" *Okay, Father,* I prayed quietly, *I give up to You all my right to win this argument. Now help me listen to her and hear what You want me to.*

Mary hesitated as a flicker of distrust was swept away by love, and then told me again how she was feeling. As she talked, I sensed her pain and began to see why this issue was particularly upsetting to her. Many tears and hugs later, we could only wonder together at the Father's love for us both.

"I don't always trust you in the moment," Mary said, "but I trust your relationship with the Father. Also, I know He loves me, and that gives me all the confidence I need that we'll work things out."

I realized that I feel the same way about Mary.

As a husband, at times I overreact, miss the point, or just plain shut down. Sometimes, I handle things very honestly, openly, and maturely, and still worry that I've done it wrong. But when I remember my Father God and surrender it all to Him, I know that we're on the same side—bonded in the Spirit, and ready to celebrate that in the flesh.

Chapter

4

How Can I Know My Man's Unique Needs?

I married my husband, Jody, because I wanted to be his lover and best friend forever. Beginning on our twenty-ninth anniversary, I spent a year writing my daughters what I have learned about developing an intimate oneness with Jody. Some of those letters were collected in the book How to Really Love Your Man *and have been adapted and reprinted here in this book, beginning with this chapter.*

No one can play as significant a role in encouraging a man and knowing his unique needs as his wife. These chapters are meant to help women, beginning with my daughters, know how to meet those needs and know their man.

—*Linda Dillow*
How to Really Love Your Man

"How Can I Know My Man's Unique Needs?" is taken from *How to Really Love Your Man,* Linda Dillow (1993).

Dear Daughters,

You have found him, your one unique man to love, an original unlike any other. You are beginning this adventure called marriage with him, and *you* are the one close to his heart who knows his deep needs. You don't have to meet the needs of any other man, only one, but it can take a lifetime to intimately know, to learn to understand, to learn to love and discover your original creation.

The more you understand your husband's uniqueness, the more you understand his deep needs, the more you can meet them. Marriage is the adventure of discovering each other so you might deeply share

- a soul intimacy.
- a body intimacy.
- a spirit intimacy.

The three intimacies together yield oneness. Sex without soul intimacy is empty, satisfying only the body. Soul and body intimacy without spirit oneness is missing God's best. God made us three-dimensional people. Man and woman are to meet body, soul, and spirit; the result will be a lover-best friend relationship.

What your husband needs will be a reflection of his longing for *companionship, intimacy,* and *significance.* How his needs will be demonstrated will be unique because he is unique. That is why, as a wife, you must make it your project to study your man. Where do you begin?

Begin by asking God. Psalm 139 declares that God understands your man's thoughts, is intimately acquainted with all his ways. The Lord is the One who can teach you all you need to know about your man. He, our Creator, was there when your man was formed and placed in his mother's womb.

Countless times I have gone to the Lord with this prayer: "Help, God. Teach me to understand this complicated man You have given me to love." Time after time, He has unraveled puzzles that I couldn't solve. Sometimes this insight has been given as I have been quiet before Him, other times through His Word or a book or the words of a friend.

How tragic that so often we go *first* to a person rather than to the One who gave our men their uniqueness. First, ask God. Second, ask your husband:

• "Honey, what is important to you in a best friend? Help me to know. Do you want me to jog with you or teach a Bible study with you?"

• "Honey, what is important to you in a lover? Tell me your dreams of all you have ever desired in a lover."

• "Honey, what can I pray for you today?"

Study your man; listen to him, talk to him, and get so bold as to ask him how he would describe his five greatest needs. One woman asked her husband to list his needs for her, and the paper he gave her listed sex five times! His answer reflects that many men find it difficult to reveal themselves. When she convinced him that she really wanted to know, he gave her his real list.

Learning to know your unique man is an art. Learning to meet his deep needs is a skill. It is a challenge that takes a lifetime.

I love you,
Mom

"The Irresistible Husband"

$\mathcal{I}$ chose to share in this chapter from Real Man *with you because it focuses on what every woman would like her husband to be—irresistible. But what is it that women want? The answer is surprisingly simple, and it's found in a man who becomes more like God, the "ultimate gentleman." We'll take a look at a scriptural course of action for becoming the kind of man no woman could resist—kind, gentle, strong, and loving—by examining the nature of God himself.*

—Edwin Louis Cole
Real Man

From the Bayou country of Louisiana comes a story of Cajun humor that carries a point we can apply to marriage.

"Wha's dat unna yo shirt?" the friend asks.

"The Irresistible Husband" is adapted from *Real Man*, Ed Cole (1992).

"It's the dyn-o-mite ah've strapped to mah chest," replies the man.

"Why you got dyn-o-mite tied ta yo chest?" the friend inquires.

"You know how Louis always come up to me and poke me inna chest all the time? Well, dah next time he poke me inna chest, I gonna blow his han' off!"

Trying to remedy an annoying situation was going to cause him more harm than good. The same can happen in marriage. A husband may try to correct situations in his marriage without using wisdom or understanding, and thereby alienate himself further from his wife and family. This happens all too often.

Recently, on a television talk show, women vented their anger toward their mates and dates. In one thirty-minute segment, remarks such as these erupted: "All men are jerks"; "He was simply more boy than man"; "All men live by their primal passions." Tragically, these comments represent what many women feel today.

Most men do not understand that a life devoid of the Spirit of Christ, lacking His grace, is coarse, whereas Spirit-filled righteousness refines character.

Sin desensitizes emotions and concern for others. The Holy Spirit, on the other hand, brings sensitivity to others' needs, hurts, and desires. The very nature of God is to work for the good of others, and that servant's heart is best exhibited in Jesus—the servant Savior for all. The same Spirit who empowered Him works in us to:

- create a servant's heart
- augment our natural talent
- maximize our personality
- highlight our awareness of people's needs and desires
- give insight into life's meaning
- deepen our understanding
- sharpen and clarify issues

This Spirit is a perfect gentleman, granting us the virtues of gentlemanliness, the fruit of the Spirit: "love, joy, peace, patience, kindness, goodness, faithfulness, gentleness and self-control" (Gal. 5:22–

23 NIV). The same virtues are also characteristics of ladylikeness, for they are without gender.

By contrast, the "works of the flesh" are sins of uncontrolled sensual passion, superstition, social disorder, and excess (Gal. 5:19–21). All of these scour our mind, soul, and body.

What does all this have to do with marriage? Simply this: God, the ultimate gentleman, is in the business of making gentlemen out of husbands. And more men need to let the Spirit do His work in their lives because the dissolution of many marriages is caused by the absence of gentlemanly qualities among husbands.

How do the characteristics of a gentleman display themselves? In such commonplace things as appearance, manners, speech, hygiene and habits, as well as in character traits.

Many husbands expect their wives to compete with the movie "sex goddesses" physically, while exempting themselves from such comparisons with other men. Although men (or women) don't need to strive for unrealistic images of perfection, men can take great strides toward self-improvement. Failure to take care of physical appearance and attire can cause men to lose respect in women's eyes. Men whose speech is profane, filled with slang and off-color humor, or limited in vocabulary and willful ignorance frequently bar themselves from more intimate relationships. Where good hygiene is possible but neglected, women are repulsed. In short, men who are indifferent to the characteristics of a gentleman diminish their stature, especially to their wives. It is amazing that, in the amount of mail I get from both men and women, such a large percentage of the complaints from women deal with the man's indifference to the common courtesies of life.

God, the ultimate gentleman, is in the business of making gentlemen out of husbands.

"Let each esteem others better than himself" is a biblical bidding for courtesy (Phil. 2:3). If a man reads the Bible for no other reason than to find a blueprint for a gentlemanly life-style, it would be a rich and rewarding experience. Just following the exhortations to courteousness, refinement, and respect for others will lead to gentlemanliness. But let's take a closer look at the fruit of a gentlemanly nature.

Gentleness, one aspect of the fruit of the Spirit, is a sign of true strength in a man, not weakness. When a man knows his strength, he can afford to be gentle. The stronger the man is, the more gentle he can be. Insecure men compensate for their lack by abusing others. Putting someone down doesn't build anyone up. King David, with his powerful war record, great riches, and reputation, wrote of His relationship with God, saying, "Your gentleness has made me great."

Kindness is a virtue that is attractive to women. Men and women were not created as competitors. Women were created to *complete* men. When men make women compete with them for attention, affection, attachment, they defeat themselves and nature. Having "brotherly affection" is to be considerate and sympathetic toward others (Rom. 12:10). This is critical in marriage.

In all fairness to men, I must admit that women seem cut from a different cloth today than in the past. It still astonishes me to hear women speak of men's "cute buns" in an aggressive manner with the crudeness formerly found mostly in men. Femininity is a woman's "stock in trade," her strength of nature, and a glory to her. Why give it up for competitive conflict?

Humility is not weakness (Eph. 4:2; Col. 3:12 KJV). It comes from the Spirit of God. Moses was called the meekest man on earth (Num. 12:3), but he was far from weak. He learned to control his spirit far off in the desert where he was disciplined by God for forty years before beginning his public ministry. And his ministry was to confront and defeat the greatest political figure in his land, then lead about two million Hebrews out of slavery and into the Promised Land. No task for a weak person!

Leadership scares many men. Unfortunately many women must bear the burden of male cowardliness. The unwillingness of men to face the realities of responsibility in marriage literally forces women into a man's role. It is unnatural, but common.

Women have risen to prominence in world leadership today. As in the Church, men have largely abdicated the roles of leadership, forcing women to fill the gap, so in the world today women politicians often enjoy more credibility than the men they have replaced. It is not strange anymore to find top social and political spots in major American cities occupied solely by women.

Houston for years had the reputation of being a "man's town." Texans to the core, Houstonians were proud of their heritage and lineage. Oil men, cattle barons, media moguls, and just plain "good ole boys" gave Houston its male aura. But no more. In Houston, the recently elected woman university president brought the number of women leading that city to six. Other positions occupied by women were the mayor, hospital chief, Chamber of Commerce president, chief of police, and school superintendent.[1]

As men have stepped aside from leadership, and specifically from the leadership of the home, they have found less fulfillment in life. Forty-eight percent of middle managers in major companies in a recent survey said their lives seemed "empty and meaningless," despite the years striving to achieve professional goals. Of senior executives, 68 percent said they had neglected their family in pursuit of professional goals, and that if they could do it over again, they would spend more time with their wives and children. Of high achievers overall, 60 percent felt they had sacrificed their identities to pursue material rewards.[2]

Recognition of others' uniqueness demonstrates strength. Women were created with a God-given uniqueness. When that uniqueness is satisfied, she is that man's wife, best friend, and the completion of his life. When the uniqueness is ignored, stifled, or simply lusted after, she is just another unfulfilled woman.

One woman in exasperation wrote me this letter: "The number one problem in marriage is not lust—it is television. My husband has been involved in church ministry for years, and all our friends have grown in the Lord, but not us. And do you know why? Because he never reads his Bible. He just sits in front of the TV every night while I take care of the children, do the chores, clean the house, and get myself ready for work the next day. I wish it would blow up!"

In a previous book I wrote about the "Video Daddy." The only thing worse than the wimp, brute, or idiot portrayed on the screen is the one glued to it. Television is actually a medium of lust. Programs and commercials are full of it. Not just sexual, but in material goods, food, and that "lust for life." Remember, sex was made for loving and giving, not lusting and getting.

A couple recently told me of the lustful marriage they had lived with for years. Jeff was an entrepreneur by nature, and they had lived in many different cities, working in many businesses through the years. Everywhere they went, Emily worked side by side with him tirelessly, raising the family as well, tending to their various houses, adapting to new communities, and providing him with everything in an attempt to satisfy him.

When the last child finished college, Emily felt herself cool in her relationship to Jeff. She was tired. Nothing she had ever done had been quite good enough. She had never worked to his satisfaction in their businesses. Their marriage bed had never left Jeff completely satisfied. Every time Jeff walked past her, he grabbed at her sexually.

She began to avoid him, became irritable, and kept him at a distance. As the marriage began to dissolve, someone gave Jeff a tape on "Love or Lust." Jeff heard more than what was on the tape; he heard God speaking to him.

Weeks later, as Jeff continued in prayer and soul-searching to hear more from God, he took Emily away for the weekend. In the car, he turned on the tape.

"This is the tape that changed my life," he said.

She laughs now that she expected it to be a trick to get her to listen to a message on woman's submission. Instead, she was shocked to hear a confrontational message of truth that nailed Jeff's every flaw. Before the tape ended, Jeff turned it down, leaned toward Emily and began to ask for forgiveness for thirty years of lusting for her, not loving her. In tears, they made a new commitment to each other and allowed the restoration process to begin.

Not only do men have appetites and desires, but women have theirs too. Though the needs are often met differently, the basics are the same for both.

According to a recent survey, nearly 50 percent of American wives "cheat" on their husbands by having extramarital affairs. This is double the number in 1948. The reasons the wives gave were:

- to force a change in the relationship
- to "prove" their desirability
- to pursue their dream of a "perfect" love
- to relieve boredom and satisfy curiosity
- to take revenge for the husband's known or suspected infidelity, neglect, stinginess, mistreatment of the children, poor personal hygiene

The underlying cause in every reason given is that the woman's uniqueness was not satisfied in the marriage relationship. Her creativity was stifled. Spontaneity was stunted. Sexual overtures were ignored. Romantic inclinations were thwarted.

Some women simply cannot stand the sight of their husbands around the home on the weekends—unshaven, disheveled, loathsome. One tip written by Abigail Van Buren was: "Don't look like a slob all weekend—unless she looks worse."

It comes back to being a gentleman.

Marriage is the second most important relationship men and women will ever have, and the choice of a mate is the second most important decision they will ever make. The most important is believing on Jesus and building a relationship with God.

The more like Jesus he becomes, the more of a gentleman he will be. Real men are gentlemen. Gentlemen are real men.

Gentlemen make real marriages.

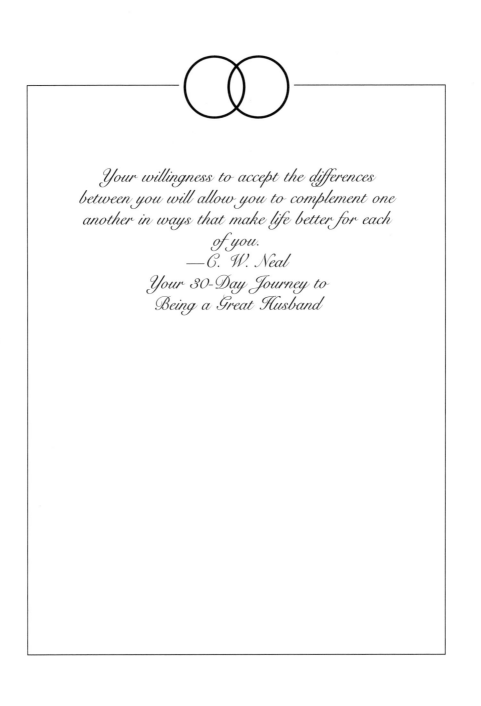

Your willingness to accept the differences between you will allow you to complement one another in ways that make life better for each of you.
—C. W. Neal
Your 30-Day Journey to Being a Great Husband

PART TWO

*Intimacy
and the
Art
of Communication*

Chapter

What Does Intimacy Feel Like?

Dear Daughters,

What does intimacy look like? What does it feel like?

Paul Stevens says that we were created with a need for intimacy, but that intimacy is not something we get through having therapy sessions or by exploring another person's body. Rather, it is the fruit of a lifetime of belonging to one other person.[1] The stage was set for intimacy when God commanded the first man to leave and cleave to his wife: "For this cause a man shall leave his father and his mother, and shall cleave to his wife; and they shall become one flesh. And the man and his wife were both naked and were not ashamed" (Gen. 2:24–25 NASB).

LEAVE   When we marry, we hope to physically leave our former homes. In many cultures, the physical leaving is not a viable possibility, but there must be a transfer of allegiance. There must also be a psychological break, an attitude that says, "My husband is now my priority and not my parents."

"What Does Intimacy Feel Like" is taken from *How to Really Love Your Man*, Linda Dillow (1993).

In the Chinese culture, when a man marries, custom requires that his mother be first and his wife second. I talked to women in Hong Kong who described untold heartaches and problems because of this failure to obey God's command to leave. In our culture, often a wife does not break the habit of allegiance to the mother or father first. To truly be one flesh, you must *leave.*

CLEAVE The word literally means to "stick like glue." Having left your former home, you bond with your spouse and become one flesh. The more you cleave, the more one-fleshed you become, a physical, mental, emotional, and spiritual intimacy. Cleaving is the process, one-fleshedness the result. Mike Mason has expressed in a beautiful way what it means to cleave:

> The Lord God made woman out of part of man's side and closed up the place with flesh, but in marriage He reopens this empty, aching place in man and begins the process of putting the woman back again, if not literally in the side, then certainly at it: permanently there, intrusively there, a sudden lifelong resident of a space which until that point the man will have considered to be his own private territory, even his own body. But in marriage he will cleave to the woman, and the woman to him, the way his own flesh cleaves to his own bones.[2]

ONE FLESH I've read many definitions of *intimacy*, but the best, most succinct, most beautiful one is recorded here in Genesis: "And the man and his wife were both naked and were not ashamed."

What does it mean to be naked? Is it only a physical condition? The first husband and wife experienced nakedness in all areas: a physical, emotional, intellectual, and spiritual transparency between husband and wife; no masks, no barriers; only communion and companionship.

They were unashamed. They enjoyed an intimacy where there was no fear to reveal, a transparency that let the other into the deep crevices of life. Neither partner feared to let the other see the good, the bad, the indifferent. They could know and be known without fear; they had no hidden agendas, no hang-ups, no embarrassments; they lacked self-consciousness.

What an indescribably beautiful provision by God! The needs for companionship and intimacy so perfectly met in a live-in lover-best friend! C. S. Lewis, in his powerful way with words, describes this intimacy experienced with his beloved wife:

> We feasted on love; every mode of it, solemn and merry, romantic and realistic, sometimes as dramatic as a thunderstorm, sometimes comfortable and unemphatic as putting on your soft slippers.
> She was my pupil and my teacher, my subject and my sovereign, my trusty comrade, friend, shipmate, fellow-soldier. My mistress, but at the same time all that any man friend has ever been to me.[3]

Perhaps no one has explained the key words *leave, cleave,* and *one flesh* better than Walter Trobisch in his book *I Married You*. Trobisch helps us understand that the marriage covenant has a public part, leaving father and mother, a personal part, cleaving, and a private part, one flesh:

> Leaving is symbolized by wedlock, that public act by which two people state they belong to each other in an exclusive relationship. Cleaving means the joining of two people in a friendship that will extend throughout their lives. One flesh is the fulfillment of the first two, when a couple expresses with their bodies the reality of leaving and cleaving.[4]

My daughters, your marriage ceremony is your Garden of Eden. Growing to become one flesh is a process that takes a lifetime, beginning when God declares you one. He declares it, but now you have to live it out, day by day, choice by choice. Now you begin to learn how to really love your man.

I love you,
Mom

Nine Myths about ~~love~~
Intimacy

We've all been taught to believe a lot of things that just aren't true about love and romance, about sex and intimacy. And those myths can keep couples from experiencing real joy in their marriages. That's why we've included this chapter from The Intimacy Factor. *When we take a hard look at these nine myths, we can see the ways in which we've loaded our spouse, or the marriage itself, with unfair expectations. We hope that exploding these myths will help ignite some new sparks in your marriage—they sure have in ours!*

—*Jan and Dave Stoop*
The Intimacy Factor

When Jan and I were dating, I had a real problem with jealousy. My insecurities flared whenever Jan spent too much time with any-

"Nine Myths about Intimacy" is adapted from *The Intimacy Factor*, Dr. David Stoop and Jan Stoop (1992).

one, even her college roommate. Obviously, we had some pretty intense discussions about my concerns and Jan's feelings of being boxed in.

The strangest thing happened. Soon after we were married my jealousy problem was cured. After some months of this noticeable shift in my behavior, Jan asked me what had changed. I told her, "Well, you're mine now that we're married. I don't have to worry about anyone else taking you away from me." Needless to say, my idea of "owning her" did not feel very good to her. In fact, that conversation produced a change in her attitude. Her insecurities were stirred up, and *she* started being jealous for the first time. For some time, I couldn't understand what she was experiencing. The problem was that we had different beliefs about marriage—some of them untruths or myths. The myth I held on to was that once we were married, we "owned" each other. Jan's myth was that somehow her husband's love would make her feel secure forever after.

What do you believe about the subject of intimacy? What were you taught? In our research for our book *The Intimacy Factor,* we discovered nine beliefs—myths—about intimacy that often keep us stuck where we are. Take a moment to assess your beliefs about relationships. Read each of the following statements and decide which are true and which are false.

1. If the other person really loves me, he/she will always know what I want or need to be happy.

2. The best indicator of a good marriage is a good sex life.

3. The level of satisfaction and intimacy automatically increases over the years of the relationship.

4. It doesn't matter how I behave, the other person should show love for me simply because we are married to each other.

5. If we are really close, we should be able to point out each other's errors and shortcomings without feeling threatened.

6. My spouse either loves me or doesn't; if not, there is nothing I can do to make it any different.

7. The more we can disclose—both good and bad information— to each other, the closer we become.

8. Keeping the feelings of romantic love alive is necessary to fuel an intimate relationship.

9. I have to feel love toward the other person before I can help the relationship become closer.

How did you answer? Did you answer true to any of the statements? If you answered false to every statement, your beliefs about intimacy are accurate. Each of the above statements is a myth.

MYTH #1: INTIMACY IS BEING ABLE TO READ EACH OTHER'S MIND

The desire to have the other person read our mind is really an extension of one of the wishes we had as a child, but it seems an innocent enough goal to have in a marriage. As children, we subconsciously longed to return to that wonderful state within the womb where everything was taken care of automatically. Now we think, *The person I love will know what I need and provide it for me even before I know I need it.*

This myth finds some positive reinforcement in the early stages of a relationship. As we are getting to know someone new, the other person can read us and know what we need at some given moment. And as that person responds to our need, our wish is being fulfilled. This gives support to the wish, and so we wish all the more for this automatic fulfillment to take place. In the early stages of a relationship, we are still far enough away from each other emotionally that we are able to see needs and respond without fear. As we get closer to each other, we find that our own fears about closeness get stirred up and blind us to the needs of the other person.

One of the most common expressions of this myth is the statement, "It isn't the same if I have to ask for it."

"If I have to tell you what I need or want," we say, "then somehow our relationship is lacking closeness, and I am disappointed by you. And if I have to ask you for what I want or need, it spoils it for me, so in many cases I would rather do without than ask."

Mary struggled with this. She was about to end her marriage with Tom because she was not willing to give up this myth. They had long, heated discussions about Tom's failure to anticipate Mary's needs. "If you can't anticipate what I need, then we aren't as close as I thought we were, and I'm not interested in being with you anymore."

Tom's response was one of frustration and helplessness. "I still do the nice things for her that I've always done," he said, "but she's gotten to where she simply expects me to do them, and they don't count anymore. I don't know what to do. I love her, but she doesn't believe me anymore. If I do something for her after she tells me, it causes worse problems than when I don't do it."

Myth #1 has become a barrier to the love and closeness Mary and Tom long for. They need to learn that no one can know what we need or want unless we tell him.

MYTH #2: SEX IS INTIMACY AND INTIMACY IS SEX

Physical intimacy and emotional intimacy are two different things. You can have intimacy without sex just as you can have sex without emotional intimacy. Yet many people still see the two as the same thing. In fact, we sometimes substitute sex for emotional intimacy without really knowing the difference.

Many times we believe this myth because we are afraid of affection. Affection makes us feel vulnerable, and when we feel vulnerable, we become afraid (there's that old barrier to intimacy again—fear). We may be afraid of vulnerability because we experienced it as a dangerous thing while we were growing up. Perhaps someone, even a parent, knew something personal about us, and used it to embarrass or somehow control us.

Physical intimacy and emotional intimacy are two different things.

The person who holds on to this myth feels reassured when the emotional aspects of a relationship are under stress that the relationship is stable if the couple has sex together. The husband or wife believing this myth wants to have sex after an argument in order to feel okay about the marriage. A more serious example is the partner who fears affection and vulnerability and, thus, uses sex to fulfill all of his or her emotional needs. Bill did this.

His major concern in his relationship with his wife was that their sex life had dwindled over the past years. "What's the national average for a married couple?" he asked me in front of his wife, Sue. Before I could answer, he answered his own question. "Two or three times a week! We're lucky if we can have sex once a month. In fact, I doubt if it's even that often."

Bill and Sue had been married only four years, and he foresaw a bleak future for their marriage. He had the statistics, he used Bible verses, he quoted previous counselors, and he even knew the average for the people in his office.

Sue finally spoke up in her own defense, saying that she was tired of simply being a sex object to Bill. She continued quickly before he could jump in and defend himself. "He wants to make love to me and then act like everything is okay. Then he's nice for a day, but he quickly gets mad if we don't have sex again. I'm tired of trying to appease him with sex. I want more out of our marriage than that."

As we talked, it was clear that Bill equated closeness with sex. In fact, he really didn't understand the distinction Sue was trying to make. "Sue told me it would help if I would just hold her without it leading to sex. I tried that, but it was never enough. She just used that to avoid sex," Bill said in his defense. "Now I guess I just ignore her most of the time. It's too painful otherwise. I mean, what's a man to do?"

Well, to start, Bill needed to give up the myth and begin to see sex as a response to closeness, not as a means to closeness.

MYTH #3: INTIMACY WILL GROW AUTOMATICALLY ONCE IT'S STARTED

There is nothing automatic about intimacy. It takes a lot of work. We are led into a false sense of security because the movement toward intimacy seems so easy in the early stages of a relationship.

At the beginning of a relationship, when the emotional distance between the couple is fairly wide, movement closer is easy. But as the distance between the two decreases emotionally, the risk of being known and the risk of being abandoned or smothered—and all of the fears associated with those risks—get stirred up and one or both partners want to run away. They can only get comfortable again by distancing themselves from one another. Two common, unsatisfying relationships develop: the pursuer-pursued cycle and the emotional blowup cycle.

The Pursuer-Pursued Cycle

In the pursuer-pursued cycle, one person wants more intimacy and "pursues" the other person in order to attain that closeness. At the same time, the other person (the pursued) feels the increased pressure and begins to back away from the relationship. But the pursued will back away only so far, because the fear of being abandoned kicks in.

Some couples develop this style of relating to the point where they can switch roles. The pursued suddenly stops, turns around, and starts pursuing. Almost as if on cue, the former pursuer begins to back away and becomes the pursued. Jan and I switched roles when we were first married, as we mentioned. I had been jealous when we were courting—I was the pursuer—but once we were married Jan became jealous of my time—she became the pursuer.

This is a "dance" couples perform. The rules of the dance require that the couple never get beyond a certain point in emotional closeness. It's as if they have a pole tied to their waists and they always stay at a predetermined distance from each other emotionally. The pole keeps them from getting either too close or too far away from each other.

The Emotional Blowup Cycle

Another style is when two people continue to move closer to each other, but as the distance between them decreases, the emotions "heat up" and one of the persons unconsciously creates a problem that leads to an emotional outburst, which pushes the couple apart.

You can imagine that this becomes increasingly frustrating. Usually, a couple will finally settle on some degree of emotional distance; this prevents further explosions but ends up being very unsatisfying. One woman said, "I'm afraid to spend too much time with my husband. If we get too close, either he picks a fight or I do." Some couples, however, continue this routine of moving closer, exploding, and then moving apart even after they have divorced and remarried someone else.

Couples who are building healthy relationships practice a variant of this last "dance." Instead of the explosion and the subsequent distancing, these couples find ways to resolve their conflict and to continue the building process. Healthy relationships follow a pattern of "waves and troughs," but with a somewhat steady overall increase in intimacy.

MYTH #4: LOVE AND BEHAVIOR ARE NOT RELATED

Often we assume that the other person can love us unconditionally. Marge was raised by a mother who constantly criticized Marge and her father. The whole time her mother was doing this, she was also affirming verbally how much she loved both her husband and her daughter. Over the years, Marge learned to filter out the criticism and focus only on the loving behaviors of her mother. "It doesn't matter what she says to me, I know she loves me."

Marge's husband, Ray, couldn't stand to be around Marge's mother, especially if any of her other family members were present. "I can't see how Marge can just overlook her mother's criticism. I think it's cruel and abusive. And now Marge is doing the same thing with me. I won't put up with it! If you can't help her, I'm out of here."

Marge sat there with a puzzled look on her face. "I don't see why he's so sensitive. He knows I love him. I wish you could help him." Marge accepted the myth that all that mattered in her relationship with Ray was that she loved him. She honestly could not understand why he was so sensitive.

Believing this myth is similar to believing the lie "sticks and stones will break my bones, but names will never hurt me." Many of us were taught this lie as children. We shouted those words at the bully, but it didn't really help then, and it doesn't help now. Names and words can wound us deeply.

Often we minimize criticism from a parent in order to hold on to the idea that that parent loved us. If we were to validate our experience of harshness and criticism, we would have difficulty believing that parent loved us. Since the injury took place when we were children, often when we were preschool age, logic and rationality were meaningless concepts to us at that age. So when we try to reason ourselves out of this myth, we must recognize that we are arguing with a part of ourselves that doesn't respond to reason.

Somehow, we need to see that when our behavior and our words do not match, we are giving a double message; usually, most people will hold on to the negative part of that message. Behavior does count, and so do the words we say. Love and behavior are related.

MYTH #5: PEOPLE WHO LOVE EACH OTHER CAN ACCEPT CONSTRUCTIVE CRITICISM

Being close does not mean we can begin the task of fixing the other person. This myth is a cousin to the previous one, but it focuses primarily on the area of "constructive" criticism. This is a myth because it works directly against intimacy.

As two people become closer emotionally, one of the big fears that begins to stir within them is the fear that once you really get to know me, you will not like me and will leave me. When one partner begins to try to help the other with "constructive" criticism, pointing out the other person's shortcomings or correcting his or her errors, the very thing we fear in a relationship is beginning to happen. The other person is noticing parts of me that he or she does not like. No one can experience this without becoming either angry or defensive or both.

You may protest that you are only trying to be helpful. However, unless the other person experiences the "constructive" criticism as helpful, it is not helpful. We often try to "help" in this way to take attention away from our own faults. We are unconsciously thinking, "If I can begin to help you improve yourself, maybe you won't notice the things that I need to improve in myself. As long as I can keep the focus on you, I'm off the hook." The one exception may be when the person has asked for the constructive help —maybe!

Over the years, my wife has been my best critic whenever I am speaking to a group. Many years ago I asked her to tell me what she thought about what I said and how I said it. Sometimes it was difficult for me to listen to what she offered, but since I really wanted to know what she had to say, it seldom was a barrier to our becoming closer. I say "seldom" because sometimes the constructive criticism was more than I wanted, and I reacted defensively. There is no room in any relationship for unrequested criticism, even if it is meant to be "constructive."

MYTH #6: SOMEONE EITHER LOVES ME OR NOT— AND THAT'S THAT!

This statement is one of the favorites of our day. I can't count the number of times someone has said to me, "I don't know why we're coming to counseling. I don't love him/her anymore, and there's nothing anyone can do about that. It's over!" Sometimes these people will work very hard to soften what they are saying. They will try to make the distinction between "loving" and "being in love." Rich had told me he still loved Kathy, but it was the kind of love he might have had for his sister. "I'm no longer 'in love' with her," he added emphatically. My standard response to these statements is "That's okay. It's not really an issue anyway."

Before I lose the couple's attention, I go on to ask, "How long has it been since either of you has behaved in a loving way to the other person?" Usually they say that it has been some time since anything like that has happened. No wonder the feelings of love have vanished.

Feelings of love usually wither and dry up in a sterile, dry environment. Love needs to be nurtured and fed. And when loving behaviors start to take place without pressure, the feelings of love are often rekindled.

When I explained these ideas to Rich, he thought for a while and then agreed to test my hypothesis. He and Kathy had been separated for more than six months by the time they came to see me, and they were starting to think about taking the next step toward divorce. But they had been married more than twenty-six years and felt they owed it to themselves and their family to talk to someone.

The feelings of love can come back if they are nurtured by the behaviors of love.

Rich and Kathy decided to test my theory over the next six months, so they started spending more time together. They were careful not to pressure each other, and they backed off when one of them felt unable to move ahead in their relationship. They also focused on doing caring things for each other.

As our sessions approached the one-year mark, it was obvious that there was not going to be a divorce. I asked Rich what he was feeling in the way of love. "It's not what I want it to be, but Kathy is more than a sister to me. I think you might be right."

The feelings of love can come back if they are nurtured by the behaviors of love.

69

MYTH #7: KNOWING EVERYTHING ABOUT THE OTHER PERSON IS AN ESSENTIAL PART OF INTIMACY

Honesty is a basic ingredient for intimacy. But we sometimes confuse honesty with knowing everything possible about the other person and revealing everything about ourselves. It is a myth that intimacy results from "telling everything," or being totally open. Our spouse may not be able to handle some of what we may disclose. Other times, our total disclosure of ourselves destroys the "mystery of personhood" that is so important to any intimate relationship.

What about when one partner betrays the other partner, as in having an affair? How much information is enough? Before we answer that question, we need to answer some other questions. Why, if we have been unfaithful, do we want to disclose this information? Are we seeking to be punished in order not to feel so guilty? Or why do we, if we have been betrayed, want to know everything the other person did? Will it really help in rebuilding the relationship? You can see that complex issues are involved here. Our efforts at knowing all about the other person, especially in this case, may not help us in our search for intimacy.

Bryan and Jill came to see me because Jill had had an affair. Initially, Bryan had no idea about what was going on; he only knew that something was wrong with the marriage. The couple had previously been to another counselor who, promoting total openness, asserted that Jill had to tell Bryan everything. Feeling guilty, Jill blurted out what had been going on and then collapsed in tears. Then, the counselor encouraged Jill to continue talking, sharing with Bryan every detail she could remember. He complimented Bryan for his forgiving spirit as Bryan listened to the entire confession. Jill and Bryan saw the counselor a few more times and felt their problem was resolved. Jill had confessed, and Bryan had forgiven.

That was over a year before they consulted me. Jill said that all was nice for about three months, and then Bryan started asking her for more details about the affair. Sometimes she told Bryan a little; at other times she insisted there was nothing else to say and she didn't want to talk about it. It didn't matter what she said or did, Bryan wasn't satisfied. He became obsessed with knowing more about what had happened, and now their problems went beyond the affair.

Bryan had found out the name of the other man during their earlier counseling sessions, so about six months before they came to see me, Bryan contacted him and pressured him into giving him some additional details. Bryan was convinced that if he could find out enough details he would understand why his wife had done this awful thing. But the more he found out, the more obsessed he was with knowing more, all in the name of "total knowing" or complete openness.

The couple's relationship deteriorated beyond anything they could have imagined. According to Jill, Bryan was always angry with her. Bryan countered with the fact that he couldn't trust her because she wouldn't be totally open with him. The more Bryan pressed, the more Jill withdrew. Their marriage was hanging together by a thin thread that seemed ready to break at any moment.

A moratorium had to be declared for Bryan and Jill to have any chance of healing in their relationship. It took some time to convince Bryan that he had more information than he knew how to handle and that any more information would only add more hurt, which he would eventually have to get over. It's been touch and go for some time, but as they spend time together and focus on where they are headed, they appear to be building some trust back into their relationship.

It's hard to know where to draw the line on full disclosure. The most important guideline you should use is to ask yourself, "Why do I want to know or share this information? What is the primary motivation?" If it's some principle of openness, or fully knowing each other—"We're going to be 100 percent honest in this relationship no matter what"—or a need to clear your own conscience at the other's expense, you'd better think again. Yes, we are to speak the truth, but it should always be tempered by love. Sometimes the total truth will destroy a relationship. Your partner may be like Bryan, who was haunted by the knowledge of Jill's relationship with another man. The ultimate test should be to ask yourself, "Will sharing this information build a greater sense of intimacy?" If not, total openness may not be appropriate.

MYTH #8: ROMANTIC LOVE IS ESSENTIAL FOR INTIMACY

Many people realize this is a myth, but they still are governed by it. Many of the books we read and the TV programs and movies we watch reinforce this myth. Yet the expectation that romantic love can and should sustain a true and satisfying intimate relationship puts an incredible strain on marriages in our culture today.

Romantic love has been described as sweaty palms, heart palpitations, obsessive thinking, and the belief that this relationship will meet all of our dreams. Think about the dichotomies in statements like "falling head over heels in love" and "I was swept off my feet." These are wonderful feelings, but no one can maintain these feelings over the years.

It's important to note here that we are not talking about romance and doing romantic things with each other. Loving interaction, as we will see later in the book, is an important ingredient in the building of closeness. But the idea that these romantic feelings can be sustained and can provide a foundation for an intimate marriage puts a strain on the relationship to the point where it undermines, rather than supports, intimacy.

Although the notion of romantic love can be dated at least as far back as the Song of Solomon in the Bible, our acceptance of it as an ideal goes back only about 800 years. Sometime during the late twelfth or early thirteenth century, Eleanor of Aquitaine and her daughter, the Countess Marie of Champagne, summoned a cleric, Andreas, to their palace at Poitiers and instructed him to prepare a manual on courtly love. The chaplain's book, *The Art of Courtly Love,* still influences the way men and women relate to each other.

One of Andreas's statements in his book gives a taste of the problem he created:

> We declare and we hold as firmly established that love cannot exert its powers between two people who are married to each other. For lovers give each other everything freely, under no compulsion of necessity, but married people are in duty bound to give in to each other's desires and deny themselves to each other in nothing.

Andreas's work was not written to describe marriage relationships. In fact, his book was designed to describe "courtly" love, illicit relationships between people in the promiscuous court of Aquitaine.

Andreas laid the foundation for the idealization of women, the importance of gentlemanly courtesy, and the emphasis on potent emotions, along with a sense of eternal oneness, undying devotion, and ecstasy. The part of his work we no longer give credibility to in our daily lives is the "agony of a love that is unfulfilled." Andreas taught that for love to be "true" love, it had to be incomplete. While two people might be passionately in love, their prior commitments to their marital partners precluded them from ever acting upon this love. Their love was expressed at a distance and was idealized; romantic love could be maintained only by distance.

The writings of Keats, Dante, and Shakespeare; the operas of Wagner; and movies like *Gone with the Wind* and *Love Story* have all shown the impact of Andreas's work. Our desire to marry out of passion is an expression of his thought, but we have contaminated his work by believing that this passion can be maintained throughout marriage. In the long run, however, intimacy and closeness are related to romance, but really have little to do with the idea of romantic love.

MYTH #9: THE RELATIONSHIP CAN GROW ONLY WHEN WE FEEL GOOD ABOUT EACH OTHER

Again, the opposite of this statement is true. A relationship will grow only as we are able to learn to work through those times when we really don't feel like doing the things that make relationships work. One of the popular songs of not too long ago said, "Loving you is easy because you're beautiful." There is no verse on what to do "when loving you is difficult because right now you look ugly to me or I feel ugly." But that's when healthy relationships really get to work.

There are two important aspects to love. One is the feeling and emotion of love. The second aspect to love goes beyond feelings and emotions to commitment: Love is also a decision.

When Jesus told His disciples that He was giving them a new commandment, "Love each other as I have loved you," He was not talking about a feeling or an emotion. You cannot demand feelings or emotions. But you can demand a decision.

When someone says he or she no longer loves another person, I often ask when he or she decided to stop loving that person. Usually there was a point at which that decision was made. That decision can be reversed, and that's where the commitment part of love comes into focus. Commitment keeps us doing the behaviors of love even when we don't feel like it. And when we act this way, the feelings and emotions of love can and do return.

These myths about intimacy all work as barriers to our finding the closeness we really long for. As you've read through this chapter it may appear to be very clear that these are in fact myths. But they still attract us. In order to break the hold the myths may still have on us, we need to understand how our personalities affect our ability to love and be loved, which we discuss in the second part of our book, *The Intimacy Factor*.

Learning the Language of Love

*H*ow do I express love?"
"How do I learn the lan-
guage of love?"

*Those are two questions that many of us don't even know how
to verbalize, let alone address. Sometimes we feel at a loss to say
and do the things that would let our spouse know how we really
feel. Through my experience as host of a Christian radio talk show
and as a pastor and counselor, I have heard the frustration and
helplessness of couples who have a tough time communicating
their love to one another, even after years of relatively happy marriage. It doesn't have to take a lifetime together to learn how to say
"I love you" in a way that your partner understands. I trust that this
chapter combined from two chapters in* Love: No Strings Attached

"Learning the Language of Love" is an adaptation of "How Do I Express Love?" and "How Do
I Learn the Language of Love?" taken from *Love: No Strings Attached*, Rich Buhler (1990).

can be a help in breaking down the "love language" barriers that keep us from enjoying real intimacy.

—Rich Buhler
Love: No Strings Attached

In fifteen years of pastoral counseling, I have sat across the desk from or shared a cup of coffee with a lot of people who are going through tough times. Sometimes it is a husband and a wife who are finally venting years of resentment. Often they are separated or getting a divorce. Other times it is a kind of in-house warfare between parents and children.

I think I've probably dealt with almost every category of conflict that can exist between people, and early in my experience I noticed something fascinating: even when people are fighting and scrapping and threatening to disown each other, love is lurking down inside of them.

I'll never forget two people whom I will call Jack and Mary. Late one night, a mutual friend of theirs had called me and asked if I would consider talking with them. This was the second marriage for both Jack and Mary, and they had been married to each other for sixteen years.

They arrived at my office showing signs of their long battle. Jack was the rough-and-tough and hard-to-bluff type. He kept his jaw clenched and had a tendency to look at the floor as he talked. Mary seemed numb. She looked as if she had completely fallen to pieces but had been hastily thrown together for our meeting.

The more we talked the more I realized that these two people genuinely loved each other. Like most of us, each had the desire to be loved and to be loving, to have a happy home, to be married to a happy mate.

I looked at Jack and said, "If you came home one evening and found the house on fire and you knew that Mary was inside, would you risk your life trying to get her out?"

Admittedly, it was a terribly emotional question, which measured more Jack's attitude about life and death than his feelings about his wife, but the inquiry produced some interesting results. Jack fidgeted in his chair, looked at me, looked at the floor, glanced at Mary, and then started trembling. He wrestled to hold his emotions, but his moist eyes and the tears that began running down his cheeks gave an indication of his answer.

I turned to Mary. "Mary, if you came home and found the house on fire, would you risk your life trying to get Jack to safety?"

With a gesture of mock disgust, Mary reached over and grasped Jack's hand. They both sat there, not quite knowing what else to say. They'd die for one another. (They just couldn't *live* with one another!) They both knew it. They had founded their marriage in love; both of them had committed themselves to love; and even in this disintegrating stage of their marriage, each loved the other. But the more I talked with them the more obvious it was that the love they felt for one another had never been truly and distinctively expressed. Their problem was not a lack of love. It was, in part, a lack of expression of love.

THE LANGUAGE OF LOVE

Unfortunately, our most sincere attempts to express love often don't succeed. One of the reasons can be found in looking at what I call "the language of love."

The language of love consists of all the ways that a person has discovered for expressing love. We learn that language from our homes, from our friends, from watching other people, from television, from films, from newspapers, books, and magazines. Anytime we have either experienced what we think is love or have seen it in the lives of others or have heard stories about it, we have added to our language of love.

Each of us has his or her own uniquely developed language of love. If you and the person you married were born on the same day in the same hospital, lived next door to one another in the same city, attended the same schools and church, and graduated from the same college, you would still be like two people from foreign countries who speak different languages. Even children who grow up in the same family come away with their own, unique languages of giving and receiving love.

> *Each of us has his or her own uniquely
> developed language of love.*

Unfortunately, few of us realize this language barrier. Since we've spent a lifetime developing a language of love, we tend to think that everyone in the world speaks the same language— ours. Everyone, that is, except the person we married!

I once counseled a couple I'll call Dan and Sue, who spent a weekend together at a marriage retreat where I was the guest speaker. The first night I arrived, one of the leaders of the group said he hoped there would be an opportunity for me to talk with them, because he felt they were having some real problems.

The next morning Dan and Sue approached me and asked to get together during the afternoon break. They had been married fifteen years, had three children, and were committed Christians, but they were going through a tough time in their marriage.

As we talked it was apparent to me that they loved one another and wanted to make a go of their marriage. They had accumulated a lot of resentment, however, and were considering a separation.

I asked Sue that important question, "How do you express your love to Dan? What little things do you do to say you care?"

She glanced at the other end of the long couch where Dan was sitting, then turned to me and said, "I like flowers and I think they are romantic. From time to time I'll go out in the garden, cut a rose, put it into a special vase, and put it on his nightstand." Then she added, "Sometimes that's my way of telling him that I'd like to make love."

"Sue, you're a romantic!" I told her. "That's a wonderful and tender thing to do."

Then I turned to Dan. "What does that mean to you, Dan?"

"Nothing," he replied.

I thought Sue was going to jump across the couch and claw his eyes out!

"What did you think whenever you saw a flower pop up on your nightstand?" I asked.

"I just thought it meant Sue liked flowers. I didn't know."

Dan was looking a bit sheepish by now. Yet he was not the only one who misunderstood his partner's language of love.

"How do you express your love to Sue?" I asked Dan. "What do you do to say that you care?"

Before Dan could answer, Sue looked at him with an "I-know-what-you're-going-to-say-and-I'm-not-going-to-like-it" look.

Dan quietly shared a story that I did not expect to hear. Sue was a professional person and worked hard; sometimes he felt bad about all the pressures that were upon her as a working wife and mother. Whenever Sue was away for the evening or had gone to bed early, Dan would scour the house, pick up all the dirty laundry, put it through the washing machine, transfer it to the dryer, and eventually fold it and put each piece of clothing in its rightful place.

It was one of the most practical ways of expressing love and care I had ever heard. "Dan, if we filled an arena with twenty thousand women, they would mob you in admiration for being the kind of man who did not come up with something corny as a way of expressing love."

Sue, however, was so flushed with anger that I could have cooked an egg on her forehead. Her frustration obviously revealed one key to their problems.

"Tell me how you feel about that," I asked her.

Sue began by telling me how capably she had fulfilled her responsibilities as a wife and mother until a few years ago when she had suffered a serious back injury and had to have surgery. She had spent almost a year in traction, completely immobilized. The doctors feared at times that she would never walk again.

The whole experience had been an emotional and painful one, she said, "But one of the hardest parts was lying in bed and being cared for by others. Day after day, month after month, I had to watch other people, family members and volunteers, take care of my children. At my worst moments I felt that I would never be needed in my home again. My family had learned to live without me."

For the past several months Sue had shown encouraging signs of recovery. Although she was not yet working, she was able to get out of bed and do a few things around the house. Two of the chores she enjoyed most were doing the dishes and, you guessed it, washing the clothes. Just doing these two things proved to her that she was recovering physically and made her feel useful as a wife and mother. She appreciated what Dan was trying to do for her, but at this stage in her life it was almost an act of thievery. "I've tried to explain this to Dan," Sue said, "but he never seems to hear what I'm saying." Here was a classic example of how one person's act of love can end up putting another person in a prison.

Love cannot be truly expressed unless we first understand the other person's language of love. I hate to pick on the husbands, but I've got to tell another classic story of the breakdown in the language of love.

One person's act of love can end up putting another person in a prison.

Several years ago I was a staff member at a large church. Shirley, one of the older women, came to me two or three times to talk about some pressures in her marriage and in her relationship with her grown children. One afternoon she said casually that in more than thirty years of marriage her husband, David, had not bought her a birthday present, a Christmas present, or an anniversary present.

I couldn't believe it.

I interrupted what she was about to say next and asked, "How does that make you feel?"

Her eyes filled with tears, and for the next several minutes, she let decades of pain and resentment flow out.

I couldn't help thinking to myself, *What a jerk her husband must be never to give any gifts on special occasions.* He was not a Christian or a churchgoer so I'd never met him, but from afar I decided not to like him!

About a year later I got a call from the husband who asked if he could make an appointment to talk with me. He said that he knew his wife had been talking with me and that he would like to do the same.

A part of our time together was spent talking about his relationship with his wife. It was natural for me to ask him my usual question and at the same time satisfy my curiosity about his unusual attitude toward gift-giving. "How do you show your love for your wife? Do you give her gifts?"

Guess what? He had a good explanation.

The man had been reared in a family where there was a lot of abuse. "Everybody spent most of their time either fighting with or enduring one another," he said. "Then when Christmas or birthdays came around we had to go through the ritual of buying gifts which, to me, seemed meaningless. I vowed that I would never give gifts just because they were expected. I wanted to give a gift when it would really mean that I cared." He had given hundreds of gifts to his wife through the years, but none of them had corresponded with Christmas or birthdays or anniversaries.

I had to admire a person who came into his marriage committed to experiencing something more real than his own childhood. Nevertheless he was wrong not to consider his wife's language of love. She had some measure of appreciation for his sincere giving, but according to her language, she was still starving for love. If this man had really wanted her to feel his love, he needed to know her language of love and use it to express his love.

There's a footnote to this story, by the way. Not only did David fall completely short of Shirley's language of love in terms of the occasions for gift-giving, but he also blew it when it came to the kinds of gifts he gave.

Shirley wanted to receive pretty cards and decorative ceramics. David didn't see much value in those "trinkets," however. He wanted to express his caring in ways that really "counted." Because he had suffered poverty as a child, this successful business-man felt that the most important thing he could provide for his wife was financial security. *Surely,* he thought, *she would appreciate that more than trinkets.* So whenever he felt like telling her of his love, he would bring home certificates of gold futures or stock options. His wife may have sat out a lot of Christmases, but she was hot stuff on the stock market!

Once again there was an element of logic and love in what he had done, but his motive wasn't matching his wife's expectations. That left her frustrated. Whenever she tried to explain how she felt, he thought she was accusing him of not loving her so he would defend his actions. Their discussions turned into arguments before they ever understood what the other was saying.

During the first years of our own marriage my wife, Linda, would occasionally tell me how much it meant to her for me to continue to observe some of the etiquette of courting. For instance, if we were getting into the car, she wanted me to take the trouble to go over to her side of the car and open the door for her. If you had asked me if I knew that was important to her, I would have answered, "Yes." If you had asked me how high on her list of ways of expressing love it was, I would have said, "Oh, about number 32."

That's because it was about that low on my own list. If you would have told me that opening the car door for her was *third* on my wife's list of priorities, I would have told you to get lost. After all, I knew my wife better than you. But it was third on her list!

I was blown away when I first learned that. It meant that if I wanted to express my love and care in a way that was important to her, a simple act like opening the car door would do it.

The sad truth is that at that time I seldom expressed my love in this way. What would I do? I'd call her from work saying, "Get a babysitter. I'm taking you out for dinner tonight."

Every girl likes to be taken out to dinner, right? Every girl likes to do something spontaneous and goofy, right? Oh, how lucky I considered her to be that her husband would brighten her evening by substituting a cozy little table for two for the family dinner table. How I grieved for all the unlucky women who did not have a sensitive and fun-loving husband like me.

And how Linda loathed it all!

After several years of this, Linda finally broke the news that although she occasionally enjoyed going out for a nice meal, and there were times when she considered that romantic, she basically didn't like dropping everything on the spur of the moment and leaving the kids in disarray.

I think all these stories are fairly self-explanatory. Each of us has a language of love that is unique, distinct. We use it to express love to others, and we expect others to use it to express love to us. When that doesn't happen we fear that love may have been lost.

But what if we feel that we are illiterate when it comes to speaking the language of love? Is there hope?

"HOW DO I LEARN THE LANGUAGE OF LOVE?"

It is a victorious day in our lives when we come to realize that our language of love is not the only one in the universe and that the person we love may be tuned in to a completely different frequency. However, that insight is just the beginning. Once I've acknowledged that my language of love and another person's language are different, what do I do about it? How can I learn another person's language of love, and how can I teach mine to another person?

The simple answer is "Ask!"

The only way we're going to find out what hidden expectations lurk in the hearts of those we love is to sit down and talk about them. It's fascinating, though, how many obstacles can stand in the way of such a conversation. One of these I've already mentioned. Because each of us has spent a lifetime developing a language of love from many sources, we miss the fact that ours is a relatively unknown language. That's why it's so easy to have the mistaken feeling that there is an accepted, authorized, universal language of love that every "normal" person speaks and understands.

It's a lonely feeling, then, if after several months or years of marriage, we reluctantly come to the conclusion that our spouse somehow missed out on the language lessons. We married a functional illiterate when it comes to expressing love. We don't want to talk about the "little" expectations we've had and the hurt that has resulted from the things our mate doesn't do to reinforce our love because, in our mind, they shouldn't have to be talked about.

It's easy to have the feeling that "If he were really a wise, sensitive husband, then he would just *know*. Nobody should have to tell him." Or, "If she were really 'tuned in' to men, then she'd respond the way I want."

We act as though talking about these things will somehow pop the bubble. The magic will be gone. We can make the choice not to open up our hearts if we want to, but we'll also be making the choice to continue living in the isolation of our disappointment and the resentment that accompanies it. What that amounts to is a shifting of responsibility. Instead of fuming over the fact that what we had hoped would happen didn't happen and holding the person who failed to meet our expectations responsible, we need to accept responsibility for our own unhappiness. We must realize that we are the only ones who can change the situation by communicating to the other person how we're feeling and what specifically can be done about it.

An experience in my own growing-up years is a simple example of what I'm talking about. One year my birthday happened to fall during the week that a bunch of us kids were at summer camp. I didn't think much about it until we sang "Happy Birthday" to one of the campers one morning at breakfast. Suddenly it struck me that in just two days it would be my own birthday, and I was fairly sure that nobody in the whole camp knew it. The more I thought about it the sadder I got.

The morning of my birthday I got up without fanfare and went through the routine of getting ready for breakfast. But on the inside I was having an absolute pity party. Here I was in the midst of total strangers, far away from home on my special day, and everyone here thought this day was the same as any other.

As I took my shower I hoped that people might really know it was my birthday. They weren't saying anything, I thought, because they were going to surprise me at breakfast.

No such luck. Breakfast that morning was the same as usual.

Maybe, I thought, *there will be a miracle. Maybe one of the counselors will have a vision saying, "Today is Rich Buhler's birthday. Be kind to him." Or maybe somebody in the office will suddenly and without explanation have the urge to go through the registration forms and notice my birth date. He or she will say to the other staff members, "Here's a poor little camper who is having a birthday today. Let's do something special for him." Or perhaps my parents are going to surprise me at dinner with a cake and some gifts they've sent from home!*

I didn't want to tell anybody. That wouldn't be right. If I told somebody it was my birthday, then they might feel obligated to say or do something. I would be arranging my own party.

By midafternoon when we were playing baseball, I couldn't stand it anymore. I let it slip to one of my teammates that it was my birthday. Within thirty seconds the whole playing field was filled with the familiar strains of "Happy Birthday." That night the campers sang to me at supper. I had learned an important lesson. I couldn't expect people around me to be mind readers, and I couldn't hold the world accountable for not knowing what I felt or what would help me feel better.

Each of us needs to realize that we must communicate our expectations effectively to those who are in the best position to respond to them.

For married couples, I recommend a valuable project, which will help each person first to discover his or her own language of love and then to share it with the other.

IDENTIFYING THE LANGUAGE OF LOVE

Initially, each person spends some time alone, putting together two separate lists. The first: The Ways I Expect to Receive Love. The second: The Ways I Communicate Love.

When you are making lists remember that little things mean a lot. Some of the greatest delight comes from soft, quiet, and almost invisible expressions of love. And some of the deepest pain results from the lack of these same little things. I've seen many couples' lists, and some of the priority items include things like a simple glance across the room or a surprise phone call at work or a hug in the middle of the night or being thoughtful enough to use deodorant before coming to bed. You may need to spend several days occasionally going back to your lists and adding anything else that comes to mind.

Once your lists are complete, go through each list and as best as possible rank each item in order of importance. What is most important to you? Second most important?

Most husbands and wives are usually aware of something that the other considers to be an expression of love. But I find that couples are constantly stunned to find out, by comparing and ranking, how important some of those things are to one another.

After you and your mate have done this, sit down and compare your lists, taking note of the top five or ten items on your husband's or wife's list. The next time your heart is in the mood to say "I love you," consider one of those ways.

A RADIO SURVEY

I once asked the persons in my radio audience to send me some examples of their own languages of love. I received more than fifteen hundred responses from both men and women, and the results were interesting.

The women appreciated things like:

My husband's bragging about me to friends.✓
His remembering a special day.
His calling from work to say "I love you."✓

His washing the dishes for me. ✓
His taking me for a special night out.
His preparing a special meal so I don't have to. ✓
His looking at me across the room at a party. ✓
His sending me a "Peanuts" card.
His complimenting me on my appearance. ✓
His realizing when I need space.

The men appreciated:

My wife's giving me a surprise in my lunch.
Her taking interest in my hobbies.
Her accepting my advice.
Her initiating sex.
Her defending my reputation.
Her rubbing my feet.

The Most Frequent Responses

There were hundreds of unique expressions, some of which occurred only once in fifteen hundred responses. For the sake of simplicity we went through the lists and arranged the responses in broad categories, such as verbal expression of love, physical expression of love (hugs and kisses), gifts, being listened to, sex, unconditional acceptance.

We were interested in seeing how often certain items occurred no matter how high or low they were on a person's list. Women mentioned hugs and kisses more than any other category; being listened to the next most often. (I've taken surveys during dozens of marriage conferences, and this has consistently been an important hunger among wives.) The third most often listed category was verbal expression of love.

The most frequently mentioned category for the men was the same as for the women: the expression of love through hugs and kisses. The second most often mentioned item for men was unconditional acceptance. (That, too, is consistent with what I have seen in similar surveys among married couples. The women have the hunger to be heard, to be taken seriously, and the men have the hunger to be accepted just as they are.)

The Top Priorities

Next, we went through the fifteen hundred responses and determined how important, on the average, various categories were. How high in men's and women's priorities did particular items rank?

Among women, the overall highest ranking category was unconditional acceptance. Among men, the highest ranking was verbal expression of love. Sex, interestingly, ranked exactly the same on both men's and women's lists—the fifth most important category out of the ten that we asked them to rate.

This survey is far from scientific, but it is interesting. I present it in order to give some examples of the languages of love and categories that are important. What you or your mate considers important may not resemble anything on this list. It is a mistake to say, "This is the way 'women' are" or, "This is the way 'men' are." You need to determine, "This is the way my wife is" or, "This is the way my husband is." Don't assume that you know!

Sex, . . . ranked exactly the same on both men's and women's lists—the fifth . . . out of the ten.

I am often asked, "What if my mate won't participate in this kind of project?"

My answer is, "Don't let that stop you from making lists of your own language of love." You will benefit from putting serious thought into the ways that you express love or should express love. You may decide to go ahead and share your lists with your mate anyway. Also, it will be valuable to realize that your mate does have a language of love, even if you have to speculate what it is.

"I always viewed my husband as an unexpressive and unaffectionate person," one woman once told me. "Your discussion about the language of love made me realize that he does a lot of things which are probably his own way of saying that he cares, but I've never viewed them as that."

The Language of Christmas

Each of us has other languages in our lives that are just as important for us to learn and to know about one another.

For example, each of us has our own language of Christmas. For me, Christmas is not Christmas without a fluffy white Christmas tree with color-coordinated decorations. However, for my wife, Christmas is a freshly cut green tree with traditional decorations. When we first married, we had to come to grips with the fact that each of us had spent our lives developing completely different Christmas customs. In her home Christmas gifts were simple, practical, and inexpensive. In my home the gifts were never lavish but they were of a different variety from that to which she was accustomed. In her home the "stockings were all hung by the chimney with care," and on Christmas morning there were gifts from Santa Claus. In my home we didn't hang Christmas stockings, and we didn't pretend that Santa was real. So Linda and I had some adjusting to do.

The Language of Sex

Each of us also has a unique language of sex. Both men and women commonly come into their marriage expecting the sexual relationship to be everything they've always dreamed and their mate to fit right into their fantasies. When that doesn't happen, many spouses feel isolated, as though they were cursed with a partner who just didn't attend the same school when it came to sex. Couples need to talk openly about their physical relationship, to know one another's language of sex, and to review together some of what has contributed to each language.

I recall counseling with a young man I'll call Ralph. He was in his late twenties and had been married for about six years. His wife had urged him to talk with me. "She feels that things could be better in our sexual relationship," Ralph said, "and we've had so much conflict over the subject that I finally agreed to talk with someone about it."

I had compiled a questionnaire on the language of sex, which I used for a couples conference. I gave copies to Ralph and asked him and his wife to fill it out and then to discuss it together.

"We've discovered some amazing things," Ralph told me later. "I guess I was influenced by things I heard my mother say when I was growing up. I actually had the impression that women just don't enjoy sex very much. I was so convinced of that, I would never really allow a free relationship with my wife. I was always afraid of doing something to turn her off, so I went the other direction and did very little at all."

Ralph said their sex life had been characterized by very brief sexual encounters, which left his wife feeling frustrated and wondering why her husband didn't want to invest more time in their physical relationship. "She started feeling like she wasn't attractive to me," Ralph said. In addition, Ralph remembered some childhood sexual experiences that had left him feeling confused and dirty and would require some good counseling to overcome. Our discussions helped Ralph realize that his reluctance toward sex with his wife was not only because of how he thought she felt, but also because of some hindrances in his own heart. Over a period of time both Ralph and his wife were able to explore the hunger each of them had to share sexually and to make one another aware of their languages of sex.

The Language of Lifestyle

There are also languages of lifestyle. For example, I have never been too particular about the kind of house I live in. I'd make a great missionary!

Linda, on the other hand, has a language of lifestyle in which the kind of house we live in makes a big difference. The kitchen window has to be in just the right place, the house has to be facing the right direction, the number of walls has to be in the right proportion to the number of windows, and so on.

Early in our marriage when we would look at a house to rent, I would be willing to take almost anything, but she would be more fussy and that used to frustrate me. I even arrogantly considered it to be a spiritual problem on her part. I'd think to myself, *If only she were flexible and able to accept whatever the Lord gives us.* The truth is, however, that she and I have two different languages when it comes to renting or buying a house. Frankly, hers is a lot more practical than mine. When I finally realized that this difference between us was not the result of a deficiency on her part, it saved a lot of heartache.

In my lifestyle gadgets are important. If it beeps and runs on batteries, I'll probably like it. I'm into computers, electronics, and airplanes. Linda doesn't understand my interest in gadgets and has sometimes even resented it.

She, on the other hand, loves to shop in fabric stores. I don't know how anyone can go into a store where there are four hundred bolts of cloth and choose which one to buy, but Linda loves it. She knows the location of every fabric store within forty miles of our house.

When we both realized how important fabrics and gadgets were to each other, we tried to understand one another's interests. In fact, I now like fabric stores because she loves them so much. And she has actually bought me a few gadgets as gifts!

It is vital that each of us steps outside our own view of things and realizes that the people we love sometimes see things differently. It *is* an act of love to take the time to learn another person's language and to use that knowledge to develop a better relationship. Instead of a couple's spending their lives together speaking Swiss and German to each other, they will develop their own new language, just as the Swiss developed a special form of German, Swiss German, which has been their unique language for centuries.

Saying to your husband, "I like you," is very different from saying, "I love you," but every bit as important.
—Patrick and Connie Lawrence
Your 30-Day Journey to
Being a Great Wife

Chapter

9

Communication

Dianne and I originally wrote this chapter for a book for engaged couples, Getting Ready for Marriage Workbook. But whether you are getting married or have been married fifty years, the importance of good communication never diminishes. And it's never too late to begin to learn to communicate with your spouse.
—Jerry D. Hardin and Dianne C. Sloan
Getting Ready for Marriage

Good communication is the art of sending and receiving a clear message. We are all continuously sending and receiving messages to and from one another. Even when we don't talk or write, we are sending a message that we want a separation from the other person. It is impossible not to communicate, but we can communicate poorly.

"Communication" is taken from *Getting Ready for Marriage Workbook*, Jerry D. Hardin and Dianne C. Sloan (1992).

The art of good communication involves the sender, the receiver, and a clear message. How many times do we experience problems because we misinterpret the messages sent to us?

You and your fiancé have learned to communicate from your families. You communicate differently because your families are different. For you and your spouse-to-be to enjoy life and grow together, you must be able to send the messages you mean and understand the messages you receive.

The most important factor in a good marriage is good communication. While finances, sex, or other issues may be the topic of heated discussions, marital dissatisfactions, and even breakups, *the inability of a couple to communicate and find a solution is the root of the problem.* So how can you and your partner communicate more effectively?

First, consider how you send a clear message. The words you use, the way you say them, and your body language add up to the total message you send someone. Communication experts have shown that only 7 percent of our message is sent from the words we say. Thirty-five percent of our message comes from our tone of voice, and the remaining 58 percent of our message is sent through our body—eye contact, facial expressions, the shrug of our shoulders.

Many times one or more parts of our message differ—our words don't match our tone of voice or our body language, so the receiver of our message becomes confused. When confused, the receiver tends to hear the nonverbal communication above all other messages. Try this experiment with your spouse-to-be. Take one of your favorite phrases, such as "Boy, do I really love you!" Then say it to each other a few times, using a different tone of voice and body expression each time. Confusing? Probably. This happens frequently in our daily communication!

Only 7 percent of our message is sent from the words we say.

A clear message comes out of your being aware of what you are thinking and feeling and being able to share that information with your partner. This clear sharing of yourself leads to a happier, healthier relationship. Here are five key steps to better communication between you and your spouse-to-be.

1. TAKE TIME FOR ONE ANOTHER

In this busy world, you will find more and more areas of life demanding your time. It is not uncommon to make time or take time for less important commitments than sharing with the most important person in your life, your spouse-to-be.

You probably will spend more quality time sharing during your courtship than you will after your marriage. We frequently hear couples in marriage counseling say, "I am just being taken for granted." What they are really saying is, "I do not feel valued when you do not ask me what I think or how I feel." It is important to begin now setting aside a regular time for the two of you to listen to and share with one another.

2. SPEAK FOR YOURSELF

Be aware of your own thoughts and feelings and be responsible for communicating those to each other. No one can speak for you, except you! Use "I" messages: "I feel sad because"; "I think we need to take this approach because"; "I am really hurting right now"; "Let me tell you how I see this situation"; "This is how I feel."

Communication gets cloudy when you begin to tell your fiancé what he thinks and feels or how she *should* think and feel. This frequently creates a defensive reaction from your partner if he or she perceives your interpretation as unfair accusation. Your partner could also perceive the interpretation in other ways—i.e., as not caring enough to listen.

Good communication comes from clearly expressing your own feelings and thoughts to each other in words, tone of voice, body language, or actions. All of these can communicate your feelings and thoughts. Just remember, speak only for yourself.

3. UNDERSTAND THAT YOUR PARTNER'S PERCEPTIONS ARE DIFFERENT FROM YOURS

You will never see everything exactly the same way because you come from different families and different ways of life. *Different* does not mean "wrong"; it does not mean "bad"; it just means "different." Sometimes you may have to agree to disagree. You may have to say, "Well, I guess we really see that differently."

It is okay to see life differently at times. In fact, it would be unusual if you didn't. Good communication comes when you value and take the time to understand your differences. When you respect the perceptions of your fiancé, you are saying, "Who you are and what you think is important to me." Couples who value one another will grow through teaching and learning from each other. Those who do not value the other's perceptions are saying, "You have nothing to teach me; my way is always right."

Different does not mean "wrong"; it does not mean "bad"; it just means "different."

Poor communication is frequently the result of our trying to prove our rightness. Ask yourself if you would rather be right or be happy. Sometimes you can't have both. If you are *not* interested in hearing your fiancé's point of view, you simply don't value what he or she thinks and feels.

4. REALLY LISTEN

Listen—not only to what is being said, but to the total message being sent. Remember, less than half of your message is communicated verbally, through words and tone of voice. It is important to listen to the nonverbal body messages as well, for those messages will frequently give you clues as to how your partner is *feeling*. At this stage in your relationship, you are probably very attuned to the nonverbal messages of your fiancé. After you marry you will need to work at staying as tuned in, for over time we have a tendency to begin assuming we know what our mates are thinking and feeling.

Take a step back and think about the ways you listen to one another. Most of us listen in three basic ways: attentive listening, passive listening, or selective listening.

Attentive listening is giving your full attention to someone. You not only listen to what is being said, but are aware of how it is said—the person's tone of voice and body. You are listening to the total message the other person is sending. You value what the other person is saying.

When you listen attentively, the stage is set for good communication to take place. You and your spouse, each, are given time to share fully your thoughts and feelings. You listen to the whole message instead of try to plan what you are going to say when it is your turn to speak. Attentive listening is one of the most difficult, yet necessary, elements of the communication process. It takes practice, patience, and respect for what your spouse-to-be has to say.

A *passive listener* may hear the words being spoken but not tune in to the rest of the message, thus missing most of it! There is little value placed upon what is being said or for the person who is speaking. When your attention is on T.V., the newspaper, or other things, you are not able to communicate effectively. If your spouse-to-be or you are involved in another activity, it is not a good time to talk, and you will need to set a time aside when you both can devote yourselves to the discussion.

We are all, at times, *selective* in our *listening*. We hear only what we want to hear and filter out the rest. During courtship you are more apt to screen out unwanted words or information. You may put little or no importance on certain things being said and a great deal of value on other words or phrases.

Selective listening has a similar effect to putting blinders around your eyes. An interesting exercise in selective listening would be to ask five to ten people who had just listened to the same speech what the speaker said. Chances are each person heard the speaker a little differently. Each person may have tuned out those things that were difficult or painful to hear. This is selective listening.

If you find yourselves repeatedly struggling with one or both of you hearing only a portion of what the other person is saying, stop and take time to find the root of the selective listening. That will help you to begin opening up your communication process.

5. CHECK OUT WHAT YOUR PARTNER IS SAYING

This process is accomplished by letting your partner know what you heard him say and asking if you correctly understood it. This allows your fiancé to correct any misunderstandings. Checking out reduces mind reading and misinterpretation—a trap many couples fall into. Remember, you can only speak for yourself. If you mind read, you are speaking for your partner! Checking out also lets the other person know you have been listening attentively and that you value him or her enough to make sure you understand what is being discussed.

Time, honesty, clarity, respect, value, and love for one another will help you and your spouse-to-be in the art of communication. Communication is a skill that can be learned and improved, but it takes time.

Remember when you were learning to drive a car. You probably had a few jerky starts and stops or fumbles as you learned, and you really had to think about what you were doing. Learning to communicate in healthy, effective ways takes time, practice, and a lot of patience. Couples who have healthy, happy, well-functioning relationships have taken the time to develop good communication skills. Do you value your spouse-to-be and what she has to say? Does he value your views? Do you take time to share your thoughts and feelings? What kind of listener are you: attentive, passive, selective, or a combination of all three? How would you presently rate your communication skills as a couple? Great? Average? Improvement needed?

The choice is yours, and the choice you make will affect the type of marriage you will have.

Chapter

Forgiveness:
The Divine Absurdity

*I*t's a truism that marriages must have communication, that husbands and wives must learn to talk honestly with one another and to listen well. A truism: almost no one is ignorant of the need. A truism: though people think, when they utter the word *communication,* they've delivered themselves of something profound; they have in fact said something nearly meaningless. Of course communication is necessary. Likewise, it's necessary to know how to handle a steering wheel before driving a car. But drunks know how to handle steering wheels; and drunks drive cars—into other people. And certain teenagers are both skilled with the wheel and rash with the car.

The most crucial issue in a marriage is not *that* a couple communicate, but *what* they communicate.

"Forgiveness: The Divine Absurdity" is an adaptation of "What Kind of Relationship Is Marriage Meant to Be? The Divine Ideal" and "What Is Forgiveness? The Divine Absurdity" from *As for Me and My House,* Walter Wangerin, Jr. (1990).

Sadly, humanity is sinful and self-centered. One may communicate very well his personal desires and satisfy himself that he's done the right thing, when in fact he's just made unreasonable demands upon his wife. Or she may communicate with exceptional facility her anger—dropping him to the floor with a verbal bullet. "We had a good talk. We got it all out into the open." Yes, and you stunned each other in the process. "I told her what this marriage needed. I told her coolly, carefully, and clearly. Things will change now." But change—if "what this marriage needs" is no more than what you *think* it needs, or what *you* need—may be that all the griefs intensify. And this may bewilder you, that good communication should have such distressing consequence.

Let there be communication, indeed.

But let the thing communicated be *forgiveness*.

THE DIVINE ABSURDITY

How long can a silence last? Long. How long could Thanne continue not talking to me—not talking, at least, of matters crucial to our spirits and our relationship? Long. Thanne had a gift for silences. And after the night when I found her awake I suffered a bewildered misery.

Oh, I was such a fool in those days. But I was working blind. What could I do, if she wouldn't talk to me?

No: I was a *fool* in those days. I did not see that even my efforts at healing hurt her. Well, I wasn't looking at these present efforts, only at past actions to find the fault; but, in fact, the fault was consistently there, in me, in all that I was doing. Therefore, I kept making things worse for all my good intentions. I was a walking fault!

At nights she always went to bed before I did. When I came to the bedroom, carefully shading the light from her eyes, doing everything possible to care for her, I always found her turned away, curled tight on her side, at the very edge of the bed. Her cheek was the only flesh I saw, and the corner of her eye—closed. Was she sleeping? I didn't know. I was scared to ask, scared to wake her if she was, and scared she wouldn't answer if she wasn't. I got under covers cursing creaky bedsprings. And my heart broke to see the cheek I could not touch. Her skin was no longer mine.

"Did you sleep well?" I asked in the morning, as casually as I could.

Thanne was growing pale, gaunt in her thinness, drawn around the mouth (from so long, so pinched a silence). Her hair broke at the ends, dry. She fixed breakfast for the children in her housecoat. Her poor ankles were flour-white.

"Did you sleep well?"

I stood by, eating toast. Ministry always grieved my stomach. On the days of difficult duties (preaching itself tore me up; counseling was forever an uncertain affair dead-ending in human sin; funerals were the worst responsibility of all) I would eat a scrap and leave.

"Did you sleep well?"

Thanne flashed me a glance as sharp as a scalpel. "I didn't sleep," she said and slapped eggs on plates. Her tone said volumes, but left the interpretation to me: *because of you.* Or, *What's it to you?* Or, *You ask me just to rub it in.* Or, *Why don't you just go to work?* I could take my pick. I left for work.

But I was not a bad man, was I? I didn't fool around with women—that's worth something in this world, isn't it? I didn't fritter away our money, or beat her, or even talk back to her. I wasn't a drunkard. What I was, was a pastor! I had given even my professional life to God. I was a good man! Then where was the problem between us?

All day I argued my defense in my own mind. All day I truly suffered a stomach pain which felt very much like homesickness, an intolerable loneliness. It prickled my back to think how much I loved Thanne, but it drew my gut into a knot to remember that we were not talking. And the knot was guilt, but the knot was self-pity, too. For God's sake, what did I do?

In the evening I planned to prove my goodness to her. I vacuumed the living room. With mighty snaps, I shook out all the rugs of our house. When the children had gone to bed (so quietly, so quietly, like mice sneaking beneath their parents' silences) I noticed that Thanne hadn't yet done the dishes. *Good!* I thought. *My opportunity!* And I rolled up my sleeves to help her out.

But when I was halfway through the pans I felt the hairs on my neck stand up—as though the Lantern had haunted our kitchen. I paused in the greasy water. I turned and saw Thanne standing in the doorway, glaring at me in silent fury, her thin arms folded at her chest.

She hissed, "You're just trying to make me feel guilty." She disappeared from the doorway and went to bed.

No—but I *thought* I was trying to help. The dirty pans beside me made me sad.

And then I pulled a trick so callous and offensive that I can only tell it here as a confession. What I did was right for the sermon that Sunday morning. I always preached sermons with a certain dramatic staging in order to serve the point, and this particular gesture was perfectly reasonable for worship. But not for Thanne. I wasn't thinking of Thanne. Or rather, I kind of hoped that a gesture so right for preaching might benefit me at home, too.

I was preaching, I think, about love. I was focusing, I think, on the necessity of gift—the giving of one's heart. Thanne and the children sat near the front of the sanctuary. While I preached, I likened the heart to the blood-red rose. And in order to signify the symbol visually, I walked to the altar and drew a rosebud from one of the vases there. Preaching, still preaching, I descended the chancel steps and moved among the congregation toward Thanne—whose mouth pinched tighter the closer I came (but I was preaching and did not notice). There, in a triumph of sermonic illustration, in front of the entire assembly, I handed Thanne my rosebud.

She took it. Instantly I knew my error. She took it, glaring at me. She took it, and her chin began to tremble. She took it, and her eyes glistened with tears—but she did not bow her head or give a single indication to the people around her that she was crying. She held her head high. She took my rose and dropped it to the floor.

That afternoon she made no dinner at all. She left the children with me and drove away alone.

She was so small. She was so independent to be driving God knows where in the car. I loved her so much, and I ached so horribly with her pain, and I was so perplexed as to why she hurt or what in the world I could do about it. I suppose that if I'd been alone, I would have panicked and gone after her, not even knowing where to look but hating inactivity more than the fruitless looking. But I wasn't alone. I had the children.

Thanne had left me with three responsibilities: to watch over the children; to cook their Sunday dinner; and to make some decision about the party we had planned for the evening. Rich and Donna Nordmeyer were scheduled to visit us for food and games and devotions. This was our regular practice; once a month we gathered to support each other. And we played a game called Risk.

Well, I cooked and we ate dinner, the children and I. But because the afternoon stretched toward the evening, and because Thanne wasn't coming home, and because games seemed alien to the mood of our household those days, I made the decision to cancel them. I telephoned Rich and explained that something had come up; we couldn't meet that night. I "fixed" it.

At six-thirty, a half hour before the time of our party, Thanne drove into the garage, got out of the car, closed the door, and walked to the house. I watched her in the evening gloom. She came into the kitchen, laid her purse aside, and began to remove her coat. The kitchen was full of shadow. I hadn't turned the lights on yet.

I said, "It's all right, Thanne. I made it easier for us."

She gave me a tight-lipped glance.

"I called Rich and told them not to come tonight," I said.

And that was the end of our silence. Thanne is little. Thanne can be as quick as a stiletto.

"You—" she whispered. "You!" she snapped. Her eyes blazing, her face broken by the final assault, one wound more than she could tolerate from me, *You always do that!* she cried. "Those are *my* friends! I needed my friends!"

With her coat half on, half off, she stood furious in the middle of the kitchen and fired at me old, old anger, a fusillade of grievances, the pain that had been eating at her, mutely, from the inside. She was frightfully articulate: God had given her a tongue, or anger had. And she did not love me then. No, she did not love me then. Each of us was very much alone. She used the word *hate*. And for the next fifteen minutes she described in particular detail what her life had been like for the last few years. She told me why she couldn't sleep the night I found her in the living room. She used the word *hate*, and she accused me as the cause of all her sorrow. And she was right.

When she was done, when the words simply ran out because there was no more to say, Thanne went upstairs to the bathroom. I stayed alone in the kitchen. And I knew one thing for sure; and one thing I guessed at. And one thing both of us wouldn't even think about.

I knew for sure that Thanne was right. I had sinned terribly against her, sins which I will name before this chapter is done, so you will understand that it wasn't a single act or a number of acts: it was I myself. I was sin.

And the thing I guessed at, while I stood beside the sink, was that I could live without love. I mumbled the words to myself in order to hear them: "I can live without love." I was, I thought, defining the rest of our lives. I was imagining our marriage as a structure containing no soul, no life nor breath. "I can live without love": a sort of a vow and a preparation. I was imagining the days we would spend together hereafter, our passage through the years with, but not *of,* each other. I was testing my resolve, I think, staring through the kitchen window to an evening darkness: I can survive; "I can live without love." Because I deserved no love! It was a righteous punishment.

And the thing that neither one of us would even contemplate was divorce. We were stuck with each other. Let the world call that imprisonment; but I say it gave us the time, and God the opportunity, to make a better thing between us. If we could have escaped, we would have. Because we couldn't we were forced to choose the harder, better road.

WHAT IS FORGIVENESS?

Forgiveness is a sort of divine absurdity. It is irrational, as the world reasons things, and unwise. But "has not God made foolish the wisdom of the world?" It is a miracle maker, because it causes things to be that, logically, empirically, have no right to be. For-give-ness is a holy, complete, unqualified *giving*.

Let me define that "giving" more clearly. Then let me speak of the source for such a marvelous impossibility.

Giving Up

Forgiveness is a willing relinquishment of certain rights. The one sinned against chooses *not* to demand her rights of redress for the hurt she has suffered. She does not hold her spouse accountable for his sin, nor enforce a punishment upon him, nor exact a payment from him, as in "reparations." She does not make his life miserable in order to balance accounts for her own misery, though she might feel perfectly justified in doing so, tit for tat: "He deserves to be hurt as he hurt me."

For-give-ness is a holy, complete, unqualified
giving.

In this way (please note this carefully) she steps *outside* the systems of law; she steps *into* the world of mercy. She makes possible a whole new economy for their relationship: not the cold-blooded and killing machinery of rules, rights, and privileges, but the tender and nourishing care of mercy, which always rejoices in the growth, not the guilt or the pain, of the other. This is sacrifice. To give up one's rights is to sacrifice something of one's self—something hard-fought-for in the world.

Giving Notice

But forgiveness must at the same time be the clear communication to the sinner that she has sinned. It may seem saintly for the wounded party to suffer his pain in silence, and it is surely easier to *keep* that silence than risk opening wounds; but it does no good for the marriage, and it encourages no change in the sinner. He, the one who was sinned against, must speak. "Giving notice" means that he will reveal to his spouse, as clearly as he can, what she has done. No, the purpose of this revelation is not to accuse: it is to impart information. Nor does he disclose the sin by acting out his hurt in front of her (that wants to punish her by increasing her guilt; but he has already separated her sin from his own hurt). With love and not with bitterness he explains both her act and its consequences, remembering always that this communication is for *her* sake, the sinner's sake, and showing always in his countenance a yearning love for her.

This, too, is sacrifice. To react in a manner opposite to vengeance (the natural desire of human nature), to risk reopening wounds, and to seek to heal the one who sought to hurt—these are sacrifices of one's self.

Giving Gifts

Forgiveness is, at the same time, a pure, supernal giving: the receiver doesn't deserve it; the giver wants nothing for it. It's not a *thanks*giving, because that's the return of one goodness for another. It's not a purchasing price, not even the price of marital peace, because that is hoping to buy one goodness with another. Forgiveness is not a good work which expects some reward in the end, because that motive focuses upon the giver, while this kind of giving must focus completely upon the spouse, the one receiving the gift, the one who sinned. The forgiver cannot say, "Because I have given something to you, now you must give something to me." That's no gift at all.

Rather, forgiveness is giving love when there is no reason to love and no guarantee that love will be returned. The spouse is simply not lovable right now! Forgiveness is repaying evil with kindness, doing all the things that love requires—even when you don't *feel* the love; for you can *do* love also in the desert days when you do not feel loving.

Only when a pure, unexpected, unreasonable, and undeserved gift-giving appears in the marriage does newness enter in and healing begin. This is grace. Only when the spouse has heard his sin, so that he might anticipate, under the law, some retribution, but receives instead the gestures of love—only then can he begin to change and grow in the same humility which his wife has shown him. Finally, gift-giving is the greatest sacrifice of all, for it is the complete "giving away" of one's self.

SACRIFICE: ARE WE ABLE?

All three types of "giving" together define the full act of forgiveness; all three must be present at once in the same act.

If one hasn't truly "given up" his legal rights and expectations, he will "give notice" and "give gifts" grudgingly. The forgiver will still expect some reward for his goodness and may grow severely disappointed if all his good efforts seem, in the end, to come to nothing.

If one hasn't truly "given notice," the forgiveness may indeed be unavailing and the sinner may never change, because she will suppose that she has a right to her husband's "gift-giving," and his love will seem no wonder to her at all—though, coming undeserved, it should seem an astonishing wonder.

And if one isn't truly "giving gifts," if one isn't loving truly (even when there's no reason for the love), then the whole burden of change is left up to the sinning one, who has just been notified of her sin. But someone sick can't heal herself very well. Therefore, newness does not enter the relationship.

Together these three elements make forgiveness a sacrifice indeed. Are the offspring of Adam and Eve able to sacrifice themselves? This is a question of crucial importance. Are we able to sacrifice our whole selves for the sake of someone who hurt us? And even if we think that we *are* able, is what we are a sufficient gift?

The apostle Paul didn't say that love bears some things, that love believes only in the best things, that love hopes for a reasonable period of time, or that it endures for a while. No, love is a divine absurdity. It is unreasonable. Paul said, "Love bears *all* things, believes *all* things, hopes *all* things, endures *all* things." Love is limit*less*. For-give-ness is to give infinitely, without end.

But look at us! We are but created creatures. There comes a point when we grow tired in a difficult relationship: there is an end to our emotional rope. The wife says, "A person can take only so much"—and she speaks truthfully. The husband says, "There's nothing left in me to give you any more. *I've reached my limit!*" He isn't lying. We are limited, after all.

This is our human predicament: we are able to sin infinitely against one another, but we are able to forgive only finitely. Left to ourselves alone, forgiveness will run out long before the sinning does.

In fact, we cannot sacrifice enough to heal the one who hurts us. We are not able to forgive equal to our spouse's sinning—not when such giving must come solely from ourselves. But if forgiveness is a tool, it is also a power tool whose power comes from a source other than ourselves. We may use it; we may carefully and self-consciously apply it to our spouses; but Jesus Christ empowers it. He is the true source of its transfiguring love. And the love of the Son of God is infinite.

Jesus Christ, the Primal Source and the Power of Forgiveness

In order to forgive your spouse—and so to heal the broken relationship—first forget your spouse. The primary relationship is between you and God; what happens there will affect what happens in your household. First, it is you and God alone.

And behold: with God, *you* were the sinner! Even before your spouse sinned against you, you sinned against the mighty God. You, like Eve, demanded the personal, self-centered authority that belongs to God alone. In your own life, you pulled God down from his throne, then sat in that seat yourself, becoming at once your own god and God's own enemy. At best you used God as your servant, making your prayers a list of demands, the good things you wanted him to do for you. At worst, you recreated the divine being in your own image, rejecting God's revelation of himself, resisting his commands as you would resist a tyrant, hating him. In either case, yours was so monstrous a sin that you should have died for it. The sentence and the consequence was death, no less than the extinguishing of your life—and no appeal.

In order to forgive your spouse . . . first forget your spouse.

When we speak in terms of life and death, we are speaking of infinities. Death is infinite, an endless separation from God and from the life that has no end. You chose, by your sinning, an infinite solitude.

But God responded with an infinite love. This is the measure of his forgiveness: that it was more than equal to your sin—and is therefore measureless.

The dear Lord God did not turn you over to death. He sent his Son into the world (into the enemy territory of your own life) to do what? To *forgive* you. And it is marvelous to note that all three elements of forgiveness (the same ones you must bring your spouse) were purely present in Jesus' sacrificial act on your behalf.

Jesus "gave up" his rights—and so removed you from the world of law to the world of mercy. Jesus "gave up" his rights. Though in the form of God, he "did not count equality with God a thing to be grasped, but emptied himself, taking the form of a servant." As a servant he lived in the flesh. Moreover, he humbled himself to death, even death on the cross. Do you die *a little* for the sake of your spouse? Jesus died completely for your sake—died the death you should have died. This is mercy, that the divine dictum "In the day you eat of it, you shall die" became "though you were the one who ate of it, Jesus died instead." When he gave up his rights, he transferred you from the world of doom to the world of life.

Also, he did this publicly; he did this in the flesh, where everyone could see it. That is, he "gave notice" both to humanity and to you: that you sinned, what your sin was, and what its consequences were—his own suffering, holy grief. The evident righteousness of Jesus' life revealed that *your* sin sent him to the cross, not his own. And just as his glance to Peter, after that disciple had denied him three times, drove Peter out of the courtyard to weep bitterly, so through his Scripture did Jesus glance at you, persuading you of your personal fault.

Finally, he did all this in grace, as a free gift for you, loving you with a love you did not deserve. "Giving gifts." He himself received nothing for the sacrifice. You received everything—though you could have paid nothing for it. You received life—infinitely. In Jesus Christ you do possess the *infinite* love which you need for your marriage. As much as you could sin, so much did he forgive you. He bore and believed and hoped and endured *all* things. This is the primal sacrifice.

Now, thou servant possessed of a measureless bank account—now remember your spouse again, whose sin against you is a pittance (however painful it may feel), whose debt is a denarius, measured in pennies.

When Christ is the single most solid reality upon which you stand; when in faith you find the source of your own life in him; when you yourself do dwell within his loving mercy and his forgiveness, then you are empowered to forgive your spouse, infinitely. Christ is the well from which to draw the water for your thirsty wife or husband. But this must be remembered: only as you know Jesus' limitless forgiveness *for you* (that first!—that personally!) are you able limitlessly to share forgiveness with your spouse (that second—but that personally as well).

But then what? Then you *become* Christ's forgiveness for your wife, your husband—for Jesus loves her fully as much as he does you. It isn't you at all who produces this forgiveness; it is Christ in you, whose divine forgiveness is forever. His was the real death, his the real sacrifice. Therefore, you do not die at all; you merely mimic the archetypal forgiveness which Jesus accomplished on the cross once for all time, once for every marriage and for every sin that any marriage suffers. Are you able? Well, if you yourself are not the one who is dying; and if you are losing nothing now (having lost it all in Christ before), of course you are able to love the one who wounded you. Of course you are able to forgive.

The Divine Ideal Revived

"Love one another," Jesus said, *"as I have loved you."* This is the love enacted on the cross, the sacrificial and self-emptying love, the love of forgiveness. Sin destroyed the image of God in human marriages. But with the gift of mercy, seized by a strong faith, sin now becomes the opportunity for the image of God to be resurrected again in human marriages.

The wife who turns her face, filled with a forgiving grace, upon her husband shows him, too, the face of Jesus. Each spouse becomes God's mirror to the other—first the reflection of God, and then the reflection of that other.

And if my wife shows God to me (especially when I realize that I do not deserve love) then my wife herself will seem to me a gift of God. She not only brings gifts—she *is* a gift! Suddenly my own love for her leaps up to a higher plane; I will handle her as a sacred, holy thing, an Eve I had no right to expect. This marriage should have died—but it didn't! That she exists at all, that I did not lose her (as rightly I should have) by my sinning, shall wring from my soul an honest gratitude. Do you understand how the very nature of the relationship is transfigured by forgiveness?

When both the husband and the wife are thus humbled by the forgiveness of their Christ, they are also humbled before each other. The individual attitude of godlikeness is gone in the true God, killed by guilt and feebleness, buried under mercy. With it goes the individual's arrogant presumption that he can himself decide what is good and what is evil: what he thought was "good" nearly destroyed them. When *both*, then, are obedient children of the same good God, the differences between the spouses are no longer threats or weapons or a shame; but, like children in innocence, they may blamelessly be naked before one another again, celebrating and sharing these differences. If one can truly trust that the other will forgive him, then he need no longer hide portions of himself under an apron of lies and hypocrisy; he can be fully honest and forthright before her. And if she believes in her own (her Lord's!) ability to forgive "all things," then she will not blind herself to the realities of her husband's character; she will not need to maintain denials or fantasies, but may see and hear and know him completely for what he is. Truth, not lies or suspicions, dwells between them. And what is the practical benefit of such clear-headed honesty? Why, that they can work *together* on the common projects of marriage, that each one, once again, is a "help" perfectly "fit" for the other.

DEUS EX MACHINA—DEUS EX VENIA

What did I learn that Sunday evening in our kitchen when Thanne broke silence and burned me with my guilt? What did I hear from the small woman grown huge in her fury, half in, half out of her coat, while the daylight died outside? I learned her grievances. I heard what her life had been like for several years, though I had not known it. I saw myself through *her* eyes, and the vision accused me.

And I learned what caused her silence in the first place, sending her out of my bed a month ago to sit in the dark of the living room and in sorrow.

"It's all right, Thanne," I said when she first came into the kitchen. "I called Rich and told them not to come tonight."

Her eyes flashed. "You—" she whispered. "You!" she snapped. *"You always do that!* Those are my friends."

"Thanne, I do not always—"

"Always! More than you know. You decide my whole life for me, but you hardly pay mind to the decisions. You do it with your left hand, carelessly. You run me with your left hand. Everyone else gets the right hand of kindness. Everyone else can talk to you. Not me. The left hand."

"Thanne! I'm not a bad person. I do everything as well as I can. What have I done to you? I try to please God. I'm a good pastor—"

"A good pastor!" she spat the words. "You *are* a good pastor, Wally. God knows, I wanted you to be a good pastor. But sometimes I wish you were a bad pastor, a lazy pastor, a careless pastor. Then I'd have the right to complain. Or maybe I'd have *you* here sometimes. A good pastor! Wally, how can I argue with God and take you from him? Wally, Wally, your ministry runs *me*, but you leave me alone exactly when I need you. *Where are you all the time?*"

I didn't answer.

Then this is what she told me in the darkening kitchen that terrible Sunday evening. This is what she made me see: that this good pastor carried to the people of his congregation a face full of pity—

—but at our dinner table my face was drained and grey. At the dinner table I heaped a hundred rules upon our children, growling at them for the least infraction. Our dinners were tense and short.

This is what she made me see: that I could praise, could genuinely applaud, the lisping song of a child at church—

—but I gave the merest glance to Mary's Father's Day card, in which there was a poem the girl had labored on for two weeks straight.

"That poem said she loved you, Wally."

Thanne said she knew how much I hated to visit the jail. But I went. And it never mattered what time of day or night. Yet I did nothing that I hated, nothing, at home.

For counseling and for sermons, my words, she said, were beautiful: a poet of the pulpit. But for our bedroom conversations my words were bitten, complaining, and unconsidered. We talked of my duties. We talked of my pastoral disappointments. Or we hardly talked at all.

"How often I wanted to tell you of the troubles here at home," she said, "of my mistakes with the children."

But I was doing the Lord's work—the Lord, Thanne wailed, whom she loved dearly. So what could she say to me through all of this? How could she find fault with a divine command? I *was* a good pastor.

If she was discontent, then, who could she blame but herself? Over and over again she had told herself that she was being petty and selfish. And that's how she endured, by accepting the blame.

But that's when the chipmunk's smile began to die on her face. And that's when Thanne began to die, a constant crab in her own eyes, truly dissatisfied and truly guilty for it. Bad Thanne. A bad person.

There were times she despised the children just for being children and for being there. And because she knew what a vile mother she must be to feel like that, she turned the despising inward.

But there was no one saying that he loved her then. There was no one pointing out her value after all. There was no one forgiving her or freeing her from confusion, from this horrible captivity. And how could someone as sinful as herself take anything away from God?

"Wally, where were you?"

She wanted me to see—but she didn't want me to see—her suffering. I shouldn't see the wickedness (yet I should, she thought, to forgive it); I should see her *need.* And I should see it on my own. If she had to show me, how little I loved her then, or how little she was worthy of my love. I should see it on my own; she shouldn't have to tell me. How could she explain what she didn't even understand? But in fact, I was seeing nothing at all those years. I didn't notice that Thanne had lost her smile— though I could smell a parishioner's sadness from halfway across the city!

"Why didn't you stop me then?" Thanne cried. "Why didn't you ask, 'What's the matter' then? *Wally, where were you?"*

I was ministering. I was a whole human, active in an honorable job, receiving the love of a grateful congregation, charging out the door in the mornings, collapsing in bed at night. I was healthy in society; she was dying in a little house—and accusing herself for the evil of wanting more time from me, stealing the time from God. I laughed happily at potlucks. She cried in secret. And sometimes she would simply hold one of the children, would hold and hold him, pleading some little love from him until he grew frightened by her intensity, unable in his babyhood to redeem her terrible sins. And sometimes she cursed herself for burdening a child, and then she wondered where God had gone.

In those days the smile died in her face. The high laughter turned dusty in her throat. Privately the woman withered—and I did not see it.

But the event which broke Thanne altogether, the little sin which was more than she could take, had occurred one evening when Rich and Donna came to our house for our monthly game of Risk. This was one month before the game I canceled. One month before she told me all her sorrow.

For me the night was no different from any other; but for Thanne it was a turning point. It shut down our marriage.

We played Risk on opposite teams, Thanne and I, so she sat across from me. The game progressed. I relaxed. I leaned back and spread myself in my chair, feeling this to be a very good party. I made jokes.

But I made them at Thanne's expense, oblivious of their effect on her. And she saw how much my very being belittled her. If she was dying, her husband was not altogether blameless. He was killing her by small degrees and scorn.

"Thanne's my little 'possum," I said. "Do you know that the woman sleeps curled up like a 'possum? And she never, never has trouble sleeping. Oh, I wish I had it so easy."

Rich laughed. Donna laughed. We all knew how exhausting was my work.

"Thanne's the best critic of sermons that I have," I said. "No one sharper nor more voluble than her, yes sir. After every sermon I ask her, 'How was it?' You know what she tells me? Every time she answers, 'Fine.' That's it. That's all I get from her. A regular Samuel Johnson."

Rich laughed. Donna laughed. Everyone knew who was the true talker of this family—and it was just like Walt to name some author no one else had read.

And when Thanne was clearly beating me at the game, I let it be known that I didn't mind. I turned that into a jolly joke as well. I said, "See how serious she gets at games? Thanne plays for keeps. Why, I remember once when we were courting—we played Hearts together, just the two of us. I absolutely infuriated her by passing her the queen of spades—twice. This woman hissed. Remember, Thanne? I think she trembled, she was so angry. Well, ever since then I let her win at games. I don't want a 'possum mad at me."

Rich laughed. Donna laughed. Thanne did not. But I didn't notice the silence. I enjoyed myself immensely that night. No, I didn't at all mind the losing. In fact, I was glad to give Thanne the gift. I went to bed quite satisfied with life and with the night. Thanne went to bed, too. But that was the night she did not sleep.

This, in the kitchen one month later, is what she told me: she heard my breathing beside her, and she realized that she did not love me. For a while she condemned herself for making too much of a little stupid humor. But it didn't matter how small the sin was. She didn't love me anymore, and that caused her tremendous sadness. She got up and left the bedroom. She went into the living room and sat curled on the sofa, alone and in the dark, and she was dead. And when I came in smelling of sleep and asking what the matter was, she didn't want to see me. Worst of all, the worst thing in the world, my touch repulsed her. My touching her made her cry.

And this, with all the pain and all the pleading of her soul, is what she demanded when she finished telling me all these things: she cried, *"Wally, Wally, where were you all that time?"*

But I could only stare out the kitchen window at the gathering gloom and answer nothing. Poet of the pulpit! I had no words whatever to say. Nothing. Oh, Thanne, I am so sorry.

"I have to hurt you," she said. The strident voice had turned to whining by now. She wasn't shouting anymore. She was just unspeakably sad. "I had to hurt you to make you notice me. I hate it. I hate it! And when you do notice me, what do I get? Wally, you are so selfish. At least I know it when I hurt you. You don't even know. I get a red flower in front of the whole congregation. Oh, Wally!"

She told the truth. All this was the truth—and now she was done.

I said, "I love you, Thanne." So little evidence. So foolish. I said, "I will always love you, no matter what."

Thanne went up to the bathroom, not to cry, just to get ready for bed. She was all done. But I hadn't moved so much as a finger. I stood in the kitchen, burning in my guilt, keeping my whole body still. How could I *not* have seen so much—especially since I did, truly, love Thanne? This was a mortal mystery discovered too late. How could she have suffered in the same house, in the same *bed* with me, and I stay so utterly ignorant of her torment? There was no reason for this, except that I am abjectly sinful—and she is right. Oh, Thanne, I am so sorry—but what good does that do? No one should grieve alone. My wife, you should never have grieved alone.

I stared out the window, and I said to myself: *I can live without love. I can because I must. I've killed Thanne's love for me. Jesus, how I miss her smile! I can because I should. I deserve nothing less than loneliness, no less than to endure the same thing she did.* Now it was dark outside, and I still did not move. I can live without love.

After that Sunday night we returned to our silences again. She cooked, and I ate her food. I always received it, those days, as a pure kindness that she would still cook for me—and that she never spoke evil of me before the children. But we didn't speak to one another, except in the gravest politeness.

I didn't so much as brush her back when I crawled into bed. And once in bed I lay stone still for fear of shaking the mattress and waking her. Did she sleep then? I don't know, though she looked sallow and sick in the daylight. For my own part, my heart hammered all night long. Sometimes she rose in darkness to pace the house; and then I cried because the bed was empty and because I could not help her in her hurt: I didn't have the right even to try. I restrained myself in silence. I played with the kids. I preached, a purple hypocrite, the poet of the pulpit. And always the tears trembled just behind my eyes, even at church. But I could live without love.

Thanne could not forgive me. This is a plain fact. My sin was greater than her capacity to forgive, had lasted longer than her kindness, had grown more oppressive than her goodness. This was not a single act nor a series of acts, but my being. My sin was the murder of her spirit, the unholy violation of her sole identity —the blithe assumption of her presence, as though she were furniture. I had broken her. How could a broken person be at the same time whole enough to forgive? No: Thanne was created finite, and could not forgive me.

But Jesus could.

One day Thanne stood in the doorway of my study, looking at me. I turned in my chair and saw that she was not angry. Small Thanne, delicate, diminutive Thanne, she was not glaring but gazing at me with gentle, questioning eyes. This was totally unexpected, both her presence and her expression. There was no reason why she should be standing there, no detail I've forgotten to tell you. Yet, for a full minute we looked at one another; and then she walked to my side where I sat. She touched my shoulder. She said, "Wally, will you hug me?"

I leaped from my chair. I wrapped her all around in two arms and squeezed my wife, my wife, so deeply in my body—and we both burst into tears.

Would I hug her? Oh, but the better question was, would she *let* me hug her? And she did.

Dear Lord Jesus, where did this come from, this sudden, unnatural, undeserved willingness to let me touch her, hug her, love her? Not from me! I was her ruination. Not from her, because I had killed that part of her. From you!

How often had we hugged before? I couldn't count the times. How good had those hugs been? I couldn't measure the goodness. But *this* hug—don't you know, it was my salvation, different from any other and more remarkable because this is the hug I should never have had. *That* is forgiveness! The law was gone. Rights were all abandoned. Mercy took their place. We were married again. And it was you, Christ Jesus, in my arms—within my graceful Thanne. One single, common hug, and we were alive again.

Thanne gave me a gift: She gave me the small plastic figure of a woman with her eyes rolled up, her mouth skewed to one side, the tongue lolling out, a cartoon face. I have this gift in my study today.

The inscription at the bottom reads: *I love you so much it hurts.*

You will need courage to forgive and lots of practice, but forgiveness is something you can learn.
—*Patrick and Connie Lawrence*
Your 30-Day Journey to Being a Great Wife

Chapter

11

Who's in Control?

In our book, Passages of Marriage, *we examine the various stages each couple must go through if they are to have a healthy, growing marriage throughout their lives together. We've included a chapter later in the book that helps couples work through the passage of marriage when toddlers and young school-age children come on the scene. This chapter deals with conflict, its presence in every marriage, and ways of handling it that are both constructive and conducive to growth in your relationship. The processes of learning to compromise, of "agreeing to disagree," and of thinking through your conflicts, aren't impossible to learn. Take the time to work through them, and you'll discover a better way to*

"Who's in Control" is adapted and taken from *Passages of Marriage*, Dr. Frank and Mary Alice Minirth, Drs. Brian and Deborah Newman, Dr. Robert and Susan Hemfelt (1992).

handle the struggle for control that is endemic to every intimate relationship—especially marriage.

—Dr. Frank and Mary Alice Minirth
Drs. Brian and Deborah Newman
Dr. Robert and Susan Hemfelt
Passages of Marriage

Carl Warden sat on neighbor Bert's front porch as Bert boasted, "Meg and I had a perfect marriage. We never fought."

"Wish I could say that," Carl sniffed. "Bess and I, we've had some go-rounds, let me tell you! We keep it honest, though, and it all worked out."

"Not us, no sir." Bert's rocking chair squeaked with every oscillation. "Meg was the proper wife of Scripture. Submissive."

Carl thought about that a few minutes and shook his head. "Bess has a mind of her own, and when she thinks I'm wrong, she doesn't hesitate a bit to point it out. I would've made some major mistakes if Bess weren't as strong as she is." Carl didn't say any more, but he reflected, *God's blessing to me that she doesn't let herself be a doormat.* And the recollections of Bess's solid, stubborn love nearly brought tears to his eyes.

THE SECOND TASK: OVERCOME THE TENDENCY TO JOCKEY FOR CONTROL

The second task of the second passage of marriage is one which will resurface off and on throughout all the passages of marriage. Each spouse will ask, "Who's in control here?" as different situations arise, from the choice of a restaurant for a Friday night date to the purchase of a new home. The source of conflict will change, as will the couple's methods of responding to it, but conflict itself is present in all relationships.

Unfortunately, too many couples think, "We must squelch conflict, lest it damage this relationship." The couple instinctively know the relationship is untested and unhardened. Yet here's an equation we've learned to be valid:

1 person + 1 person = conflict.

Its corollary:

1 person-in-love + 1 person-in-love = conflict anyway.

Conflict is inevitable, no matter what the ages or back-grounds. The new couple are not far enough into their relation-ship to know that conflict, because it is inevitable, is nothing more than a normal part of marriage. How the couple deal with that conflict, however, can make or break the union. Often their ability to handle conflict is stifled by their fragile egos and dreams.

Fragile Egos

If the couple as well as the relationship are young in years, they don't know themselves well yet. An older couple such as Louie and Marj Ajanian won't have such fragile egos. The sum of their years is more than a century; they know by now what they can do and who they are.

Even the well-established ego gets bruised at the beginning of a marital relationship.

Both parties are equally affected, of course. The man, too, enters marriage with a lot of insecurities. "Will she get tired of me? Continue to love me? Can I satisfy her—and keep on satisfy-ing her? Can I handle this new responsibility? Especially, can I provide financially for her?"

One of our clients voiced those insecurities: "I felt vulnerable. If I flubbed up, if I didn't do everything expected of a man, my ego would really take a beating. I wanted to be the dream hus-band, the Clark Gable of married men."

Fragile Dreams

Not even Clark Gable the actual man could equal Clark Gable the dream image. No matter how well the partners think they know each other, when courtship becomes marriage, some disil-lusionment sets in.

Debi Newman explains it from experience. "Brian was so romantic! In July, six months before our wedding, he sent me six red roses. August, five months before the wedding, five roses. And so on until one rose a month before. January when we got married, nothing. And for the next three years I got nothing.

"Brian was still very nice and thoughtful toward all the other people in his life. I felt sort of left out. We've each given on this issue; he's more attentive, and I've learned to be content in his love, without a rose a month."

Not just expectations transfer from courtship into marriage. So does every unresolved issue. Conflicts the couple thought would disappear, little things in their engagement, blossom into big things in the marriage.

ATTITUDE ADJUSTMENT IN CONFLICT

The couple in the throes of Young Love, not yet fully comfortable with each other, will instinctively guard what they say and do. They know (although they might not articulate that knowledge) that the greater the openness, the greater the potential for conflict. What they may not realize is, the greater the openness, the greater the potential for improved intimacy.

In forty-three years of marriage, Bert and Meg never achieved anything near deep intimacy. Although Bert would tell you quite truthfully that he loved his Meg, he could not tell you what Meg thought, how she responded to a situation ("Oh, I don't know, I guess she just sort of accepted it"), what she felt or when ("Frankly, she got to be something of a cold fish after a while"), or whether she even had any hopes and dreams ("Never mentioned them, so I guess she didn't have any"). And yet, every human being not only possesses a wonderful capacity for deep intimacy, but every person craves it. Intimacy feeds happiness and contentment. We were made for it.

When Carl said he and Bess "kept it honest," he referred to their mutual desire to avoid dirty fighting. Conflict approached wrongly causes not intimacy but pain and alienation. Separation. It's a lady-and-the-tiger situation. In a famous short story, a man must choose between two doors. If he opens the one, a willing and lovely lady awaits him. Behind the other door waits a hungry tiger. The story is an allegory of life, and it also typifies conflict. Behind one door, intimacy. Behind the other, separation. But there's an infinite difference here. The man could not know in advance which door hid what. You can.

Causes and Symptoms

Boy, do you feel rotten! Sneezing, a runny nose sore from so much blowing, no energy, aching all over. . . . You take cold medicine, but unlike many medicines, cold medicine does nothing to cure the cold. All the king's horses and all the king's men have not been able to cure the common cold. The medicine alleviates the symptoms somewhat—the nose does not run so fast and so far, the sneezing lessens, the aches abate. But the causative agent, the cold virus, follows its merry course unhindered.

The germs cause the symptoms. Instead of that nasty cold, should you contract one of certain treatable kinds of pneumonia, the appropriate antibiotics will stop the cause—the pneumococcus germs—and thereby the symptoms as well.

Married couples assume that conflict in their union causes separation. Actually, conflict is usually not a cause; it's a symptom. The wedge has already been driven in somewhere, somehow, and conflict has resulted. We've learned that if you can find and deal with the issue causing separation—the germs, by analogy—the conflict, the symptom, takes care of itself.

Not always, though, can you do that. Sometimes you can merely treat the symptoms. However, if you handle the conflict well, improved intimacy and contentment result, and the cause emerges, to be healed.

"Aha!" you say. "So if I let 'er rip and encourage conflict, my marriage will grow stronger. Good! I love to argue."

That's not what we're saying at all! We're saying that you can turn the friction inevitable in any honest union into an asset. Food is a good illustration. We must have it; eat or die. And yet, used wrongly, food becomes the center of all sorts of problems, from anorexia to obesity.

As the marriage matures, moving from passage to passage, the couple's attitudes toward conflict will change. The symptoms—the conflicts themselves—will change somewhat. So, therefore, will the means of dealing with them.

Conflict is usually not a cause;
it's a symptom.

Frank Minirth puts it this way: "Part of the idealism in the first stage is, 'We're not supposed to be fighting.' I was small as a child, and very lonely growing up. I met Mary Alice, and she was the most beautiful thing. She looked just like Snow White. How can you fight with Snow White?

"Also, fighting is a fearful thing. You just know it will destroy that fragile relationship. At first we didn't know how to handle it. We learned together how to argue without hurting each other, to grieve the past, and take up the new."

THE RESOLUTION

Although the couple's attitude toward conflict matures and changes, the three ways to handle disagreement remain the same: a) compromise, b) agreement to disagree, and c) love gift.

Compromise

Everyone gives in a little. That's what Frank and Mary Alice Minirth decided to do when they purchased a vacation home. A friend of the Minirths' tells about their compromise: "Frank is a country boy. He likes animals; he likes rural living. Mary Alice is strictly a city girl. They have a property in rural Arkansas—I mean, *very* rural Arkansas. Cabins, horses, wild land. As you approach, you see no power poles, no hints of modern conveniences at all. It looks like a hundred and fifty years ago. But inside the cabins are up-to-the-minute kitchen appliances, right down to the dishwasher and microwave. The outside is Frank's concept of country living; the inside is Mary Alice's. It's a lovely compromise and works beautifully for both of them."

Agreement to Disagree

Early in their marriage the Newmans agreed to disagree. Brian remembers one incident clearly: "Debi was making pancakes for breakfast, shortly after we married. She tossed the flour into the blender, and then an egg and some milk. That just floored me! That's not the way you do it. You mix the dry ingredients thoroughly and separately. You blend the egg into the milk. Then you slowly add the dry ingredients to the egg-and-milk until you get a perfect batter."

Debi adds: "I could have backed off and done it his way, but the potential was there for me to bury my anger—to be resentful. That wouldn't have done either one of us any good. I stuck with my way. We didn't resolve it by compromise or giving in. We simply agreed to disagree."

Brian continues: "Her pancakes turned out just fine. You know, though, a strongly controlling man might not be able to eat them when they weren't made the way he thought was 'right.' "

The symptom in that case was a disagreement over method. The cause was, again, a family-of-origin habit. Brian grew up with a certain concept of what's "right." Debi didn't mind a bit taking shortcuts.

Debi explains: "When one spouse is very controlling, it's important that the other not constantly cave in just to avoid conflict. That's an open door to unhealthy polarization. The controlling spouse becomes all the more controlling, and the other begins to lose identity and self-esteem. The situation—giving in, I mean— certainly generates anger, and that's not good for either the spouses or the marriage."

Does that mean one should never give in? Not at all!

Love Gift

A love gift is, essentially, exactly that: giving in. A love gift says, "For whatever reason, I'm giving on this issue. I may feel as strongly as you do, but I'm willing to give."

Obviously, a love gift must be given without anger or it will not be a healthy response.

Debi Newman recalls this illustration: "A situation came up when we were engaged that nearly wrecked us before we even married. I wanted to apply for a job as secretary. Brian worked as a janitor in the same building. He saw how the men treated the position of secretary—their attitude—and the way they flirted with the secretaries. He felt extremely threatened and insecure, and he thought a couple just starting out shouldn't be in a threatening position of that sort. I wanted the security of a steady job, and didn't feel I had many options.

"For a while we thought it really was the end of the relationship. Compromise wasn't possible; either I took the job or I didn't. I finally made the decision to give in on this issue. I didn't understand everything Brian was feeling; I definitely didn't agree with him, but I chose not to apply for the job out of love for him.

"God worked in all of this. He helped us with the anger and forgiveness, and I got an even better job. Surviving that crisis put us on a much deeper level of intimacy."

None of these three is appropriate to every situation. Sometimes, for example, compromise is wisest; at other times it's not possible. Should a couple become locked into one of these three approaches to the exclusion of the other two, problems follow.

Carl's friends Bert and Meg illustrate this. Meg gave in every time. And that's where a love gift became, with time, a cop-out, no longer either love or a gift.

THE NUTS AND BOLTS OF CONFLICT RESOLUTION

There is no cookbook method to deal with conflict, and for good reason: In the heat of disagreement, when your very self is on the line, you don't think of following rules. And if you do think of it, you don't want to anyway, lest by following the rules you lose.

There are, however, some guidelines to prevent conflict from causing separation.

As you consider those guidelines, use as a specific example

the last conflict you suffered with your spouse. It needn't be a big one—maybe it was an argument over how you spend your time. Sometimes one spouse or the other acts as if he or she is still single. The person hasn't made changes in his or her relationship with single friends as we suggested in the last chapter. "You're not playing golf again with the guys this Saturday," the wife moans. "You played golf twice this week after work. We never spend any time together." And there begins an argument.

As we go along, apply the guidelines to the particular instance you select. You'll study who said precisely what (it's amazing how often statements are misheard and misread), what the underlying feelings and needs are, what went wrong, and how you might handle the situation better when it pops up again. Because most conflicts are born of the same problems they do keep popping up, again and again.

Know Thyself

First, understand and be aware of what's going on inside yourself. Divide a piece of paper in half vertically. On one side list the things you say out loud, such as:

"I see you less now than I did when we were dating."
"Who's more important to you, the guys or me?"
"I don't matter to you; you don't really love me."

On the other side of the paper list the thoughts you are thinking:

He wishes he wasn't married.
He'd rather be playing golf with the boys than spending time with me.
I feel lonely (abandoned).
I have no control over this situation.

Often you won't admit these thoughts, but you know they are there and now's the time to own up to these feelings.

Now think about why you might have felt that way. For example, at a pause in a wild argument, when vitriol had reached an emotional level, one of our clients suddenly sensed his old inadequacy fears kicking up. He was deeply, viscerally afraid of seeing himself as a loser. The self-revelation forced him to yield somewhat simply to beat down that ogre from his past, inadequacy.

Can you remember the last time you felt that way? *(For instance, if you felt lonely during the argument, perhaps you'll think, "I always felt lonely when my parents went on long business trips and left me at home." Or, "My father was a workaholic and he never spent much time with me.")* Are the two situations similar? If so, how? *(For instance, the feeling is the same: "I feel as if I've been abandoned. Those feelings from childhood might be making me feel worse now.")*

You obtain insight into conflict in marriage through this type of introspection, through feedback from others, through willingness to grab hold of nuggets of truth others give you. You may have to wade through a lot of dross to find those nuggets. You don't have to buy it all, but do look for them. As you open yourself up to understanding, you set a precedent for how you'll resolve conflict.

Brian did that. "I told a friend about the pancake incident not long after it happened. 'Brian,' he said, 'that is an amoral issue. There is no right or wrong. Don't let amoral issues become bones of contention.' He said a lot of other things, too, but that stuck with me."

Think

Have you ever analyzed a television series episode? Try it sometime. You'll find an unvarying pattern. For example, there's the one-hour adventure story: In the first two minutes, a lot of attention-getting things happen. They want you to stay at that spot on your channel selector. The plot gets rolling in a hurry, drawing you into the story. The first commercial break happens at, literally, an odd moment. The second, though, will occur on the half hour. Just before this break, the hero will be in the utmost danger, the ultimate pits—whatever—for the producers want you involved enough that you won't switch channels during all those commercials. If there is any character development, it will happen during the third segment, "garbage time." After the third commercial break, just as it appears the villain might win, the action will lead to a flip-flop as the hero comes out on top, an exciting finish, and the wrap-up. Every time.

This is one of several reasons Americans no longer feel any strong need to think. Television, by rote formula, does all the work of thinking for us. Some shows even do the philosophizing for us in the wrap-up. We need not bother to look for deeper meanings; they are clearly explained. Yet unless people are trained in the ability to look at options and to think, they can't resolve conflicts.

"Okay," you say, "so what's to think about?" For starters, think about what your spouse's position really is. Use debating skills. Anyone surviving a high school debating course knows that you must be able to debate either side of a question, if you're to present your own side effectively. You must know where the other side's strengths and weaknesses lie. Take a moment and mentally fill in these blanks: "My spouse kept saying *(you don't appreciate all I do for you or how hard I work)*." "His (her) position has some merit, in that *(he does work hard and some of the times he was playing golf he was with clients)*." "He (she) seemed to be feeling *(angry, afraid)*."

Often the husband realizes that the wife is right. He has been spending a lot of time playing golf. So he becomes defensive because he feels guilty. He is, in fact, having difficulty making the adjustment to a married relationship where he has to consider someone else's desires.

Finally, think about whether some other situation could be feeding your husband's or wife's anger, *such as, a difficult situation at work or a domineering mother who tried to control every minute of his or her time.*

Frequently we are so busy formulating our own position and mentally framing the perfect riposte, we miss the other person's position completely. This type of introspection forces us to think also of just how our own side looks. (For instance, Charles Darwin, when making major decisions, would list all the pros and cons side by side. He used the method only to clarify his thoughts, and not as a guide, for although the cons far outweighed the pros, he boarded the *Beagle* anyway, and became one of the best-known figures in history.)

While you're enumerating various sides, study your own. In your recent fight, for instance, what did you say more than once? *("You don't really love me, and I'm not sure I even love you.")*

Do you really know that your husband or wife doesn't love you? Do you have the power to read his or her mind? We always advise couples to stick to the facts, not their assumptions, which might well be inaccurate.

Think about the second part of that statement now: "I'm not sure I even love you." How might that have been misconstrued? *("He or she might see those words as rejection and a threat to our marriage.")* Do you say these same things at other times when you and your spouse fight?

It's natural to throw grenades back and forth in an argument. If both parties know themselves, however, they can call a halt to general accusations and talk about their true interior feelings. This will *never* happen if you speak in absolutes:

"You *never* stay home with me."

"You would *always* prefer playing golf with the boys rather than spending time with me."

Absolute statements usually guarantee defensiveness because they are so overstated. A husband might play golf with the boys on Saturday and once or twice during the week, but the other four nights he is at home with his spouse.

We also advise couples to be wary of character assassinations. The wife in this example might say, "You're a totally selfish person. You never think of anyone but yourself."

We suggest that couples ask themselves an important question as they are fighting: "How would you feel if your spouse said these things to you?" If you can take a moment to do this, you will readily see that you were caught in the trap of making absolute statements or dealing in character assassination.

Evaluate your own need to control. At the heart of the golfing argument is that question, "Who's in control here? Who sets the schedule? What time is mine? What time is yours? And what time is ours together?''

And much of each spouse's reaction is motivated by fear. It's scary to yield some control of your life to someone else. It's difficult to work out time-sharing in a marriage.

If you have by nature a strongly controlling personality, your potential for conflict is greater, for you feel the urge to control what you cannot control—your spouse's attitudes, feelings, and actions. We find this equally true for men and women.

And what about your husband's need for control? In the golfing example, the husband is probably feeling, "You're trying to control every part of my life." He's just as afraid as you are.

Finally keep a clear head about just how big this fight really is. Not all disagreements are created equal.

If you were looking at that fight from the perspective of six months from now, would it rate as an enormous barrier or an insignificant pothole on the road to happiness?

Stick to the Basics

Think also about the basics. Vince Lombardi watched his Green Bay Packers lose several games and decided to go back to basics. He waved a pigskin aloft and announced, "This is a football."

Julia Karris wanted to buy her stepdaughter, Kinsley, the latest shoes for school. Jerry insisted that $69 was too much for a pair of shoes the fourteen-year-old was going to outgrow by Christmas.

Julia explained the prestige attached to that particular brand.

Jerry remained unimpressed. He lauded frugality.

So far, both were sticking to the basics.

Then Julia pointed out how much Jerry spent for fishing equipment. He countered with the amount of "free" time she gave the department store. She complained how stingy he was, and he fumed that she shared the same spendthrift ways that alienated him from his first wife. Basics had just gone out the window.

Caught in the middle, young Kinsley felt certain she was the cause of her parents' fight. She could not see, nor could they, that they had strayed from the basics. They were dragging in issues from the past, things which had nothing whatever to do with the wisdom of purchasing a pair of shoes.

When Carl and Bess "kept it honest" as they fought, Carl meant essentially that they thought about the basics. *They kept to the issue at hand.* If the price of a pair of shoes were at issue, they argued the cost and value of the shoes. And that brings up another key point Julia and Jerry were missing.

Keep Your *Self* Out of It

Keep out of it? But we're the ones fighting!

Issues and persons are two different things. *Argue over issues, but never allow your conflict to get personal.* As much as you can, keep emotions out of it. Given its own way, the need to win will gain full control of your emotions and rob your rational processes. Disagreement then becomes a brute dogfight, invariably shredding love and egos. Dogs don't fight in support of ideas. They fight each other. A constant equation is

Conflict – rational processes = explosion.

Brian Newman says: "We see it constantly in couples we counsel. Once a conflict becomes emotional, reason goes out the door and the conflict is never going to be resolved. We help the couple keep it from becoming personal, by any of several ways."

Get Creative

Part of being creative about conflict is being able to see options. There is, for example, the obvious but rarely used option, to simply cool off a while.

Never allow your conflict to get personal.

Debi explains: "So very frequently when we talk to Christian couples, we hear the passage, 'Be angry, but do not sin; do not let the sun go down on your anger.' The man and woman interpret it that their anger has to be resolved quickly, and so they deny their anger. Or else, they take it to bed with them. Lights out may be the first time the couple is really together.

"We try to help them see that dealing with anger does not always mean getting rid of it or resolving it right away. That's simply not possible in every instance. By all means, address the anger before the sun goes down. But you might have to address it by agreeing not to deal with it now; you'll deal with it tomorrow. Then set a definite time tomorrow. You may not be able to sleep any better, but it gives you breathing space."

Breathing space. Time out. Most people need to dispel the physical rush with which anger and frustration can overload the rational circuits. Throw rocks, mow the lawn, do something physical to sap off the adrenaline that anger ignited. Indeed, you may have to postpone discussion more than once if the flame isn't banked right away.

Cooling off time is not wasted time. There are many helpful things a couple might want to do during such a time out.

Write your spouse a letter. Don't mail it. It serves its purpose just by being written. Flush it down the toilet with military honors.

Defuse the Situation

One couple hit upon a diversion by accident. In a particularly acrimonious set-to, the bride of seven months wailed, "All I know how to do is love!" Now one or the other will pop that quote into the middle of an argument and they both end up giggling. Situation defused.

Another couple take their clothes off if argument rains hard and heavy. It is very difficult to argue angrily in the nude. The sheer incongruity of the situation works against anger.

Reflect now on that fight we've been picking apart in this section. Should something have been done to prevent its escalation? Consider what you could have done (for example, "*I could have called time out by going outside to do some yard work* or *I could have given up trying to control the situation*).

Sometimes fights are the only way two people express their true feelings. In the golfing argument, that is exactly what happened. Both spouses had a problem that needed to be aired and resolved. Did that happen in your incident? The next time the issue surfaces, what are three different ways you can redirect it—making it not a fight but a negotiating point?

For instance, if the couple in our example argument worked through their fears—his about her controlling him as his mother did and hers about being neglected as a child and the natural fear of giving up some control of their lives in the intimate relationship of marriage—they can then negotiate a workable solution. The wife might say, "If you play golf once—or at the most twice—a week, then you and I also need to have a date where you are investing some time with me." Unless their underlying fears are shared with one another, however, this healthy resolution will never occur.

Think about your incident now and consider what you can do next to redirect the argument to make the experience beneficial to you and your spouse.

Although you cannot always expect perfect resolution, you must always look toward eventual resolution. The alternatives are easily seen in these mathematical equations:

$$\text{Conflict} - \text{resolution} = \text{separation.}$$
$$\text{Conflict} + \text{resolution} = \text{intimacy.}$$

That's Not What I Said

*ove doesn't end after you say
"I do." And one of the pri-
mary ways you keep it growing and blooming is by good communication. I'm sure you'll agree that men and women are different
creatures, which means we communicate differently.*

*By following a few simple principles (yes, they really can be
very simple to practice) in this chapter adapted from* Courtship
after Marriage, *you can learn to communicate in a way that will
ensure a long and happy courtship for the two of you.*

—*Zig Ziglar*
Courtship after Marriage

The fiftieth anniversary is a very special occasion, and in the
small midwestern community everyone wanted to honor this couple, so the city really rolled out the red carpet. The festivities in-

"That's Not What I Said" is adapted and taken from *Courtship after Marriage*, Zig Ziglar (1991).

cluded a breakfast celebration where the mayor spoke; one of the local service clubs sponsored a noon luncheon; friends of the family gave an afternoon tea reception; and an anniversary dinner with just the family participating concluded the activities. At about ten o'clock that evening as the big day was drawing to a close, the man and his wife were finally alone.

As was his custom, the husband went to the kitchen, prepared a piece of toast and a small glass of milk, and called his wife to announce that it was ready. She walked into the kitchen, took one look at the snack, and burst into tears. The husband was naturally puzzled and concerned, so he embraced her and asked what the problem was. She tearfully explained that she had thought that on this most special of all days he would have been more thoughtful and not given her the end piece of bread. The man was silent for a moment, and then he quietly said, "Why, Honey, that's my favorite piece of bread."

The irony is that for all those years he had been giving her what he considered to be the best and she had been accepting it with the feeling that it was the worst. The tragedy is that had they just been talking and listening while sharing their likes and dislikes, much pain could have been avoided. The natural question that follows is this: How many other "misunderstood moments" had occurred throughout the marriage because they did not share their feelings about a thousand and one different things?

Of course, that's a simple example, but an amazing number of husbands and wives really do not do a very good job of communicating.

SHARE THE DETAILS

Now, this will not come as a great shock to you, but men and women are different. Beyond the obvious differences, there are many subtleties. However, there is nothing subtle about the differences in the area of verbal communication.

Studies involving hidden microphones on little boys and girls prove quite conclusively that at an early age, not only do little girls talk more, but they are substantially more skilled and effective in their communications. They enunciate more clearly, and their words are more easily understood.

It has been estimated that in a typical twenty-four-hour day, the average woman voices some 25,000 words while the average man verbalizes 10,000 words. Unfortunately, the man invests about 9,000 of his words in his typical workday, and his wife invests about the same number in her workday. When they get back together in the evening, his verbal bank account is approaching bankruptcy while her verbal bank account contains a surplus that must be used by midnight or lost forever.

The woman often *needs* to talk and *needs* to hear her husband invest part of his verbal bank account by telling her on a daily basis of his love for her. As a matter of fact, somebody once asked when a man should tell his wife he loved her. The wit responded, "Before someone else does!" Yet another man confessed in bittersweet irony that he loved his wife so much that sometimes it was all he could do to keep from telling her. In yet another case, I heard of a man who hadn't told his wife he loved her in over twenty years and then shot the man who did!

Behind these slightly humorous/slightly truthful "slices of life," there is a serious message. Talk, listen, and communicate with your spouse. It is a fact that on average, women do talk more than men, and on average, they need to hear more from men.

Yes, I know averages are often misleading. For example, if you were to put one foot in a bucket of ice water and the other foot in a bucket of boiling water, on average, you would not be comfortable. I also know you can drown in a river that has an average depth of only seven inches. However, I can say with considerable confidence that in the communication department the average American woman is more interested in details and "small talk" than the average American man. (But who wants to be average?) Actually she has a real need, and a sensitive husband meets that need by investing a solid part of his verbal bank account in significant *and* insignificant small talk. *And* he listens with interest as his wife shares her feelings and invests her verbal bank account in him.

NO ONE IS IMMUNE

Probably the one area in which The Redhead and I have had the most difficulty throughout our marriage has been the area of communication. Most people would assume that since I earn my living primarily by speaking, writing, and doing video and audio training programs, I'm the bubbling, detail-oriented conversationalist at home. My wife will assure you that such is not the case.

I well remember a meeting with the executive staff at our company that lasted over four hours. We went into many of our plans for advertising, marketing, direct mail, and an overall approach to a new system of distribution. The meeting was lengthy and exciting. When I arrived home, The Redhead naturally asked the question, "How did it go?" I responded, "Really fine." She said, "What did you talk about?" And I replied, "Well, we got involved in some details of advertising and direct mail; we talked about a couple of new products, and some new ideas on marketing, and that was about it."

She looked at me with that "Now, come on, Zig, you can do better than that" grin and said, "Honey, you were in a meeting that lasted several hours. You have now spent less than sixty seconds telling me what took place." Normally, I talk a little more than that, but the point is the same. Women want more details than men do, and in this area all of us could improve if we really started thinking in terms of what will meet the other person's needs and make him or her happier in the process.

DIFFERENT INTERESTS AND PERCEPTIONS

An important facet of building a healthy marriage is understanding that not only are men and women "different," but they have different interests and perceptions. For example, about five years ago, my brother, Judge, and his wife, Sarah, were visiting in our home and for some reason a convention we had attended in Daytona Beach, Florida, in 1952 was mentioned. In order to put a handle on circumstances and the event itself, Sarah said to Jean, "You remember that convention, Jean. That's the one Sybil Small wore the blue dress with the white collar and belt. She had the little blue-and-white hat to go with it, as well as blue-and-white shoes." The Redhead acknowledged she remembered. I looked at my brother; he looked at me; we both broke out in laughter at the same time. I then said to Judge, "You remember that one, Boy! That's the one where Earl had on the brown suit, the brown-and-white tie, and brown-and-white shoes." And, of course, we laughed even louder.

Question: What man would remember what someone else had been wearing thirty-three years ago? My only point is this: Husbands and wives must clearly understand that there are vast differences—and that those differences don't make one any better or any worse than the other—differences simply mean each of us is unique. When husbands and wives learn to deal with those differences in a kind, loving, and gracious manner, our chances of having a romantic relationship all our lives will be greatly enhanced.

THEY'RE ONLY "WORDS"

Words were important to Thomas Carlyle, but he didn't realize just how important until after the death of his wife, whom he sometimes neglected in life. In his diary was found what has been termed by some the saddest sentence in the English language. Carlyle wrote, "Oh, that I had you yet for five minutes by my side, that I might tell you all."

C. S. Lewis in *Reflections on the Psalms* wrote,

> It is not out of compliment that lovers keep on telling one another how beautiful they are. The delight is incomplete 'til it is expressed. It is frustrating to have discovered a new author and not be able to tell anyone how good he is, to come suddenly at the turn of the road upon some mountain valley of unexpected grandeur and then have to keep silent because the people with you care for it no more than for a tin can in the ditch, to hear a good joke and find no one to share it with.

IF YOU CAN'T TALK, WRITE

A poet once said that those who do not show their love do not love. I'm not certain that's completely accurate, but I know there are many husbands and wives who are loved but have no assurance of that love. In those cases, the mate is so non-expressive that whether or not they are truly loved is pure guesswork. There are many people who will protest that they are "just not very good at expressing themselves," and that they show their love in other ways. While every act and evidence of love is important, a mate needs verbal reassurance (a note is pretty good, too) on a regular basis of being truly loved. (It literally takes only one second to say "I love you," and you can emphasize each word in three seconds.) In most cases, the man is not the expressive one and does not verbalize his feelings or demonstrate his affections unless he wants to express them through sexual involvement with his wife. This causes his wife to feel used, not loved.

For people who do not verbalize very well, I would like to remind you that you apparently verbalized well enough before you were married to persuade your mate to marry you. This indicates that your *ability* to communicate is not the problem. Your lack of interest or even unwillingness to communicate is the major problem.

The sad truth is, many times husbands and wives, even after years of marriage, still have difficulty discussing everyday involvements ranging from painting the front porch to deciding who takes out the kitty litter. One of the reasons for the breakdown is that many times the mate who opens the conversation has been interrupted before completing the thought or feeling. On occasion one mate finishes the sentence, word, or thought for the other one. Incidentally, the offending party might not be fully aware of this annoying habit. This thoughtless habit definitely is irritating and too many times closes the lines of communication. Oftentimes the one who opened the conversation feels a "what's the use" attitude and then stubbornly refuses to make any further effort to continue the conversation.

If you recognize any signs of communication problems in

your home, let me urge you to write a letter to your mate and either mail it or place it in a spot where your mate will be sure to find it when you're not around. This gives you the advantage of being able to carefully—and less emotionally—state how you feel without fear of either interruption or rejection. Written communication also demonstrates a willingness, even an eagerness on your part to solve the problem and open those lines of communication.

I encourage you not to bring out a laundry list of perceived ills or problems, but to lovingly and factually state your desire to draw closer to your mate by being able to express your thoughts and feelings. Be careful not to attack your mate personally. Instead, address your concerns, your feelings, and the problem as you perceive it. Use phrases like:

- "I always feel bad when we hit a roadblock in our communication efforts."
- "It's amazing how each of us communicates so well with others, and yet we seem to have difficulty communicating with each other."
- "Would you help me to understand why this happens and what I can do to help us find a solution?"
- "I'm not blaming you. I'm just saying there is a problem, and we certainly want to solve it so we can get on with loving each other."
- "I feel bad when I am unable to express my concern in an acceptable manner, especially about some things that mean so much to both of us."

Trying to just say the words I have written here will come across as "patronizing" and won't solve the problem, so put these statements in your own words and share them with complete sincerity. If you will carefully choose *your* words prior to the "moment of emotion," you will be much better prepared to handle the situation.

IF YOU'RE WRONG, APOLOGIZE

Be courageous and apologize when you make a mistake! For example, "I know I should have called you last night to let you know I was running late, but a phone really was not handy and driving out of the way to find one would have delayed my arrival even more. Next time I will do better so that you will at least know that I am alive and well and headed in that direction. Why don't we sit down tonight and just talk about this communication problem?" You might write a short note saying, "I apologize for not picking up the bath mat this morning, and I understand that upsets you. I'll try to do better next time. P.S. Thank you for the delicious meal last night. You really outdid yourself on that one!" Only insert that last line if the facts are obviously true. Insincere flattery will not help your case at this point.

You can disagree without being disagreeable.

Actually, in many cases, when you acknowledge that you have made a mistake, you are encouraging and laying the groundwork for a more open and loving relationship with each other. A gentle, loving attitude is the key. People who are *"brutally* frank" and "let it *all* hang out" are courting disaster in any relationship. Honesty *and* compassion are important companions. All of us disagree from time to time, and it's a sign of maturity when we can disagree without being disagreeable.

For what it's worth, when you are wrong and admit that you made a mistake and ask forgiveness, you clearly establish the fact that you're wiser today than you were yesterday. I don't believe your mate would hold that one against you! Remember the biblical admonition found in Ephesians 4:32: "Be ye kind one to another, tenderhearted, forgiving one another" (KJV). We need to also remember that until we forgive each other, God is not going to forgive us (Matthew 6:14–15). Kindness and gentle communication are often the keys that unlock the door of forgiveness.

ARE YOU LISTENING?

There's another crucial ingredient in communication. In fact, in some ways an even more important ingredient than saying the right thing is *listening!* Many marriage counselors say that not listening is the number one problem in families today. Studies show that poor listeners have less satisfying marriages as well as less successful careers. (You *can't* respond to a message if you didn't "get" the message.)

The results of a widely publicized survey stated that 98 percent of the women surveyed wished for more "verbal closeness" with their male partners, and the most frequently cited cause of women's anger was "He doesn't listen." Seventy-one percent of the women surveyed said they had given up and no longer even tried to draw their husbands out. That's sad *and* a sure sign of a "sick marriage." Fortunately the illness need not be fatal, and it won't be if you practice the communication techniques we're covering.

HERE'S HOW

Mastering the skill of listening is not nearly as difficult as some would believe. Here are some specific steps you can take to become a better listener immediately!

1. Give the speaker your undivided attention. When you make eye contact and focus on your mate, you're saying, "You are important to me. Your words and ideas have meaning in my life." When you read the paper at the breakfast or dinner table, look around the room, continue watching a television program (or change channels with the remote control), or "doodle" while your mate speaks, you send a very different message. It's simply wise to listen carefully and from time to time nod your head or inject a word or thought to make absolutely certain your mate understands that you are giving him or her your undivided attention.

2. Show your attentiveness with your body language. Sit up and lean forward when talking with your mate. If your manager or the President of the United States were to visit with you, your posture would be different than it often is with your spouse. Why? Your mate will, over the years, have a much greater meaning in your life than *anyone* else. Don't "slight" him or her because of familiarity. Do show respect by being a "well positioned" listener.

3. *Rephrase or restate key statements.* If you will feed back what you think you are hearing, in your own words, you will show an interest, and you will increase understanding. Use phrases like, "So what I hear you saying is . . ."; "Do you mean to say . . ."; "And that made you feel . . . (angry, happy, sad, glad, etc.)." On those occasions when either of you is frustrated and has a tendency to unload in an impetuous, impatient, dogmatic way, it's certainly a sign of maturity if the other person will quietly say, "I can understand why you're so upset, Sweetheart. Johnny forgot that he had been potty trained and not only ended up with dirty pants, but managed to soil the rug, the bedspread, and the bath mat. And you already had more to do than any two people could handle. Most of all, after all the time you spent on his training, I know how disappointed you must be. No wonder you're so upset!"

Verbalizing the problem clearly shows that you are listening, that you understand and are sympathetic, and that you appreciate all her efforts. Most important, you communicate that even though *things* did not go well, *she* is A-O.K. This approach diffuses a lot of the hurt and anger and preserves her worth as a mother and a person. In most cases, a sympathetic ear, a loving hug, *and* a helping hand will solve the problem of the moment— and firmly implant another brick in the building of love on which your marriage rests.

4. *Let your mate finish the sentence.* Interrupting with your thoughts or finishing a sentence for your spouse is a fast way to quash communication. Listen—pause—and listen! When you are planning on being married a lifetime, there is plenty of time for you to respond. Listening is just as important as talking. After all, God gave us two ears and only one mouth. We are often guilty of thinking about our next sentence while another person is talking rather than listening carefully to his or her exact words. This is particularly harmful with a spouse. When you're in a conversa-

tion with your spouse, try to clear your mind of all your pet personal preferences and prejudices. Make an attempt to view the conversation in the clear light of day. Listen from your mate's frame of reference. What has he been through today? What is her general emotional state? Listen with your ears and your eyes.

5. *Express your feelings.* One of the most important, and easily the most neglected, components in effective communication involves the simple expressing of feelings. That's sad because in order for real intimacy to develop, partners must be able to express their emotions to one who listens. "Feeling" or "gut level communication" occurs most often with the use of the phrase "I feel . . ." because "I feel" messages convey honest emotions. Incidentally, it's good to be honest about your true emotions, but it's even better to keep them under control. Never say anything derogatory about your mate's character or personality. And eliminate such phrases from your vocabulary as "you never," "you always," "I can't," "you should," and "you shouldn't."

6. *Be careful about supplying solutions.* Particularly if his wife does not work outside the home, a man may make a fundamental mistake of thinking that when he arrives home in the evening and his wife proceeds to dump part of her frustrations of the day on him, she wants him to play Solomon and give her the benefit of his incredible wisdom. For her, it's been "one of those days." She's been doing battle with an infant and a rambunctious three-year-old, and in his mind she wants him to offer an immediate solution to the problem.

In most instances, that is not the case. She understands that in the majority of these situations there is no immediate solution. What she really wants is an *attentive* ear, a *sympathetic* listener, a *caring* husband, and some *assurance* that she is a good person, a good mother, and a good wife.

One man put it this way: "I was working in a job that required me to quickly, efficiently, and effectively discover answers to problems. That was a real help to me in my job, but a problem in my marriage. When my wife was concerned, harried, upset, or ready to give up on our children, me, herself, or the family pet, the 'world's greatest problem solver' was on the spot with exactly the right answer . . . at exactly the wrong time. Time management, goal setting, appointments to be set, chores to be prioritized, anything and everything she needed was available—except the most important thing of all: SENSITIVITY. She needed a listener, not a talker; she wanted care and concern, not direction. The more my wife failed to heed my words of wisdom, the more I demanded to be heard. My desire to help became a millstone around the neck of our marriage."

Listening is especially important when your mate is frustrated and has had it "up to here." A listening ear, combined with genuine interest and concern and a little hugging, will go a long way in building or rebuilding a relationship.

Listening is loving.

---

7. *Remember: Listening is loving.* A wise man once said that talking is sharing, but listening is caring. For this reason, a wise husband will carefully listen to the woes of the moment and myriads of details and incidents that make up his mate's day. He understands that duty makes us do things well, but love makes us do them beautifully. The exciting thing is that what occasionally starts out as "something you should do" will turn into "something you want to do." Interestingly enough, over a period of time, you will be amazed at how exciting some of those details can be.

THE "HEART" OF LISTENING SKILLS

Good listening is a skill that requires *practice, empathy,* and *true concern* for the other person. There is no greater security you can give your spouse than to carefully listen and verbally encourage with words such as "I know what you mean"; "I understand"; "For goodness sake!"; "You don't mean it!"; "You've got to be kidding!"; "He said WHAT?; "That's great"; "My goodness." Of course, "I love you" will fit into just about any conversation.

IT TAKES TIME TO COMMUNICATE

Amazingly enough, many couples make time for just about everything—and everybody—but each other. I'll have to confess that I am possibly the most guilty person alive on this one, or at least I *was* very guilty. I still am to a degree, but not nearly as much as I was a few years ago. In the past, when acquaintances or business associates would pass through town and say, "It's my only night here," or "I'm just here for the weekend," I would expect my wife to "understand" that I had to see my friend or business associate and that she would have to forget what she had been planning all week. Basically it was a "me-first-and-you-and-the-kids-can-have-what's-left over" approach to marriage. That *is* communication, but unfortunately it's the kind of communication that eliminates any possibility of a loving marriage.

I'm pleased to say that now, in most cases, I have my priorities in order and explain to my business friends that I'd love to get together but prior commitments make it impossible. I will confess that I'm still having to work on turning down some of those intrusions on family time because sometimes they just seem so important. However, in the final analysis, when you make one exception, you'll open the door to rationalizing the second; and as former President Ronald Reagan would say, "There you go again." Now I make appointments with The Redhead, and since my relationship with her is by far the most significant relationship I have, with rare exceptions I keep those appointments. That *communicates*, loudly and clearly, how I really feel about her.

YOU'RE VERY IMPORTANT, BUT I'M BUSY

Even as I was writing this chapter on communications, the sound of The Redhead's voice broke my concentration. "Honey, can you come help me with this?"

My first thought was, "Now, she knows I'm in the middle of writing this book on courtship after marriage"—and then before I could finish the thought, the irony caused me to stop and laugh out loud. Isn't it fascinating how we instinctively and instantaneously rate what we are doing as being more important than what our mate is doing?

In this case, what I was doing was clearly the most urgent and important. After all, a book on the family—and specifically on courtship—would rate somewhere in importance between the Bible and *The Decline and Fall of the Roman Empire.* And what was The Redhead doing that was so important she dared interrupt me to ask for my help? Nothing—except wrapping Christmas presents, preparing dinner, and setting the table for this family for which I was so passionately declaring my love (and especially my love for her) in this book.

The first time she will know why I was grinning so big when I responded to her call for help will be when she reads these words in this book. When the impact of my own hypocrisy hit me, I laughed at myself and responded to her call. The "interruption" took all of three minutes (counting the hugging time), and I was "back to the drawing board"—a happier and hopefully wiser and more sensitive husband. By responding to her call for help, I had communicated my love for her and her importance to me.

THIS IS A BIG ONE

One of the best and most effective communication steps The Redhead and I have ever taken took place on January 1, 1989. To give you a brief background, let me state that on July 4, 1972, I made my commitment to Jesus Christ. The Redhead had made her commitment much earlier. Beginning January 1, 1989, we took another giant step in our relationship when we each acquired the New International Version of the *One Year Bible.* That simply means the Bible is divided into 365 portions and each day's reading includes something from the Old Testament, something from the New, something from Psalms, and something from Proverbs.

Almost without fail, we discuss what we've read that day. If I'm in Dallas, we read the Bible together; and when I'm on the road, we each will have read our Bibles, then we pray together before we discuss the message. It's uncanny how God seems to almost always reveal the same things to each of us from His Word each day. There are also those exciting times when He has shown each one of us something of an entirely different nature than what the other has seen. I can tell you that we feel even closer as a direct result of sharing God's Word on a daily basis.

Over the years I've noticed many times when a particularly moving event takes place in our lives and we are drawn closer and closer to God, we are invariably drawn closer and closer to each other. When you learn to love through Christ, the sweetness of that love is beyond belief, and those communication barriers begin to come down.

COMMUNICATE WITH QUESTIONS AND HUMOR

A sense of humor is critically important if romance and fun are to be permanent parts of the marriage, and humor is a needed ingredient in effective communication. Neither men nor women are attracted to grim, humorless members of the opposite sex. However, we need to make certain our mate thinks that what we say about him or her really is funny and is *not* a put-down in any way. For example, I never tell a joke where my wife is even involved in the scene without clearing it with her first.

Never will I forget one Friday evening when I returned from a tough week on the road. The Redhead met me at the airport, and she was dressed "fit to kill." As usual, she had on some of the good, sweet-smelling stuff that I especially like.

As we were waiting for my bag to come down on the carousel, she snuggled up real close, slipped her hand into mine (she's powerfully friendly, anyhow!), and said, "Honey, I know it's been a long, tough week for you, so if you want to we can stop by the store on the way home and pick up a nice steak or some seafood. While you relax with the paper, I'll prepare a nice dinner for two. Tom is spending the night with Sam, so we'll be by ourselves. Then, Honey, after we've had a nice dinner, I'm certain you won't want to get involved in cleaning dirty dishes and greasy pots and pans, so you can just relax and catch up on some of your reading while I take care of cleaning the kitchen.

"It shouldn't take me more than an hour, hour and a half, two hours at the most. (Pause) Or the thought occurs to me, Honey, that you might be more comfortable and enjoy the evening more if I were completely free to devote all of my time and energy to you. I could do this in a really nice restaurant. Of course, Honey, it's entirely up to you. What do you prefer?" (That Redhead does have a way with words.)

I don't really think it's necessary to tell you we did not stop by the grocery store or cook that dinner at home.*

Not only is humor important and effective in communications, but gentleness, kindness, and thoughtfulness are also of paramount importance. The guideline for effective communication is for husbands to be just as gentle, kind, and thoughtful in conversations with wives as they are with secretaries or complete strangers who stop them on the street and ask for directions. Wives should be just as thoughtful and considerate of husbands as they are of their coworkers, their employees, or even their hairdressers.

BE SENSITIVE

When your mate is tired, is devastated over a disappointment, is frustrated or angry, is physically ill, just "blew" an assignment, or did something he or she perceives as a "dumb mistake":

DON'T: make amorous advances; press him or her to make an important decision or even involve him or her in sharing important information unless it's almost a life-and-death issue that must be dealt with at that moment; be critical of anything your mate has done in the past or bring up something that has to be done in the future.

DO: be gentle, loving, supportive, and kind; be empathetic and understanding; adopt the servant's attitude and gently ask if there is anything you can do to lighten the load; affirm personal worth; express your love and support; say, "You are number one with me," and hug, touch, or hold hands.

* From *Secrets of Closing the Sale* (Fleming H. Revell, 1984), reprinted with permission.

Timing is vital, and when it coincides with genuine sensitivity and empathy, it builds a marvelous base for real friendship and helps build a love that truly will last a lifetime.

COMMIT—COMMUNICATE—CARE

I want to emphasize that if you practice every communication skill and follow all the suggestions in this book and every other book on the subject, there will still be those occasional miscommunications. In short, I don't believe there is any such thing as a trouble-free marriage with no disagreements. As I said earlier, though, you can disagree without being disagreeable. In our case, The Redhead and I have had, and do have, our difficulties. However, I believe one of the reasons our love has grown through the difficulties, and our marriage is more stable and solid than ever, has to do with the way we have dealt with each other when we disagreed or miscommunicated.

Basically, when we have crossed wires, we have always treated each other with respect. Not once has either of us been vindictive and called the other by some names we would later regret. We've never attacked each other personally, and that's important. We try to remember that failure is an event and not a person, and that we're going to be together a long time. In short, when we made the commitment to marry, we made the commitment to stay together. When we made the commitment to stay together, we knew, as a practical matter, that it would be more fun if we communicated and respected each other. To paraphrase a prophet of old, I encourage you to "*stay* and do thou likewise."

Chapter

13

Keeping No Record *Rom* of Wrongs

Dear Joy and Robin,

I was thinking today about Ephesians 4:32: "And be kind to one another, tender-hearted, forgiving one another, just as God in Christ also forgave you." How wonderful our marriages would be if we could apply just this one verse!

As husbands and wives, we need the healing touch of forgiveness. Where else could there be more opportunity to annoy, insult, or offend than in the most intimate of relationships, marriage?

Dr. Ed Wheat affirms that newlyweds need to develop the "skill" of forgiving each other. Forgiveness is not a feeling but a choice we make, and often it goes against every self-centered fiber of our being. This choice is vividly seen in this story told about Clara Barton, the founder of the American Red Cross. One day she was reminded of a vicious deed that someone had done

"Keeping No Record of Wrongs" is adapted and taken from *How to Really Love Your Man,* Linda Dillow (1993).

to her years before. But she acted as if she had never heard of the incident! "Don't you remember it?" her friend asked. "No" came Barton's reply. "I distinctly remember forgetting it." A conscious choice to forgive a vicious deed, a conscious choice to continue forgiving when reminded of the deed. By replying, "I distinctly remember forgetting it," Clara Barton was saying, "I remember choosing to forgive, and I still choose to forgive."

Did her choice eliminate all pain caused by the horrible act? Certainly not; but her words portray a woman at peace, a woman who was able to love because she forgave. First Corinthians 13:5 maintains that "love keeps no record of wrongs" (NIV). To love and forgive, we must

1. Choose with our free will to forgive.
2. Make the promise to lift the burden of guilt from the person as far as the wrong against you is concerned. Remember the person's sin no more, never naming it again to the person, to others, or to yourself.
3. Seal it with your behavior, demonstrating love with tender-hearted kindness.
4. Trust God to allow you to forget and to renew your mind with new attitudes.[1]

The following story has been an encouragement to me to follow these four steps:

When missionaries first went to the Eskimos, they could not find a word in their language for forgiveness so they had to compound one. This turned out to be ISSUMAGJOUJUNG-NAINERMIK! It is a formidable looking group of letters but an expression that has a beautiful connotation for those who understand it. It means "Not-being-able-to-think-about-it-anymore." I have this huge word "ISSUMAGJOUJUNGNAINERMIK" posted in large letters on my refrigerator. I get some strange looks when people see it but it reminds me to forgive freely and forget, to not be able to think about it anymore.[2]

My prayer for you, my daughters, and for me is that we might be faithful to choose to be good forgivers; that our marriages might be characterized by forgiveness, kindness, and tenderness.

Much love,
Mom

Leaving my side of the road to come to yours is
what caring is all about.
—David Ferguson
Intimate Moments

PART THREE

*The Art
of
Sexual Intimacy*

14

Learning to Say the "S" Word (or Building a Creative Love Life)

*Y*ou're probably chuckling at the title of this chapter, but isn't it strange that grown-ups like us—married grown-ups, no less —have a hard time discussing a topic that is so important to married life? It shouldn't be that difficult, should it? Didn't God create sex for our pleasure as well as procreation? We're delighted to present this chapter from our book, The Marriage Track, as a means of getting couples like you to be honest with each other about your sexual relationship, to take a look at past attitudes or experiences that may hamper freedom in your sex life. We have also included a chapter on building a Christian marriage, that is sure to help your marriage last a lifetime. And we're hoping that you can laugh along with us as we share stories from our own marriage. Being creative can go a long way toward experiencing

"Learning to Say the 'S' Word (or Building a Creative Love Life)" is adapted and taken from *The Marriage Track*, Dave and Claudia Arp (1992).

the freedom in married love that God intended for us. Have fun!

—*Dave and Claudia Arp*
The Marriage Track

Sex! There, we've said it. . . . We've said the "S" word.

Why are people so hesitant to talk openly about the sexual dimension of life? When we stop and think about it, we realize sexual thoughts and feelings are prominent throughout our lives.

· In the teenage years, we dream about it, and if coming from a Judeo-Christian value system, we do all we can to use self-restraint.

· In our twenties and thirties, as the children begin to arrive on the scene, we dream about the day we'll once again have the energy for it and fewer interruptions.

· In our forties, as our own children become teenagers, our thoughts about sex focus on our kids and on our hope that they will not experiment with it.

· In our fifties and sixties, the nest empties, and "we've forgotten how!" as one friend said, or might add, we're just too busy.

· Our seventies and eighties allow us time for sexual fantasies vicariously lived out through watching the soaps on television. For many of the elderly the "S" word is again a dream.

While sexual thoughts and feelings are close to the surface during all the stages of life, why is it so hard to say the "S" word? Recently, while we were leading a class for parents whose children are entering adolescence, the "S" word came up in a discussion of sex education. Members of this group were definitely in the "worrying about our own kids" stage.

Their fears are not without foundation. Our world grossly misuses God's positive gift of sex. Sex is used to sell just about anything. After all, what does the kind of detergent we use have to do with a fulfilling sexual relationship? Does a mouthwash or toothpaste really give sex appeal?

When we were growing up, the culture applauded fidelity. Today young people are told to have "safe sex," and the media presents sex as total ecstasy with no responsibilities or consequences. No wonder the parents in our group were scared. "I don't want to tell my child about sex because I want her to remain innocent," said one concerned parent.

We were amazed at this parent's naivete. First, if this eleven-year-old didn't know about the "S" word, we would be surprised. Secondly, what attitude was this parent unintentionally passing on to her daughter? If no knowledge of sex equals innocence, does an understanding of the sexual dimension of life equal guilt? This kind of fallacious thinking is the source of some of our own inhibitions and hesitations to use the "S" word.

Think back into your own childhood with us. What were your earliest impressions of sex? Did you believe the "birds and bees" story?

One girl asked her grandmother, "Where did I come from?"

The grandmother replied, "Honey, the stork brought you."

"But what about my mommy? Where did she come from?" she continued to probe.

"We found her in the cabbage patch."

"What about you?" the granddaughter asked.

"My parents found me behind the rosebush."

The next day at school the little girl reported to her class, "There has not been a normal birth in our family for three generations!"

Claudia's earliest memory of any conversation about sex was in the third or fourth grade when an older friend told her what boys and girls do to each other to make babies. It didn't sound like fun, and at that point Claudia decided to be an old maid! Dave also got his initial impression about the "S" word from friends—just as inaccurate and confusing.

Take a minute to recall the first time you talked about sex.

Whether our parents used the "S" word or not, our being here is evidence our parents had at least some interest in sex. Is that hard to believe? Probably all kids at some time are convinced that their parents really "don't do it!" It's especially hard for teenagers to think about their parents as sexual creatures.

What do you remember from your home of origin? If your parents were comfortable with the "S" word and were open and honest and positive about sex with you, count yourself among the very fortunate. If, more typically, your parents choked on the word *sex* and left many unasked questions unanswered, you may have entered marriage with a confused picture of sex. For instance, growing up did you hear comments like "Don't be loose" or "She's a fast girl. Don't be like her!"? You weren't sure what "loose" and "fast" actually meant, but you knew they weren't positive.

God created sex for our enjoyment and pleasure.

Then your own hormones began to "click on." You met that special girl or boy, and sexual feelings you didn't know you could ever have began to surface. Not only did you try your darndest to use self-restraint, but you began to feel guilty for having all those feelings!

Those who grew up in conservative homes may have gotten the impression that sex is sinful. Certainly God intended the sexual union to be experienced within the framework of marriage, but the Scriptures also teach that God created sex for our enjoyment and pleasure as well as procreation. Many overlook the fact that sex was God's idea.

The Bible discusses sex openly and matter-of-factly, acknowledging that it is a precious gift from God. Consider Proverbs 5:18–19:

> Let your fountain be blessed,
> And rejoice with the wife of your youth.
> As a loving deer and a graceful doe,
> Let her breasts satisfy you at all times;
> And always be enraptured with her love.

Look again at Genesis 2:24–25: "For this cause a man shall leave his father and his mother and shall cleave to his wife, and they shall become one flesh. And they were both naked, the man and his wife, and were not ashamed" (NASB). God put His stamp of approval on the sexual union in marriage. He not only approves of it; He originated it! It is to be an expression of love between husband and wife, fulfilling and enjoyable. Why then is it so hard to say the "S" word?

Back to Our Dating Days

In recalling our dating days, we have to admit that our relationship was far from platonic. We were quite familiar with each other, but did manage to save the big "S" for marriage. Even with the culture working with us, it wasn't all that easy. Once we read a book on how to handle sexual impulses. The author suggested that when we felt tempted, we should get out of the car and run around it five times. That was about as helpful as taking cold showers! Then we finally made it to that big day—our wedding day—only to discover that "doing what comes naturally just wasn't enough."

Think about it. First, you've got all these conflicting messages. For what seems like an eternity, you have been working your hardest to avoid the "big sin." Suddenly you say, "I do," and it is now God's good gift to you. It is now okay to experience the big "S." And then you begin to realize that instructions for sexual fulfillment were not included with your marriage license. Maybe, like us, you felt a little let down when you discovered that here is another learning experience in which you slowly develop expertise and new skills. For us it didn't happen instantly as it does on television. Our marital camera didn't fade into instant ecstasy!

We must admit, we got married thirty years ago, and getting any kind of counseling before marriage was still the exception. Today, premarital counseling may help, but face it—you can't learn to swim until you get into the water.

The problem with the "S" word is that we talk about it with friends and with each other before marriage, but once we say "I do," talking about sex becomes a "taboo." When things don't instantly click in the sexual arena, many conclude that sex is overrated—it's okay but not what you had hoped it would be. So you compensate in other areas of your relationship and relegate the "S" word to an inactive vocabulary file. Some cover up even with their mates: "Honey, I'm just too tired . . . too busy . . . the neighbors will hear us." Before long the sexual part of marriage is buried under your inhibitions, lack of knowledge, and boredom. Whatever happened to all those sexual feelings you had trouble controlling before marriage?

With today's statistics, we can't leave this subject without addressing those who tried using self-restraint before marriage but just didn't make it. You feel guilty and wish you could go back and wipe the slate clean. Added to the dilemma of overcoming inhibitions, boredom, and lack of knowledge is a big hunk of guilt.

Maybe you regret that you had several previous sexual partners before you met your mate. This could have been before you embraced the Christian faith or—even more guilt producing—you may have slipped while you were trying to follow the Lord. Maybe as a child you were the victim of sexual abuse or incest or have gone through the trauma of rape.

Whatever your past, there is healing, forgiveness, and hope. While *The Marriage Track* is not adequate to deal with deep-seated problems, we encourage you to get help if your past is blocking your future. Do not hesitate to seek counseling from a qualified professional. If you don't know where to find one, begin by consulting your pastor. Help is available, but it's up to you to take the initiative to find it!

THE NEWLYWED GAME—LEARNING TO SAY THE "S" WORD

Let's move on to our early marriage days. Our initial disappointment became a challenge to learn and develop expertise. We decided to tackle building a fulfilling sexual relationship with all the gusto we could muster. We were still in college and as poor as church mice. Our major form of entertainment was working on our sex life. We made some basic commitments to each other that helped us to get our sexual relationship on the right track, and thirty years later we are still tracking together. Some of the discoveries we made in those first years of marriage follow.

We had to *talk* about it! We had to develop our "S" word vocabulary. How would the other know what feels good unless he or she was told? In some ways it was like learning a new language and was awkward at first. For years we had tried not even to think these thoughts, much less verbalize them! We also had to be willing to talk about our fears and inhibitions. One of us was much more inhibited than the other, so a major part of "talking it out" was the willingness of the other to listen!

The Bible gives us the utmost freedom to be creative in marital lovemaking.

We had to *become explorers!* In this arena, talking just isn't enough. We actually had to explore each other's bodies and discover what felt good and what we didn't like. Doesn't that sound simple? Yes! Was it simple? *No!* Remember, before marriage we felt guilty if we "over" touched. Guilt is accompanied by a fear that we can't perform or won't be exciting to our mate. One discovery we made that helped us and can help any married couple is to plan times of "nondemand touching," exploring each other's body to see how good we can make the other feel. The goal is not sexual union—as a matter of fact, for this exercise sexual intercourse is forbidden! This helped us to relax, took off all the pressure of performance, and allowed us to get to know each other in a more intimate way.

We became *readers and learners.* Thirty years ago there weren't many "how-to" books, but we managed to find a few. We liked the ones that had illustrations. This helped us to be brave enough to try different positions for lovemaking. Not all were successful, but along the way we began to learn what worked for us. The Bible gives us the utmost freedom to be creative in marital lovemaking. There are no rules, no regulations, and no instructions on positions, foreplay, or frequency of sexual intercourse. The guiding principle is that it is pleasurable for both. Hebrews puts it this way: "Keep the marriage bed undefiled" (13:4).

We learned to be *"others centered."* In the sexual side of marriage it's easy to become "me centered" and lose our sensitivity to our partner. We forget that the best way to really please ourselves is to please our mate. Jesus said it is more blessed to give than to receive. This is true in the sexual relationship as well as in the totality of life. We found that when we focused on pleasing the other, we were less self-conscious and even overcame some of our inhibitions. We tried to learn all we could about what turned each other on. We found that Dave tended to be visual while Claudia responded to tenderness and talk.

How Long to Adjust?

We have heard that it takes up to six years for a married couple to adjust sexually and up to twenty years to enjoy each other fully. How long have you been married? Six months? Five years? Twenty years? Let's say you have been married for five years. Do you have five years of expertise in this area or one year's expertise repeated five times? Is your sexual relationship growing? What are you doing to make your marriage a love affair? If you're not at the love affair level with your mate, we'd like to help you put romance into your love life.

Think back to your wedding night and the first years of your marriage.

Can you identify with some of our memories? Perhaps you identify more with our friends who are both highly sexual people. They can respond to each other sexually even in the middle of a serious conflict. Their sex life holds them together and requires little effort to make it run smoothly.

On the other end of the spectrum are the couple so disappointed with sex that they relegated it to the back burner and chose to work on other areas in their marriage and never made it past those initial adjustments. Maybe children arrived quickly or they just never got around to working things out.

THE "S" WORD IN THE TWENTIES AND THIRTIES

About the time things began to settle out for us sexually, the kids started arriving, and we started dreaming about that day way in the future when there would be fewer interruptions and much more energy. We handled our sex life and the first baby without too much stress, but when our second child arrived, things got complicated.

Psychologists tell us that the two times of greatest stress on a marriage are when you have toddlers and again when you have teens. If you have both, you have an extra challenge to keep it all together!

For us the hardest time in our sexual relationship was when we had three children ages five and under. Dave, the night owl, eagerly looked forward to lovemaking after the baby's late night feeding. Claudia, the morning lark, barely survived feeding the baby, and all she wanted after that was sleep—blessed sleep. Missing each other's expectations just made us grumpy in the morning. Actually Claudia would have been more up for sex at five in the morning, but Dave was asleep and the baby was crying. We both began to wonder if this was "natural" birth control.

Maybe you find yourself in a similar stressful situation. Your children are draining your energy, or maybe you don't have children but you're both working extremely hard in your careers. Time for loving is elusive and rare. Fortunately for us, in those stressful years we could still talk about the "S" word and both wanted to find a solution to our dilemma. Maybe some of our helpful discoveries will also help you. Yes, there was a solution, and things did get better.

A Fulfilling Sexual Relationship Takes Understanding

We don't marry into an instant understanding of each other. Before we were married, we felt we knew and understood just about everything about each other. But later we discovered there were new discoveries and areas we had to work at in understanding each other. Our friends Helen and Pete love each other and want to have a good sexual relationship, but they need help in understanding how they are different. Check out this scenario:

Helen decided to make this night special. Lately their sexual relationship had been sort of bland, and she decided to spice it up. "First," she thought, "I'll pick up Pete's favorite Chinese food, pull out the china and silver, and even use linen napkins and light the candles." She followed her good intentions with action and even splurged on a manicure. When Pete walked in the door, soft music played in the background, and Helen was ready!

What about Pete? The main thing on his agenda was getting home to see the NBA final on television. At lunch Pete and his management team had talked about the basketball final. He knew his team had a great chance to win it. His agenda was to get home, turn on the TV, pull up a TV tray, and watch his favorite team take the championship!

Helen and Pete had different expectations for the evening— neither good nor bad but definitely conflicting.

When Pete arrived home, Helen was ready for a passionate kiss and bear hug. Instead she got a quick peck as Pete headed straight for the TV. Talk about expectations! They were in conflict, but neither understood the other's hopes. The evening went downhill from there. Pete was so into the ballgame that he was missing Helen's act. A drama was being played and he didn't even know he was the villain!

Later as they were preparing to go to bed, Helen began to undress. Pete is a visual type of guy, and just seeing his wife undress caused his blood to flow. As he began to show a little loving initiative, Helen ran out of the bedroom in tears!

What was Pete's crime? He and Helen failed to understand their expectations and the different way they responded to each other. Pete was stimulated by sight. If Helen had been a "total woman" and met him at the door in a raincoat (only), he might not have made it to the NBA final on TV. On the other hand, if Pete had given Helen the tenderness and chatter she desired, her response could have been different too.

What about you? What puts you in a loving mood? Take time to talk about this with your mate.

A Fulfilling Sexual Relationship Takes Time

Too often what happens is that other things take precedence over the sexual relationship. You want to work on it but don't set aside time to spend alone together. Remember, it takes time to communicate, to work through conflict, and to build a creative love life. Ten minutes after the ball game on TV just won't do. Let us encourage you to commit yourselves to taking the time and making the effort to make sex a growing, exciting part of your marriage. It can happen!

We started by carving out a regular time each week when we could be alone without the children. Having an office in our home proved advantageous. One year we instigated our "Monday Mornings." All three children were in kindergarten or Mom's Day Out and we had full run of the house. We discovered that there is nothing sacred about making love at night. Monday mornings were great! Your schedule may not be as flexible as ours, but you need to find the time that works for you and plan it! For example, maybe you can hire a baby-sitter to take your kids out for a couple of hours Saturday mornings.

We also started the tradition of going off alone together. We began to realize we needed extended times alone together—more than just a morning. So we began to look for opportunities to plan just-for-two getaways. We couldn't afford to hire a sitter to come and stay with our children for an extended time, and our parents lived too far away. But we did have friends—very good friends—who offered to keep our three Indians. We reciprocated by keeping their two girls, and we're sure we got the better deal!

Years later two of our early getaways stand out in our memories, but for very different reasons. The first was a weekend we went to a cabin in Alabama. This was our first weekend to get away alone, and it was "love city" from the time we got there to the time we left! Dave remembers the Alabama weekend as very fulfilling. Claudia remembers being oh so exhausted.

The second getaway we especially remember is the week we spent at the beach in Florida. Claudia fondly remembers the slow pace of life, the long walks on the beach, romantic interludes, candlelit dinners for two, and shopping together and buying a new dress. Dave remembers it as a great week too, but years later confided he was a little disappointed that we didn't make love every day we were there.

Make your marriage . . . a love affair.

If we could live those years over again, we would talk more about our expectations and what is realistic for us. The key is to find balance and to come up with your own unique plan. While you're parenting toddlers, a fulfilling sexual relationship is not going to happen spontaneously!

You may want to take a few minutes right now and talk about your unique situation and what you can do to make your marriage more of a love affair. Take a tip from the Arps and do talk about your expectations. When you plan a getaway for two, you may want to talk about which of our getaways you identify with more—the cabin in Alabama or the beach in Florida? Where in your weekly schedule can you carve out some just-for-two loving time?

SEX IN THE LATE THIRTIES AND FORTIES

Let's jump ahead a few years, past the late-night feedings. The "S" word is still around. Now our own teenage fantasies and sexual dreams become nightmares and fears for our own teenagers. We pray daily they will have the self-restraint that was so difficult to find in our own dating and premarriage years.

That elusive and subtle fear may enter our bedroom. We may become more guarded around our adolescents. After all, we don't want them to get any ideas from us about how enjoyable sex is. Because we are so fearful that our children will become sexually involved, we may, without realizing it, lower the priority of the "S" word.

Please don't misunderstand us. We don't advocate parading

our sex life (or lack of it) in front of our kids. But we can pass on positive attitudes about sex to the products of our family planning. Whenever the "S" word came up in family conversations, we openly told our sons that sex in marriage is one of God's greatest gifts. It's okay to let your kids know that you know skin on skin feels good. At the same time we stressed that they were not adults. The "S" word is reserved for marriage and for adults! We were encouraged when one of our sons filled out a high school form and put "not before marriage" in the blank that said sex.

We do know that attitudes are caught, not taught. It's not so much what you say as what you model. Do you openly give and receive physical affection? In *How to Really Love Your Child*, Dr. Ross Campbell talks about the importance of filling your child's emotional tank with hugs and kisses. This is just as important for mates—especially when you have teens! One of Dave's best childhood memories is seeing his parents out on the balcony kissing and hugging each other. In the days of epidemic divorce, kids feel secure when they are assured—not just by words—that Mom and Dad really do love each other.

The adolescent years can add stress to any marriage. So we found some ways to combat that stress in our sexual relationship.

We needed to protect our own attitude toward sex. Even though sexual activity was not appropriate for our adolescents, we affirmed it was still right and appropriate and important to our marriage relationship.

We made a commitment not to let our teenagers crowd out our "alone time." Some of the ways we found that time were:

1. Use times when your adolescents are at school activities. (You don't have to be at every ball game they sub in!)

2. Look for alone time—like when your teens sleep in on Saturday morning.

3. Soundproof your own bedroom. A stereo system or radio provides a noise buffer and adds to your privacy.

Don't let your teen's problems totally overwhelm you. Sometimes we can get too caught up in our children's situations. After all, this is a temporary stage. They do grow up and they do leave home. You want to nurture and enjoy your sexual relationship with your mate all of your married life, so don't let the stresses of life with adolescents short circuit it!

Develop a sense of humor. Sometimes in family life you have to either laugh or cry. When faced with that choice, we tried to laugh. Laughter dispels tension and actually helps us relax. During those years we tried not to take ourselves too seriously and to realize that much we were experiencing was temporary.

Do the unexpected! During these intense years, you can add the element of surprise by doing the unexpected. We've been known to do some zany things ourselves. Claudia will never forget the day Dave came in with three red roses and said, "Pack your bag. We're leaving in thirty minutes!" Remember, Dave is the romantic!

Off we went to a wonderful little hotel in the Vienna woods about thirty minutes from where we lived. Claudia wondered why they looked at her so curiously when we checked in. Dave had previously chosen the hotel and told them he had a very special lady friend he wanted to bring for a getaway. To this day, Claudia is convinced that the staff didn't think we were married. Dave's reaction? "If you're going to have a romantic affair, have it with your mate!" And that's just what we did.

Now think about your marriage. What are you doing to build a creative love life? Waiting for the children to grow up and leave home is not an appropriate answer! Or if your answer is, "It's just not that important to us," we'd like to challenge your thinking. Take it from us, this part of marriage can grow and become more enjoyable and fulfilling every year!

LOVE LIFE IN THE FIFTIES AND SIXTIES

One friend said, "By the time you've gotten to the empty nest, you have forgotten how to spell the "S" word. We are now in the empty nest. For years we have looked forward to the extra freedom and flexibility we would have in our sexual life when our last son left home. It does have its benefits!

We hadn't forgotten the "S" word, but we had developed the habit of work, work, and more work. Some of the time vacated by our son was swallowed by more book deadlines, marriage workshops, and parenting groups. The whole house was now available to us. We could venture out, but our lifestyle was too busy to take advantage of our new freedom. We simply tried to do more!

Again we needed to work to add some creativity to our love life. We tried to slow down and even reclaim our den with the fireplace. Old habits die hard. If you are a driven workaholic, your love life may suffer. Here are some ideas we have found helpful.

Try new things. Move your lovemaking to new settings. Try out all the rooms in your house and see what appeals to you. For instance:

· Maybe one of your kids who flew the nest left a waterbed behind.
· Consider that swing you just added to your secluded screened porch.
· Why not initiate the new carpet?
· Love under bubbles in a candlelit bubble bath?
· A whole evening of nondemand touching.
· A game in which the loser must strip—one game you can both win!

All these suggestions are not from the Arps. We heard some of them at a follow-up group of one of our Marriage Alive Workshops. The workshop had taken place eight months before and this particular group had gotten together each month to share and encourage one another to stay on the marriage track. That they had been successful was evidenced by this particular evening.

Each couple had been asked to bring one thing that represented their marriage. One couple brought a beautiful green potted plant to suggest a healthy and growing marriage. Another couple brought a devotional book and shared how they were now having devotions and praying together. This, they said, had deepened their commitment to God and to each other.

Amazingly, over half of the group shared something about adding creativity to their love life. From hotel receipts to whipped cream—this group was creative. But one couple took the prize. They brought a tuxedo apron, a chef's hat, and a bottle of lotion. They were in the empty nest and both worked outside the home. On this evening the husband had volunteered for kitchen duty and begun to prepare dinner. The wife, exhausted, stretched out on the newly carpeted living room floor and fell asleep. Imagine her surprise when her husband woke her up wearing only the tuxedo apron and chef's hat, with lotion in hand all ready to give her a body massage! Creativity was alive and well at their home.

Another couple took a picnic basket full of goodies to eat and checked in at a local hotel. The money they spent on the hotel was a great investment in their marriage team.

Another thing we have discovered about this stage of life is the importance of doing what we can do to stay healthy and physically fit. We didn't come up with this on our own. Several years ago, Claudia hurt her back. For several weeks she was out of commission. It wasn't fun, but one benefit of this "down" time was our new determination to improve our physical condition. We used to play lots of tennis, but somehow had just let it slip. So we started walking together and even doing some weight training together. Now we definitely have more energy for the "fun" things in life!

A friend of ours decided to take an empty nest inventory of her clothes, especially her underwear. Out went the dowdy duds and lace was back in.

You may not like all of our suggestions, and that's fine. But we hope you like some of them. If you seriously want to deepen your sexual relationship, make this area a priority. Begin by checking your schedule. Make sure you guard your "together alone" time. You'll never add creativity to your love life unless you have some uninterrupted blocks of time alone.

Also let us encourage you to be sensitive to one another.

Have you ever been on a diet? What do you think about all the time? Food! When we aren't sensitive to our partner's sexual needs, we are putting him or her on a diet—and guess what he or she thinks about all the time. That's right—sex!

A friend of ours asked her doctor what he felt was the major sexual problem in marriage. He said half of his patients complained that their mates never bothered them about sex, while the other half complained that their mates bothered them too much about sex. He said that if only he could reshuffle the couples, everyone would be happy!

Perhaps you don't agree with each other about the frequency of sexual intercourse. Discuss this area openly, but remember that the key is to be sensitive to the needs of the other person.

SEX IN THE SEVENTIES AND EIGHTIES?

Recently we visited an elderly couple, both in their eighties, both hard of hearing. It was hard to have a conversation with them over the television. They didn't want to miss their soaps, and on this day the soaps were hot and steamy! From the hot tub, to the waterbed, to the beach, the "S" word was acted out with passion and fury. We began to realize that sex is still a focal point even in the senior years! But most elderly are experiencing it vicariously.

We plan to be the exception, and if we are we'll write a book about it! In the meantime, we're going to keep working on our sexual relationship. To be honest, we are not to the soap opera stage. With all the "soap" passion and excitement, we wonder why those characters don't have heart attacks right and left! If sex is all that great all the time, the Arps are missing out, and probably you are too!

We conclude by confessing to you that our lovemaking is usually fine, sometimes fantastic, but always enjoyable. As the years go by, it keeps getting better, and we look forward to enjoying each other in our sixties, seventies, and eighties. If we have heart attacks, we can only say, "What a way to go!"

What about you? It's your choice. Your sexual relationship can be as fulfilling and exciting as you want to make it. You will find it takes time and work. But it's worth it; it can become better, more intimate, and more wonderful as the years go on!

Sex

*W*e are never too old to love!
Neither are we ever too old
to enjoy God's gift of the outpouring of love—sex.

This chapter was included in my book "I Don't Know What Old
Is, But Old Is Older Than Me" *after much discussion and thought. I
re-present it here for all the reasons I first wrote it and for the
younger generations who may be reading this book, with the hope
you will find you have something wonderful to look forward to in
your later years.*

—Sherwood Wirt
"I Don't Know What Old Is,
But Old Is Older Than Me"

After long deliberation Ruth and I came to the conclusion that
this book on ageing should include a chapter on sex. That is to say, *I*

"Sex" is adapted and taken from *"I Don't Know What Old Is, But Old Is Older Than Me,"*
Sherwood Wirt (1991).

came to the conclusion. Actually Ruth's reaction was "The world may be waiting for a chapter on sex, but I'm not sure that I'm all that ready." That is why there was a long deliberation.

So allow me to explain to you and to her the theological reasoning behind this decision.

First, I felt it would help to sell the book. On this point I received substantial support from my publisher.

Second, specific Christian literature on sex is not very extensive, and Christian literature on sex among older people is practically nonexistent. Therefore, this chapter could very well come under the heading of original research.

Third (and this reason is clearly theological), I am adopting the premise that we Christians are far better qualified than most to discuss sex because we know the One who invented it. We make this claim modestly, with full recognition of the massive secular research being conducted in the field. But we not only know who invented it, we know why He invented it.

We know what human sexuality is designed for and what it is not designed for. It is designed to give us joy. Not just to propagate the race, not just to alleviate concupiscence, not just to follow some blind primitive instinct, but to provide us with a touch of ecstasy and a foretaste of Heaven. God never intended sex to be an instrument for self-gratification, or immorality, or unnatural practices, or crime.

God is a God of love, and love, unhindered, always expresses itself in joy. Thus in God's ordered universe, evil activities invariably cause their own misery and punishment. The terrible current scourge of social diseases is, whether we want to admit it or not, a silent witness to what happens when God's design is violated.

Yes, we Christians know where it all started and where it will end. Where did it start? In the Garden of Eden, somewhere in Iraq, in the area that used to be called Mesopotamia, or the Fertile Crescent. It must have been a beautiful setting, since it was specifically called a garden. Probably there were tall, waving palm trees, a charming brook bordered by yellow daisies, with butterflies and multicolored birds flying about. Imagine a shady grove in the midst of all that beauty. In the late afternoon a small table is set with a white tablecloth. On it are a pair of lighted beeswax candles in golden candlesticks, two crystal goblets, and a bottle of Grapillon (also known as sparkling cider). There are two chairs, and seated in them are a man and a woman. Soft music is coming from somewhere in the background. The couple are facing each other and holding hands. She is attractively dressed in a summer frock of white muslin. He is wearing tennis shorts and a T-shirt that says "Surfers of the World, Unite!"

That's not the way it was, of course, but the point is that the people who lived in the garden were happy. God saw to it that something was going on in that garden, and it wasn't tiddledy-winks.

For centuries the world has had the wrong impression about God, Christianity, and sex. For example, many people claim the Bible teaches that sex is wicked (though how they could arrive at such a conclusion after reading the Song of Songs is beyond me). They believe that when the preacher tells people to repent of sin, what he really is saying is "Repent of sex." We Christians are supposed to shy away from sex, to treat it as a no-no, an unmentionable subject, something we put up with in order to have children. We older ones especially are supposed to put away childish things such as sex, and content ourselves with sitting in our rocking chairs, knitting sweaters for our grandchildren, and watching television, or (if we are male) pulling hairs out of our ears and reading the paper.

I'll be honest and admit that some believers may seem to talk and act that way. It makes you wonder how, with such a doctrinal handicap, Christians ever managed to populate such a large section of the earth's surface. Perhaps the truth is that over the centuries most Christians have been laughing up their sleeves at the bad press some theologians have been giving the subject of sex. They (the Christians) have just gone to bed and enjoyed it, and not talked about it. In doing so they fulfilled God's original purpose, which was that they should be fruitful and multiply. They created families, built homes, reared sons and daughters, and ignored the "saints" who insisted that the whole depraved sex system was built on original sin. And what is more, they kept right on enjoying it long after anyone suspected they were capable of it.

That leads us quite appropriately to the subject of sex and ageing, which is the primary interest of this chapter. Because of the exalted nature of our discussion, I will not attempt to quote statistics, but rest assured they are available in any bookstore or public library. If you want to investigate, you can find surveys conducted by psychologists of married couples in their seventies, eighties, and nineties, all of whom appear to be willing to contribute their personal experiences to the sum of human knowledge about sexuality and ageing. What can I, a retired and ageing journalist, possibly add, particularly since I have no great love for surveys?

I shall defer all questions to my wife, to Dear Abby, and to Moses. My wife respectfully declines to comment. Dear Abby recently carried a letter in her newspaper column about an eighty-seven-year-old husband and his seventy-something-old wife who were having a frequent, satisfying intimate relationship. And as I mentioned earlier, the Holy Scriptures give us the facts about Moses, who at the ripe young age of one hundred and twenty years was thus profiled in the original King James translation: "His eye was not dim nor his natural force abated."[1]

Let the record show that the Bible further relates a number of rather amazing stories of sexual activity among aged people, and as one who accepts the Bible without reservation as the Word of God, I must say that I have no trouble believing those accounts.[2]

Some say the biggest error caused by the modern sexual revolution has been the openness with which society now talks about healthy and legitimate sex. But that is not an error at all, nor is the new openness contrary to biblical teaching. There is modesty in the Bible, but the prudishness of the Victorian era is nowhere to be found, for the Bible teaches that sex is a creation of God and an excellent thing to be enjoyed within the bounds God has set for it.[3]

Neither is there any error in removing the cloak of shame that we (not God) have thrown around sexuality. Sexual activity outside of marriage does deserve shame, because it is a sin that flaunts God's love, violates His commandments, and stains the purity of the wedding vow to "cleave only" to the beloved. The Bible calls extramarital sexual activity "fornication." I have heard Billy Graham say that God especially hates this sin because it takes a person's mind off the things of God faster and more thoroughly than anything else we do. With that I agree.

The Bible teaches that sex is a creation of God and an excellent thing to be enjoyed.

Sex, however, remains a living force in God's good creation to be used or misused. To speak of misuse, *the really gross error of the sexual revolution has been its separation of sex from true love between human beings.* This bifurcation has caused the human race unimaginable distress and suffering.

The Darwinian revolution, rather than the sexual revolution, may be ultimately responsible for this tragedy.[4] By classifying *homo sapiens* as a creature descended from primates, certain protagonists of the evolutionary hypothesis on our anthropological faculties are encouraging people to regard themselves as little more than animals. It's true that we are possessed of certain animal characteristics, for which we can also thank God. Many Christians, however, have come to recognize that sex remains one of the clearest evidences of the working of a divine hand in the creation of human life. In other words, in the glory, the joy, and the miracle of the sexual relationship we have evidence that humankind is not only a work of the Creator Himself, made and shaped in His image, but also that God continues to be involved actively in the workings of His creation.

What impels a raccoon to have sexual intercourse with another raccoon, I am not prepared to say, but defer to the specialists in animal husbandry. Everything, however, that I know about sex among human beings tells me that the sexual relationship goes with love or it doesn't belong anywhere. In fact, it goes bad. Here is where the divine hand can be seen at work. God, as the traditional marriage service declares, established marriage for the welfare and happiness of humanity. In His wisdom He put a strong band of protection around sex to make sure it would be an instrument of joy and not of misery and that it would produce good fruit. That band of protection is known today as a wedding ring.

The ring itself is not a sign of legality. It is not a government stamp. Many years ago a Seattle superior court judge told me, "I'm not married to my wife because the state of Washington said I could be." In other words God established marriage; the state merely confirms it. The wedding ring is actually a signet denoting God's welcome into the bliss and promise of the married state.

It's pitiful to see and hear of millions of people attempting to find what they call "sexual fulfilment" in every kind of relational activity imaginable, but never discovering real happiness. Instead, by engaging in free sex, they so often open a Pandora's box of horrors compounded by guilt, jealousy, cruelty, revenge, crime, disease, and increasingly in recent years, death. Every night on the newscasts we see the frantic responses of people who are trapped and harmed by their own sexuality.

As long as sex and love are separated, the Devil has a holiday. Love between a man and a woman is, in fact, the only guarantee of "good sex." In this context I am discussing love within marriage as God ordained it. Yet even within marriage, unless love is present, sex can be frustrating and disappointing. Unless there is tenderness and affection and responsiveness and trust and mutual caring, sex can be about as worthless as a bag of peanut shells, a drag.

What good are all the directions about foreplay and afterplay and in-between play if down inside a husband is nursing a bitter grievance over some nasty remark about his behavior made at breakfast? What good are taking showers and trimming fingernails and dimming lights if a wife cannot forget how her husband insulted her in front of friends? All the sex instruction books in the world cannot turn a black eye or broken ribs into a loving heart. All the psychological remedies for impotence and frigidity are ineffective against the damage done by mental or physical cruelty in the home.

*Love between a man and a woman is, in fact,
the only guarantee of "good sex."*

As people grow older their tempers calm down. They are not upset as they once were, nor do they react to things the way they did when they were younger. Perhaps that is partly the reason why today, secure within the bonds of Christ, ageing married couples by the thousands are finding a continuing and increasing source of joy in their sexual relationships.

I am not going to underrate sex. Of course it's fun, but *fun* cannot begin to describe it. Sex is a wonderful experience that cannot be compared to anything else. No poet has adequately reduced it to iambics; no music can truly convey its quintessence. And yet from everything I learn about the subject, millions of people never come near to knowing, sensing, or feeling its magnificence. For many it has become a quick fix, a ten-second high, or a casual, routine, and often boring exposure to what one woman described to me as "stifling intimacy." Sex is thought about, talked about, dreamed about, and written about as no other subject; but for all that it remains for a host of people, including older people, a fleeting goal, a disappearing rabbit, or else a rainbow whose pot of gold was never found.

But there is hope!

Amid all the sordidness and pain and misery brought about by the sexual revolution, one change for the better has taken place. Bookstores, particularly Christian bookstores, are now carrying excellent manuals on sex and marriage that offer factual information and practical guidance to young and old who are planning to marry, or who are already married and feel their sexual relationships need improvement. Never doubt that there can be improvement! Sex should never fall into a rut. Married love can be an increasing source of new pleasures, even for older couples. If you have not found them, start looking now.

Much of the help needed can be found in simple applied

Christianity. For example, both the wife and the husband can begin thinking of each other rather than of themselves and their own inhibitions. Believe it or not, most husbands would like their wives to be bolder and more aggressive during the time of wooing. Most wives, on the other hand, would like their husbands to think of something besides their own pleasure while making love —in other words, to show real love by taking time to give the wife her enjoyment. A male chauvinist of a few decades back said that wives shouldn't expect pleasure from sex; they get their pleasure, he explained, from their children or from being mistress of the home. What a delightful bedmate he must have been!

It works in other marital relationships as well. Right now, what would be most pleasing to the other party? Ask yourself, what can we do together that would cement our relationship? Perhaps there is something about your spouse's behavior that is particularly bothersome. What can you do about that? I'll tell you: Shut up about it! Learn to live with it. Pray about it. Nobody is perfect. "You can't change anyone," I was told years ago, "but *God can change you.*" There are things you do that bother your spouse. If you keep quiet, perhaps your spouse will not mouth off about you. Then you can get back to sweet talk and hugs in the kitchen. It's worth a try.

If any one thing will kill sexual pleasure fast, it is a domestic argument. There are no arguments in our house. I just give in. (Copy editor, delete that last sentence, I was kidding.) The truth is that Ruth and I are having too much fun to argue. Anyway, arguments are a waste. A jingle I heard years ago put it right:

> I'm a lover, not a fighter—
> kind of like it that way;
> If you want a sparring partner
> why don't you live with Cassius Clay?

God made us for love. While we are on earth He provides us with sex and holy matrimony to enjoy as part of that love. They are not for sale and are not for everyone. Many celibate people live wonderful lives. Jesus was a celibate. My wife, Ruth, was single and celibate for sixty-one years before we were married.

"Did you feel you missed out?" I asked her once.

"No," she said quietly, "God had other things for me to do."

Strange developments are taking place among older people in today's society. Financial considerations are such that single men and women are living together without marriage rather than take a drop in individual incomes that marriage would cause. I understand that certain churches are thinking of blessing these arrangements. I question very much whether God is blessing them. Scripture cannot be broken, and Hebrews 13:4 states, "Marriage is honorable among all, and the bed undefiled." The Greek word for "bed" here is *koite* (κοίτη), which doesn't mean "bed" at all; it is identical with our *coitus,* and the dictionary defines *coitus* as "the act of sexual intercourse." However, my calling is not to judge any more than it is to argue. My business is love, and so is yours; so let's get on with it.

I told you at the beginning that we Christians know where the sex relationship will end. We have it on the authority of our Lord Jesus Christ that there is no marriage or giving of marriage in heaven.[5] That may well rule out sex. Does it trouble you?

Relax. Heaven is going to be so much better, so much richer, so much more thrilling and enjoyable than anything we know here that you won't miss a thing on earth. As the apostle Paul reminded the brothers and sisters in Corinth, in 1 Corinthians 2:9:

> Eye has not seen, nor ear heard,
> Nor have entered into the heart of man
> The things which God has prepared for
>   those who love Him.

*A gentle touch or countless other tender
expressions of "I care" separate love
relationships from mere acquaintances.
—Holly and Chris Thurman
Intimate Moments*

Chapter

16

Roru ✓

Can My Husband Really Sense My Sexual Attitude?

Dear Daughters,

When I wrote *Creative Counterpart* in 1977, few Christian women were talking about the sexual relationship in marriage. Your father had written *Solomon on Sex* the same year, and with two books dealing with sexual issues, I felt I was labeled as one who speaks and writes about "those things." At one point I told your father that I thought I would hide in the house for several weeks so people wouldn't stare at me. I was sure they were whispering together and saying, "I bet she even *does* those things she and her husband wrote about!" This is just one of the joys of being an author.

I felt it was important to talk about the physical aspect of marriage in 1977, and I feel it even more strongly now. At the end of the chapters on sex in *Creative Counterpart*, I talk about the importance of a wife being available to her husband, aggressive

"Can My Husband Really Sense My Sexual Attitude?" is adapted and taken from *How to Really Love Your Man*, Linda Dillow (1993).

toward him sexually, and creative in their lovemaking. I end with this statement:

> There are many creative things I can suggest, but you must start thinking and come up with your own. Remember, special times together are important and cannot be stressed enough, but the most important thing is your ATTITUDE. Does your husband know you are available and excited about him as your lover? God gave him to you as your beloved and your friend. Let him in on the secret!

What attitude does your husband receive from you about your love life? I remember a friend stating it like this: "When he walks out of the shower, what attitude does he sense from you? Do you walk up to him and put your arms around his slightly wet body, kiss him, and tell him how good he looks to you? Or do you run the other way in fear that if your attitude is positive he will get 'ideas'? Does your attitude say, 'I am excited about you and moving toward you,' or 'I am not excited about you and am moving away from you'?"

Remember, an attitude is an inward feeling expressed by behavior and can be seen without a word being said. Attitudes are expressed by our body language and by the looks on our faces. What are we expressing to our lovers and best friends?

I can just hear you saying, "But, Mom, is a wife *always* supposed to have a positive attitude about sex? What about when she is tired, depressed, or hurried, or she just plain isn't in the mood?"

In my letters to you about communication, I stressed the importance of honest, open sharing. This is true in every part of your relationship, including the sexual. The question is: How are your honesty and openness expressed? What *attitude* is communicated to this man you love?

• "I'm too busy for you. Can't you see I have other things on my mind? Is sex all you ever think about?"
• "Honey, I'm whipped. The day has been awful. I don't think there is any way my body can respond to anything but a hot bath

and sleep. But I would love to love you. . . . Let me make you feel good. Tomorrow will be another day, and I'll be ready for you to pleasure me and be a full partner in our lovemaking."

Both statements are honest, but one is selfish and one is loving; one presents a negative attitude, the other a positive. Whether we are aware of it or not, an attitude is being projected; our men *sense* either our love or our rejection.

I must clarify. In the letters I wrote about sex, I said that the wife should be a full partner in the lovemaking, be totally involved and responsive, and that it was just as important for her to be satisfied as it was for her husband. What I have just said in this letter does not negate that. Both are true. The norm is that both are always involved; the exception is that one can satisfy the other in a loving and caring way.

Let me share with you the story of one woman. I will call her Jenna. I came to greatly respect Jenna as I grieved with her, wept with her, and watched her choose a beautiful attitude that so honored God.

Jenna had no sexual feelings. She was married to a wonderful and loving Christian man. She was terrified that because of her inability to respond, he would tire of making love to a "board" who just lay there unresponsively (that was her description) and turn to another woman.

Jenna knew why her sexual feelings were locked up. When she was twelve, her older sister had become pregnant. The distraught mother held Jenna across her lap and begged Jenna to promise her that she would never do anything like her sister had done. Jenna promised, and when she began to date and had sexual feelings, she rejected them. From her perspective, sex was something that brought pain and an unwanted baby. Besides, she had promised her mother.

Years of rejecting her God-given sexual feelings resulted in them being so deeply buried that she couldn't find them when both she and her husband desperately longed for her response.

Thus far, professionals had not been able to help, so Jenna

had come to me. After sharing all I knew from Scripture, praying, suggesting, I said, "Jenna, I don't know what God will do. I know He can release you, but I can't promise you He will. I can only tell you what my choice would be if I were in your place. If today I knew that I would never have another sexual feeling, would never experience again the joy of sharing heights of pleasure with my man, with God's help, this would be my attitude.

To choose to become an incredible, fantastic, and creative lover to my man. To seek to know and understand his needs, his dreams, his desires, and to meet them. To become all he had ever longed for in a lover. To emotionally enter in to lovemaking with every fiber of my being, and to trust God for the physical feelings. If the feelings did not come, I would be at peace that I was loving my man with all I had to give.

As I shared this with Jenna, I told her that I knew what I was saying was difficult, very difficult. Several months later, she said, "I still don't have feelings, but I am more at peace. You're right. I don't have to be a board, and giving so much emotionally and physically to my husband has given much to me. Attitude does play a big part. I just pray I can continue to have this positive attitude and trust God for the feelings. My husband sure likes the 'new me.'"

Well, my daughters, my observations tell me that you are not lacking in sexual feelings. (That's why I've spent the last years on my knees!) But you will have choices to make because you will be tired, there will be times when you want to crawl into bed alone, so how will you be honest and still love your man?

You can suggest that you wait until another time when you are more alert, you can say you want to love *him* but don't feel like you can respond, or you can say, "Lord, You know how I feel, blah. But I love this man, and I want to show him my love even though I don't feel like it right this minute. Teach me to love him. I choose to love him now."

Attitude isn't everything, but it is a lot. It's been said that a woman's sexiest organ is her brain. When I choose to dwell on loving my man, regardless of my feelings, amazing things happen.

Some of our most beautiful times together have been when "I wasn't in the mood."

> *I love you,*
> Mom

17

How Your Family
Controls Your Sex Life

The title of this chapter may have you thinking that you need to put deadbolt locks on your bedroom door to keep your children out at inopportune times! Though that might be a good idea, it's not the subject of this chapter, taken from Restoring Innocence. *Rather, we're taking a look at how our family of origin has influenced our ideas and attitudes about sex. Our family is the single most powerful influence in shaping the way we relate to others, as you will see. Unfortunately, too many of us received either mixed signals about sexuality, or were loaded with shaming messages about something that is supposed to be free and beautiful within the context of marriage. It takes courage to look inside our families of origin and face the pain of a wounded heart. But when we know where the pain comes from, we are that much closer to restoring*

"How Your Family Controls Your Sex Life" is adapted from *Restoring Innocence*, Al Ells (1990).

the innocence God intended for healthy sexual expression in marriage.

—Al Ells
Restoring Innocence

"My family didn't have any genitals," said Ann.

The statement surprised me. I had never heard someone describe their family in such a way. "What do you mean?"

"I was watching a videotape of families when the narrator said some families acted as if they had no genitals. It instantly made me think of my family. No one in my family ever told risqué jokes or mentioned the words *sex, penis,* or *vagina.* I think we all acted like sex and sexual parts did not exist. But Ryan's family is just the opposite. They're always talking and joking about sex, so much so that I don't feel comfortable around them."

"Does that mean that sexual territory is embarrassing to you?" I asked.

Ann did not respond right away, she seemed lost in thought.

"What are you thinking?"

"I was just realizing how embarrassed I must feel about sex. Even talking to you makes me uneasy. Ryan says I'm too inhibited. He thinks I should desire it more, but I don't feel I need sex that often. He also complains that I'm too squeamish about sex because I don't like foreplay or too much touching. He thinks something's the matter with me when I say I could probably live without it." Ann hesitated, "Do you think there's something the matter with me?"

I did not want to answer, knowing it would probably hurt. "Yes, Ann. I believe you may be experiencing a condition described as inhibited sexual desire, which means sex just doesn't hold for you the pleasure and fulfillment God intended."

Her expression changed. A few soft tears dropped from her cheek. Dabbing her eyes with the tip of a tissue, she said "I have always known it, but it's still hard to hear the words." She paused a few moments, adding, "Is it because of my family?"

"Probably. But not only because of your family. Sexual problems can have more than one contributing factor; but since families do establish the foundation of sexual expression, I am sure your family has contributed to the problem. Are you willing to explore how they may have done so?"

I asked for her permission because many people are hesitant to look closely at their family. Some people feel disloyal if they examine family weaknesses or share family business with anyone outside the family. As one family member in a therapy session aptly put it, "We just don't talk about those kinds of things with other people. We keep our business to ourselves."

It isn't necessary to broadcast family "sins and secrets" to the world. However, it can be unhealthy never to discuss family relationships when it keeps you from facing the truth about yourself and your family. Health requires reality, and an honest appraisal of our own and our family's deficiencies is part of the reality of life. They must be faced if we are to truly let go of the past and move on.

FAMILY POWER

Family is the single most powerful influence in shaping the way we relate to others because it develops within us:

- our self-concept
- our framework for love
- our view of others

Let's look at each of these in detail.

Self-concept

Self-concept is the sum of all the thoughts, images, beliefs, and perceptions we have of ourselves, and it is formed, in large part, by how our family related to us. If a family treats a child with neglect, ignoring the child's presence and needs, a feeling of not being worthy or important is created. In contrast, caring, attentive parents say by their actions, "You are special. You count. You are valuable."

How we see ourselves has a lot to do with how we relate to others. It also has a lot to do with what we expect from sex. Most women who have few sexual boundaries come from families that did not validate their self-worth. When this self-worth is lacking, there can be a tendency to give sex to gain validation—doing whatever is demanded in order to receive the love and approval so desperately needed. Tragically, this can invite sexual abuse and victimization. In the same way, those who place a lot of emphasis on sex and sexual prowess also usually come from families where self-worth wasn't validated appropriately. Acceptance and approval had too much to do with being sexually accomplished. People raised in these environments give love to get sex, wanting the validation that sexual prowess provides to counteract the insecurity felt deep within. This is what compulsive sex is. It can also lead to deviation and the violation of others.

How families validate, accept, love, discipline, or reject members can powerfully influence their inner self-concept. And this self-concept will greatly influence how one views body parts, sexual identity, sexual competence, and sexual expression with others.

Framework for Love

Family life imprints in each of us a framework for love. Your concept of what love is and how you give and receive it all come from family patterns of interaction. If the "I care" messages between Mom and Dad were devoid of any touching or affection with each other or you, two things may happen. You may have difficulty with touch and affection, feeling uncomfortable giving and receiving. And sex may not be easy or fully pleasurable. This is because sex is the total touching of two bodies, merging two people into one. It is the most encompassing physical expression of love that is possible. And where touching and physical affection were rigidly regulated, sexual constriction may follow.

Family life imprints in each of us a framework for love.

The other possibility is that you may overcompensate by needing or giving touch and affection too much, and for the wrong reasons. Ryan gave and needed a lot of affection, but he always connected it with sex. He could not distinguish between non-sexual and sexual affection—which are both needed for a healthy relationship.

When someone needs touch and affection too much, boundaries will be violated and the touch of the needy person will become more sexually oriented because sex is so sensual. The sexual needs may then supplant the common need for affection, leading to a pattern of giving attention to get one's sexual needs met. All the while, though, the real need for loving affirmation remains unmet. If the need for affection is not openly dealt with in a relationship, it can distort the fulfillment of other needs, causing a continuing void and resulting in compulsion. Sex is meant to fulfill our deep needs for affirmation and affection; but when it becomes the *only* means, it becomes too powerful and yields less fulfillment—not more.

View of Others

Our families also imprint us with a view of others and how to relate to them, determining what we will do with and for others. If your family treated men better than women, or sons better than daughters, then you will tend to value maleness over femaleness. If you are a woman in such a family, then it is possible that you will see your role as valuing the desires of men over your own. If your partner wants sex and you do not, then you will tend to defer to his desires rather than your own. The end result is that you will never consider your own sexuality or sexual needs.

If your family's unhealthy values offended you, however, then you may react by overcompensating. You may value women over men, femaleness over maleness, daughters over sons, and have difficulty being considerate of your husband's desires.

Either way, your family's perception of others will influence your relational and sexual choices. Sex will tend to be one-way rather than mutual.

ONE-WAY SEX

When sex is not mutual, when one partner is giving more than the other, one of the partners is usually giving sex for the wrong reasons:

- to not anger or offend the other person
- to make the other person like them or be happy with them
- to keep the partner from seeing them as deficient

Women who fake orgasms are protecting themselves from being viewed as deficient. Also, women who only give sex to get love are in the same trap. Good sex requires self-honesty and honesty with the other party; it requires mutuality. Not mutually perfect performance or desire—few couples have perfectly attuned sex—but mutual commitment to enjoy the gift of sexual intimacy that God has offered, and mutual commitment to foster a climate where both come to enjoy sex by embracing it for themselves and sharing it with the other.

Sex given for the wrong reasons lacks this quality of in-depth honesty. In short, true intimacy is missing.

Intimacy is the profound feeling of enrichment that comes from the total sharing of one's inner being with another and the acceptance of what was shared. It comes from the Latin word *intimus,* meaning "innermost." This pictures intimacy as the touching of two souls, the joining of two spirits. Intimacy becomes the soothing balm of our aloneness. When we taste of it, we are somehow less alone, less pained, and more whole.

In sex, we have the physical act of intimacy, which can bring an even deeper experience of oneness. Our physical nakedness reflects our emotional honesty, and our physical embracing shows our emotional acceptance. Profound and intimate sex does not require great expertise, but rather deep exposure of one's self and loving acceptance by the other.

With intimacy as the goal of our sexual expression, we can even experience differing desires and practices and still have healthy sex. A wife can still desire sex less than her husband, yet both can find great fulfillment.

When sex is given for the wrong reasons, however, the partners cut themselves off from the vulnerability of honest self-exposure, and they withhold the precious commodity of total acceptance. Sex then becomes more a reflection of the need for the partners to face themselves more honestly. These couples must ask themselves these questions: Am I embracing my own need for sexual expression? Am I providing true sacrificial love, love with no strings attached? How vulnerable have I been?

But with the idea of sacrificial love must come a word of caution. When sexual and emotional vulnerability are offered and total care and acceptance are not returned, sex becomes damaging. Sexual vulnerability demands a sacred response, or it will shame and wound. Abusers, adulterers, and sexual addicts violate boundaries and degrade sex. They, too, are wounded individuals who need to seek their own healing. The person in relationship with these people must realize that sacrificial sexual love will not fix them. Only God can. This person's continual sexual surrender will only feed the problem, not diminish it. One-way loving is rarely helpful or healthy.

COMPULSIVE OR OBSESSIVE SEX

"I can't stop thinking about sex. It's always on my mind, even during church. My eyes and mind wander, looking at the buttocks of every woman in front of me. I used to think this was normal—that all guys feel this way—but now I'm beginning to wonder."

Ryan raised this concern during one of our sessions. Sex for him had become an obsession. Obsessions are ideas or thoughts that haunt us and cannot be shaken off. For the sexually obsessed, sex thoughts and fantasies continue for hours on end or throughout the entire day. While the unobsessed individual may have fleeting urges or thoughts, the sexually obsessed have let the fantasies take control. For them, sex has become so consuming that it is a constant companion in their thoughts, even the focal point of their lives.

Many families promote this kind of sexual preoccupation. They may joke or jest about sex or make frequent sexual innuendos. Or, on the other extreme, they may prohibit any sexual discussion and overreact to any sexual display. Both positive and negative over-emphasis make sex too important. It will result in either sexual obsession and compulsive practices or cause children to want nothing to do with sex because it has been made too scary or powerful for them.

Also, when the family does not meet emotional needs adequately, children may resort to sexual self-stimulation in order to experience comfort. Sexually compulsive individuals admit to feeling lonely all the time. This loneliness comes about in two basic ways. One is by not giving children enough attention, love, or affirmation, so they grow up seeking it through sex. And the other way is to give children too much love, care, or attention through enmeshment. When this happens, children will grow to adulthood craving that immediate intimacy they experienced, seeking it through sex when it isn't available.

SHAME

Perhaps the single most hurtful legacy many families leave their children is shame. This painful emotion is at the root of most one-way and compulsive sexual practices. Where guilt says, "I made a mistake," shame says, "I *am* the mistake." Shame is often an excruciating and punishing awareness of one's own insufficiency and inadequacy, and it is probably the most painful emotion one can experience.

Where guilt says, "I made a mistake,"
shame says, "I am the mistake."

Not all shame is bad, however—a small amount is probably healthy. It can help remind us that we are fallible humans with a sinful nature and keep us from being a law unto ourselves. And it's also a valid emotional response when we have violated healthy laws and boundaries.

But too much shame can assign us to a life of fear and self-hatred, creating an enemy within that condemns and criticizes us. It starts an inner war that we rarely seem to win.

Both the sexually compulsive and the person who gives too much have that enemy within—a deep inner voice of rage, rejection, shame, or doubt that prohibits them from being at peace with themselves and their sexuality. And both have tied their inner feelings of inadequacy to their sexual practices. Sexually compulsive individuals try to feel better about themselves through sex, with some displaying an aura of machismo to declare outwardly what they wish was true inwardly. Individuals who give sex to get love or approval also try to conquer their shame, but they do it by avoiding the anger of others or trying to win others' approval to reinforce their approval of themselves. Neither will be emotionally or sexually fulfilled until the hurts and pains of the past are resolved and the shame released.

Shame also adds to sexual dysfunction by increasing sexual inhibition. We feel too embarrassed about ourselves to be totally naked—physically and emotionally—with someone else. Our blemishes, fat rolls, and imperfections interfere with our acceptance of self and others, making us too self-conscious to be able to abandon ourselves in passion. Sometimes the fluids of sex can become embarrassing—the act of sex is then perceived as "dirty." Shame will declare too many do's and don'ts and restrict natural sexual expression.

On the other hand, a person may react against this powerful negative feeling by becoming shameless. Shameless sexual practices—promiscuity, prostitution, rape, incest, masochism, voyeurism, and pedophilia—violate personal and moral boundaries and cause hurt to one's self and to others.

Contrary to public perception, individuals caught in these vicious traps of compulsion and obsession carry a lot of shame, which is why many of them keep their sexual practices secret. They know their behavior would not stand the test of public scrutiny, they fear what others would think if their life-style became known. This causes them to resist facing their practices, which only increases the hold the desire has over them. Secret lives always breed shame and more sickness. The more shame, the more avoidance of change and the deeper and more secret the practice becomes. Bondage thrives in darkness. It wanes when exposed to the light of truth.

Shamelessness can also be seen in those who are overly open and vocal about their sexual practices. Those who loudly proclaim the virtue of unrestrained sex are probably reacting to their past, where sex has been embarrassing or shameful. These individuals are desperately trying to avoid feeling the pain of this very powerful negative emotion. This can also be true of homosexuals who participate in public protests for "gay rights." The protester believes that if others can be convinced that homosexuality is acceptable, then his or her shame can be removed. However, public acceptance cannot totally remove one's shame; only a profound experience of God's forgiveness and love can release one from its bondage.

Shame is, however, lessened by acceptance. The inner feelings of inadequacy you have are tied to how others validate you. If you experienced rejection as a child, you may become very shame-based, meaning that shame becomes a major motivation for what you do or do not do. All of us need acceptance and affirmation as children in order to experience worth as adults. Healthy inner beliefs about self and others allow us to be guided by conscience rather than emotional neediness and keep us from violating ourselves or others.

NEXT STEPS

Shame is at the root of a hurtful family legacy and one-way or compulsive sex is the result. We need to revisit the shaming events of our lives in order to be healed. This means that both the shameful acts of others against us, as well as our own shameful ways, need to be brought to the light of God's healing and grace.

"But I can't go to God and ask him to help me. I've failed too many times. I'm powerless over my addiction. I may never be able to stop this thing. I would feel like a hypocrite."

Those were Ryan's desperate words of hopelessness when I confronted him about his need for God. Many who are trapped in vicious cycles of compulsive behavior feel this way.

The victims of someone else's sexual practices can also feel hopeless and unworthy of God. Sandy, a victim of incest, doesn't feel God could ever forgive her even though she did not initiate or desire sex with her father. Because of what happened, and especially because there were parts of it that felt good, she feels dirty and undeserving of God's care and love.

Guilt and shame are sensitive territories to navigate. To get through them, you will need to separate the acts of the past into two categories: those acts committed against you—for which you had no responsibility; and those things you have done for which you do have culpability. It is very difficult to sort out this territory on your own because the feelings of guilt and shame are so powerful, powerful enough to cause denial, confusion, or exaggerated reaction.

If shame or guilt is part of your hurtful family legacy, you will probably need someone else to help you sort through these feelings and facts. Often this is your only assurance of not deceiving yourself and continuing in your shame and self-defeat.

So, your first step has been to recognize the shame.

The next step is to ask for help.

This takes courage because you will not want to relive the shameful feelings by telling someone else, but there is no other way. You have to be willing to revisit the shame in order to be healed. Choose a trusted and competent person who understands shame and also knows Jesus—the lifter of our shame. A spiritual awakening in Christ provides the experience of God's love, which is a powerful balm to the deeper inner pain of shame. For many, the fear of God keeps them from his love. But Jesus will come to you no matter what you have done or what has been done to you. He is the healer of broken hearts and the mender of hurtful pasts. We have only to ask.

Chapter

Sexual Fidelity Restores Trust

*I*t would seem that a book on
Christian marriage shouldn't
even have to mention marital infidelity. Doesn't the Bible make it
clear that God meant for marriage to be one man, one woman?
Don't the traditional wedding vows themselves call for faithfulness,
"forsaking all others . . . till death do you part"? Of course we
know what the standards are. But why did God insist on exclusivity
in marital sexuality? This chapter from Broken Vows focuses on the
"whys" of marital fidelity and also examines the damage that can
take place when those vows are broken. In discussing the causes
as well as the consequences of adultery, we'll also see how broken
vows don't have to mean the end of a Christian marriage. There is
hope for those who have made mistakes, and we hope these pages
will make that hope a reality for those who hurt.

—*Les Carter*
Broken Vows

"Sexual Fidelity Restores Trust" is adapted from *Broken Vows*, Dr. Les Carter (1991).

"Look, let's be reasonable. Maybe you don't like the fact that I fooled around a little, and I guess I can understand your feelings. But don't be so old-fashioned. Having sex with someone else isn't the end of the world. It's not nearly as bad as you're making it out to be."

Michael was giving his wife, Janet, his very best sales pitch, but she wasn't buying it. Tears rolled down her face as she cried, "How could you be so insensitive? When we married you vowed that you would never forsake me for another, but now that means so little to you. I feel like I don't even know you. How can I possibly believe that you really love me?"

Was Michael's wife living in the Dark Ages with outmoded, petty, or unrealistic beliefs? If the modern scorning of puritan morality is accurate, perhaps he had a good point. Sexual excursions outside marriage might be considered an impish game, not moral decay. Yet if the Bible is still true and therefore trustworthy, Michael was flippantly winking at a deeply serious subject.

I believe the Bible to be God-inspired and thus without error; therefore I conclude that Michael's attitude was in need of repair. Sexuality is not to be entered into lightly or shrugged off with free-spirited notions. Christian principles of sexual fidelity within the marriage have deep spiritual roots. Contrary to humanistic ideology, sexual fidelity is not an archaic, arbitrary teaching passed on by rigid, judgmental prudes. Sexual behavior is intricately linked to the commitment of pure love God offered His human family. An understanding of the importance of sexual purity is found by thinking through the following series of questions about God's plan for our lives.

WHY WAS MARRIAGE INSTITUTED?

When Adam was given life, he had a perfect personality with a perfect ability to relate with God. He had a high sense of dignity since God had gifted him with dominion over all created things. Yet God knew that Adam would feel incomplete if he had no one of his own kind to love—Adam was created in God's image with a natural desire to receive and give away love. A wife was given for the purpose of more deeply experiencing godly love. As Adam and Eve shared human love, each became more appreciative of spiritual love with God.

Today, when a husband is kind to his wife, she is much more inclined to receive spiritual truth. When a wife supports her husband, he is more likely to be open to words from the Lord. Conversely, when there is tension or alienation, spiritual truth is more difficult to digest. From mankind's beginning, God's plan has called for marital harmony to be a conduit for spiritual wholeness.

This notion of marital love as a precursor for spiritual depth is captured in a brief phrase at the conclusion of 1 Peter 3:7. Peter had already instructed wives to be submissive, chaste, and respectful toward their husbands. And he had directed husbands to be understanding toward their wives, giving them a position of honor. Then he explained *why* they were to live in such a manner: "that your prayers may not be hindered." Peter was fully aware that if the relationship between a husband and wife is pure, so is the ability to commune with God. Marital love, above all other relationships, has the special designation to be an embodiment of spiritual love.

WHAT ROLE DOES SEX PLAY IN GODLY LOVE?

Adam and Eve sealed their commitment toward each other by becoming one flesh (Gen. 2:24). God ingeniously devised the sex act as a symbolic, intimate covenant with the mate, knowing that commitments gain depth when a sacred ritual is exercised. Sexuality is a husband and wife's "contract" which expresses the exclusivity of their love for one another, thus providing an experiential picture of God's exclusive love for His creation.

When Michael expressed his lighthearted ideas about sexual play, Janet questioned him, "Doesn't our marital commitment mean anything to you? When I married you, I determined that no one else would hold that position of honor in my life."

Later I talked privately with Janet and mentioned, "You really expressed some impassioned emotion regarding your feelings about sexual exclusivity. How did this affect Michael?"

"Well, I was pleased because that evening he told me that he had never really thought about sex as communicating so much. Morality was not taken seriously in his background. He had never been challenged to think deeply about the meaning of fidelity."

Many scoff at the idea of sex as a contract. However, it is intriguing to observe the intense bonding that develops when two people have engaged in sexual intercourse. No one can deny that sex creates a hold, a knitting together of spirits, that cannot be logically or casually explained. Sexuality is the most powerful demonstration of commitment. For that reason possessiveness becomes part of the relationship once the line of sexuality has been crossed. This produces feelings of security and significance for marital partners, but for nonmarital partners it produces confusion.

Exclusive marital sex affirms the couple's commitment to God's ways and to the specialness of their relationship. A couple communicates to each other, "I honor you with a position held by no one else," and "I respect your need to feel significant." This enhances a mate's ability to discover dignity from the Lord.

Sexuality is the most powerful demonstration of commitment.

One particular woman cried as she learned of her husband's love and sexual devotion to her. Her husband's best friend told her, "One evening at the gym the guys were discussing their various sexual conquests. Roger was real quiet, so they started needling him. They discovered his exclusive sexual interaction with only his wife and had some bellowing laughs at his expense." Determined not to succumb to their locker room crudeness, he remained quiet and went his way. As this friend related the incident, he noticed the wife's tears. Assuming her to be hurt, the friend asked if she was angry. Her response said it all, "I'm not angry at those men for being so rude. I'm crying because my husband loves me so much that he won't compromise his morals for anyone else!"

Why Does God Place Such Emphasis on Exclusive Sex Within Marital Bounds?

God is very insistent regarding fidelity for two major reasons. First, God is an intensely personal God who desires intensely personal commitments. He craves one-on-one relationships with each human. This is why Christ's teachings emphasize individual responses to God. Our Creator is not interested in seeing organizations, families, or countries come to Him. He relates to individuals. He has given every person a conscience which prompts him or her to assume personal responsibility to make an account to God. He has provided His Holy Spirit to stir the heart and mind of each individual, prompting each person to either affirm or deny a commitment to Him. This underscores the idea that His love is to be internalized rather than generic.

Even in the Old Testament days God instituted a ritual that demanded a very personal response to prepare lost mankind for Jesus Christ. When He chose Abraham and his descendants to represent Him to all the families of the earth, He required the males to commit themselves to God by giving one part of the body, the sex organ, to Him. The rite of circumcision served to represent an exceedingly personal contract with God. Abraham's nation was blessed because of this commitment to God.

Because marital love was designed to depict God's pure, complete love for each individual, He asks that we enter the same kind of personal commitment. When spouses reserve the sex act solely for each other, they demonstrate an understanding of God's intimate nature. The mandate for exclusive intimacy is neither petty nor arbitrary. Physical love, like spiritual love, is most complete when contained in a deeply personal and exclusive relationship.

The second major reason that God desires exclusivity in marital sexuality is related to mankind's deepest struggle resulting from the Fall. In essence, sin produced the overwhelming desire to have it all. Rather than desiring submission to God's scheme of right and wrong, each person is driven to indulge self's cravings. This trait was engendered in Adam and Eve when Satan enticed them to be as God. It is natural for each of their descendants to seek their own means of self-will, including sexual behaviors. God's requirement of sexual fidelity is one of many instructions intended to stem the tide of self-preoccupied living. This commandment can be construed as part of the process of being restored to Him, since restraint and self-denial cause us to become available to His indwelling presence.

Couldn't It Be Said That Sexual Exclusivity Limits Individuals in the Sharing of Love?

The rise of pop psychology in the last generation initiated an increasingly permissive view toward sexual love. Grounded in a humanistic philosophy, which believes that morality is not an absolute, many have concluded that sexual love can and should be freely shared. This thought was recently romanticized by the unlikely duo of Julio Iglesias and Willie Nelson who melodiously honored the many women who had been the objects of their sexual passions. "To all the girls I've loved before . . ." This philosophy presumes that sexual love, shared as broadly as possible, is the ultimate expression of personal wholeness.

Let's examine the implications of this notion. Sharing sex with multiple partners necessitates a brief commitment as compared to the lifetime commitment with an exclusive marital partner. Persons who jump from one partner to the next face each sexual interlude with an attitude that it will end whenever the thrill is gone. The security of each relationship is tentative—there is no guarantee of a commitment, only ultimate rejection. Love is based on performance, not on a mind-set of giving. Sexual interplay is reduced to an external function that has little to do with a person's innermost spirit. Such activity is grounded in a "what's in it for me" motivation with little concern about the act's long-term effect on the other.

I asked Michael in a private session: "What did you think Janet's reaction would be once she found out about your sexual excursions?"

His answer told me that he either used much denial or was not at all contemplative: "Oh, I'm not real sure what I thought. I mean, I figured she would be mad, which is why I hid it from her. But I didn't really think she would be so distraught."

"In our last joint session she clearly expressed a feeling of rejection. It seemed pretty evident that exclusive sexuality means a great deal to her."

"Yeah, maybe I'm learning this too late. As soon as I went after another woman, she interpreted it as a rejection of her. I didn't think of it in that way, but I guess that's what my behavior implied."

"Let's be optimistic and turn this thought around. If she knows that you willingly put aside your temptations to become sexually involved with another woman, the feeling of rejection could diminish and your love would be heightened."

"Maybe so . . ." he nodded. I could see the wheels turning in Michael's head. He and Janet were going through their greatest crisis to date, but it was causing him to think about the outcome of his behavior as never before.

In the long-term, multiple sexual relations degrade human dignity. Sexual partners are reduced to objects of indulgence, and the person engaged in such behavior learns to live with a mind-set of usury and manipulation. Humans are made to relate to each other in the image of God, not by animal instinct.

RESPECTING GOD'S PLAN FOR SEXUALITY

If we understand that sexual fidelity within marriage is a sacred part of God's plan for mankind, several truths become clear. By embracing these ideas, restoration can occur.

Adultery Is Sin Against God

I recently talked with a retired couple who was struggling with grief and pain because their son-in-law had left his wife and three children for another woman. They made a statement that is frequently expressed by people in their position: "We know that this is really an issue between our daughter and her husband, but it feels as if he has completely turned his back on us as well!"

Later I talked with the son-in-law, and he expressed that he had no idea that his wife's parents would feel so personally rejected. He also gave a commonly heard response: "I knew my wife would be hurt and that they would side with her, but I didn't really anticipate that they would see it as an issue between me and them." This man failed to realize that when he sinned against his wife, he also sinned against those who loved her.

God is the Creator and sustainer of each life and loves each person as His own child. When someone sins against one of His children, he or she sins against Him. Our heavenly Father deeply cares about the needs of each of His children. When we feel pleasure, He feels it with us. When we feel pain, He feels it too. No act goes without His notice and an emotional response from Him. He is intricately linked with humanity.

Unfaithful spouses, like Michael, expect God to be mad not hurt. Michael told me, "I felt a little guilty about my behavior after I had done it, but I never really thought about it as hurting God. I assumed He would be mad, so I tried to run from Christianity and my guilty emotions. I purposely overlooked my religious beliefs because they clouded the issue."

Once an unfaithful spouse admits that he has purposely grieved the Lord, I try to help him filter his attitudes and behaviors through an understanding of God's desire for his life.

"Michael, God is just. He holds absolute standards of right and wrong. But He is also loving. No law given by Him is primarily for the sake of making a person feel devalued. God loves Janet and wants you to be a conduit of His love for her. He has given you a wonderful role to play in her life."

"So if He feels disappointed with me because of my affair, it is caused by His love for her, not His dislike of me."

"God wants the highest for you too. He knows that if you follow His plans you will be a happier person."

Michael was capable of genuine change as he considered how his sin against Janet affected her relationship to God. It caused him to realize that restoration would occur when he would look beyond the behavior itself and face God who prescribed the ways of right and wrong.

An analogy: I may speed in my car because I am attempting to get around a slowpoke. But I may be apprehended by a policeman, a representative of the county and state, because I violated laws created by the state, not the slow driver. I will then face a judge who will expect me to demonstrate a loyalty to the ones who make and enforce society's laws.

An unfaithful spouse may reject the spiritual significance of adultery, but his or her subconscious mind is aware of this truth. Paul told the Romans:

> For the wrath of God is revealed from heaven against all ungodliness and unrighteousness of men, who suppress the truth in unrighteousness, because what may be known of God is manifest in them, for God has shown it to them. For since the creation of the world His invisible attributes are clearly seen, being understood by the things that are made, even His eternal power and Godhead, so that they are without excuse (Rom. 1:18–20).

Innately, the adulterer knows that the sexual sin is not part of God's master plan, so the decision to act out is a specific rejection of that plan and of God who designed it.

Adultery Is an Act of Arrogance

When an individual first seriously entertains the notion of committing adultery, an inner voice speaks a warning against such action. A mental struggle then ensues as that person weighs the moral reasons to refrain from sin against the personal craving to indulge in sensual desires. A decision to pursue the adulterous relationship means that the person has decided, "I'm above the rules that God has given mortals."

In a joint counseling session, Janet expressed her strong anger toward Michael. "How can you dare have the audacity to go out with that woman and then expect our family and friends to take us back into their circles! Don't you realize how high and mighty you've been acting?"

"Now, wait a minute. I may have a lot of flaws but high and mighty isn't one of them. You've got to admit that I conduct myself humbly most of the time." He then looked to me for reinforcement, hoping I would bail him out.

"Don't discount too quickly what Janet is saying. When we consider the subject of arrogance or pride, there may be some subtleties worth looking into."

For the most part, adulterers do not think of themselves as arrogant. Arrogance is open conceit or bragging, they reason. Since they have many moments of social appropriateness, they claim innocence of this trait. But another definition of arrogance is "blatant disregard for authority," which is not necessarily accompanied by loud clanging or pompous strutting. Instead the adulterer relegates God's ways to second-class status.

Adultery Always Has Consequences

God gifted mankind with an innate desire for free will, but He also instituted a system of consequences as protection against unrestrained abuse of freedom. Consequences create feelings of guilt and frustration in the sinner which are part of God's plan to highlight the futility of sin and draw individuals back to His higher order of life. Solomon, the wisest man who ever lived, saw the benefit of such reproof. "Do not despise the chastening of the LORD, nor detest His correction," he said, "for whom the LORD loves He corrects, just as a father the son in whom he delights" (Prov. 3:11–12).

Consider the analogy of a broken leg. God allows pain so the person will be prompted to seek immediate attention. If God had not created a system of pain, He could be considered cruel, since greater damage would surely follow.

Similarly, to communicate His displeasure with sexual misdeeds, God allows the parties involved to experience a wide range of painful emotions. There will be struggles with guilt. Feelings of self-doubt and insecurity will abound. Formerly healthy relationships become strained. Communication with children and other family members is difficult. Life will not continue as normal because God does not want His loved ones to think of infidelity as a normal activity.

Some find it difficult to accept consequences that will be natural by-products of unfaithfulness. After giving up his girlfriend, Michael was angry when Janet still had difficulty trusting him. "Why is it so hard to convince my wife that our marriage will be fine? She doesn't seem willing to let bygones be bygones!"

Janet blurted out, "Michael, think about what happened! You completely violated my trust in you. I'm not going to stand idly by and let you assume that all can be normal."

"What price am I going to have to pay?"

"Well, for starters, I'm not going to just jump back into a sexual relationship with you until I can trust you."

"But Janet, that's not fair. Don't you think my confession is proof enough that I'm sorry?"

In our next session I tried to show Michael that Janet had every reason to feel hurt and angry. "You have to understand her hurt and anger and let those emotions run their course."

Michael had forgotten that any transgression carries consequences, and sometimes those consequences are powerful and long lasting. Rather than scorning them, Michael needed to remember Janet's negative reactions when he felt tempted to seek sexual pleasure outside marriage again.

For some, the consequences of infidelity spread beyond immediate families. Some lose jobs. Others forfeit church positions. Some live for years with a badly stained reputation. Others experience deteriorated relationships with children, in-laws, or former friends.

The fact that such consequences are so common indicates that sexual behavior is closely linked to a person's integrity and trustworthiness. It is not only the act of sex that causes others to have doubts about the unfaithful spouse, but also the fact that a vow was not honored and manipulation was used.

An Adultery-Torn Marriage Will Not Heal Quickly

Common sense tells us that it takes longer for a patient to recover from open-heart surgery than from a tonsillectomy. The heart is more vital than the tonsils, therefore the body is much more intricately affected by tampering with it.

Likewise, sexual purity is so central to God's plan for our lives that when adultery is committed it takes time to heal. Often persons mistakenly push to get the problem of infidelity out of the way in an attempt to return to normal living. Doing so minimizes the seriousness of the act.

Michael and Janet had been separated for three months when Michael confessed to the adulterous affair. When Michael wanted to return home, I applauded his decision, then I suggested that they consider a step-by-step plan to help them ease back into full marital relations. However, Michael insisted on moving home immediately. Janet agreed, thinking that she should not risk alienating Michael further.

Within a few weeks Janet was back in my office, telling me how miserable she felt. She still believed that her husband wanted to work on their marriage, but it became painfully evident that he had not taken time to think through his emotions and guiding philosophies. They had attempted to patch the marriage too hurriedly.

I encourage couples to allow for a three- to six-month time period to "let the dust settle." For some couples this period may be shorter, for others, longer. Once painful emotions have eased, couples need another six months to establish healthier forms of relating to one another.

Often persons mistakenly push to get the problem of infidelity out of the way in an attempt to return to normal living.

Only after Michael fully realized the extent of Janet's hurt did their marriage turn the corner. After much counseling he accepted that there would be some fallout from his affair. Janet was persistent in keeping emotional issues before him, so he developed patience and a new understanding of her needs. Janet and Michael remained under the same roof as they gradually witnessed a return of their love for each other. In retrospect they admitted that they should have reconciled at a much slower pace.

In a particularly uplifting session Janet told Michael, "One of the problems that led to your affair was your desire to have it all. Now I see your willingness to set aside your old tendency to be in control, and I am feeling more comfortable with you. I sense a real change in your attitude."

"Well, it wasn't easy for me to accept the slow approach toward reconciliation, but I finally decided that I would do whatever it took to prove that I'm different. If time is part of the equation, I'll give you all the time you need."

Adultery Requires a Spiritual Solution

Whenever I counsel individuals who want to end an adulterous relationship, I suggest a number of lifestyle changes. For example, the other person needs to be considered off limits, with all contact coming to a complete halt. Accountability measures need to be put in place. New efforts to win back the spouse need to be implemented. Overloaded schedules need to be reduced to allow time for family matters. Communication styles need adjustment as do strategies for handling emotions. These solutions and many more need to be set firmly in place so the old lifestyle of deception can be replaced by a new lifestyle of wholesomeness.

These solutions will have little depth, though, if there is no effort to get one's life right spiritually. It is possible to implement all the externally correct behaviors and still remain vulnerable to the repetition of the old life of deception. All behavior is an extension of the unseen spiritual self—any restructuring that does not address the inner self is merely window dressing.

I talked privately with Michael, then with Janet, about their spiritual paths the past several years. Michael was quite candid when he said, "I've been taking advantage of God's grace. I was saved in college and had some real spiritual growth for several years. But then I let some bad habits creep into my life which I rationalized by saying that God would forgive me no matter what.

"I quit reading my Bible. I didn't really want other men to know of my salvation. Church was just a place to fill time on Sunday mornings. That was all a part of my demise. Now I'm committed to reestablishing my relationship with the Lord. I enjoy my daily devotional time. I hunger for the Bible instruction I receive at church. I truly want to talk openly about the Lord, both with Janet and with my friends."

Janet's thoughts were different. "My Christian habits haven't really changed. For years I've been consistent in my Bible study, daily devotions, and church participation. This whole incident has made me realize that I haven't been willing to let Michael share these with me. When he shunned his faith several years ago, I was too quick to write him off. My greatest adjustment will be to be more open with him about the Lord's presence in my life."

I suggested that this couple write out their spiritual goals, including the study, prayer, and church habits they discussed with me. Then I asked them to read those goals to one another as a commitment to meeting them. We prayed together and each of them committed to rely on God to give them the wisdom to be a conduit of His traits to each other.

Guilt is the emotion that prompts healthy spiritual introspection. Some humanistic thinkers suggest that guilt is outdated, but it is nonetheless a healthy emotion for anyone wishing to make amends for misdeeds. Healthy guilt is a true sense of remorse and shame, which leads to corrective changes in thought and deed. It prompts persons to compare the deficits created by sin with the gains created by virtuous living. And it acknowledges how the only true source of good is God Himself. When guilt is successfully worked through, people find peace in the lifestyle provisions prescribed by the Father who wants the best for His children.

Paul gives the Galatians a detailed distinction between the life that does not respond to the Holy Spirit's prompting and the life that does. The traits of the one who has not found spiritual depth include immorality, impurity, sensuality, disputes, and carousing.

When God's voice is heard, the traits love, joy, peace, patience, and self-control become prominent (Gal. 5:16–23). A person who is not committed to the call of God will much more readily fall to the baser elements than the one fully committed to His ways. Without the Lord's guidance we have only human power and influence to guide us.

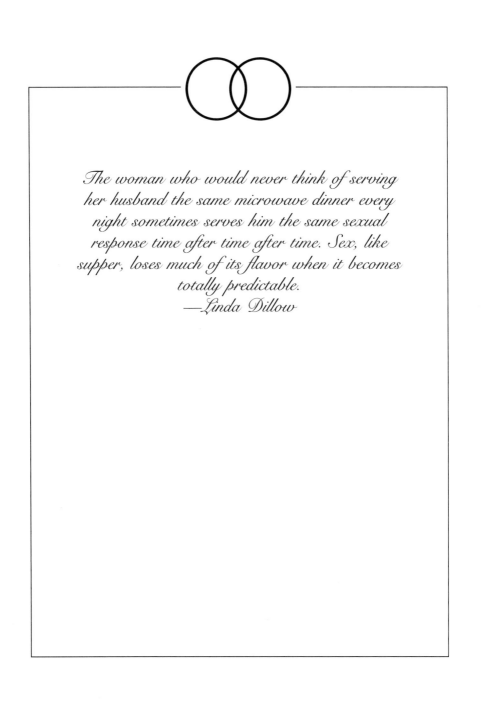

The woman who would never think of serving her husband the same microwave dinner every night sometimes serves him the same sexual response time after time after time. Sex, like supper, loses much of its flavor when it becomes totally predictable.
—*Linda Dillow*

PART FOUR

All in the Family

Chapter

19

Our Parents' Impact on Our Ability to Trust

*A*ll of us have fears. It's a normal part of being human. But two basic fears are related to childhood issues with one or both of our parents: fear of abandonment and fear of being consumed. These two fears deeply affect our ability to trust.

The Fear of Abandonment

Children who grow up in a family in which the mother and/or father is either not there or is emotionally unpredictable and inconsistent will often experience feelings of abandonment. These children have a very critical attitude toward themselves, often blaming themselves for not having their needs met by their parents. They feel somehow at fault. This leads to feelings of insecurity and badness, and a sense that their needs are greedy, way out of proportion to what they should be.

"Our Parents' Impact on Our Ability to Trust" is adapted from *The Intimacy Factor*, Dr. David Stoop and Jan Stoop (1992).

As these children become adults, they sometimes give up on ever having their needs met by another person. Some of them choose to withdraw into a lonely, isolated world of their own, as Chris did, where no one is close enough to hurt or disappoint them. Some of them still have a private fantasy of what it would be like to be close to another person and to be nurtured, but they have given up hope of ever experiencing it in this life. A more common pattern, however, is for these adults to work very hard at doing everything right, for then they may earn the right to be cared for. They become perfectionistic, trying harder and harder to serve the needs of the other person in the relationship, believing that eventually the other person will take care of them. Usually, though, their fears of abandonment will take over and they will blame themselves when the other person does not show caring.

Fear of abandonment and fear of being consumed deeply affect our ability to trust.

Marianne was afraid of being abandoned. Her boyfriend had been paying a lot of attention to her girlfriend, and when she confronted him about it, a huge fight resulted. She was angry, and she let him know it. But as soon as he left, her anger turned to panic. She had thoughts like, "I'm sure I was wrong. I just overreacted. Maybe he'll never talk to me again. I really blew it this time. I've got to get control of myself in these kinds of situations. It's all because I feel so insecure, just as he says."

She baked some of his favorite cookies and drove around looking for him so she could apologize for her terrible behavior. We asked her what she had done about his flirting with her girlfriend.

She had to think for a while before saying, "Oh, that. I guess it was my fault for not being understanding. I guess I just made too much of it."

The problem is nothing had changed. Her boyfriend's behavior would continue, and Marianne would keep blaming herself and apologizing in order to make peace. And everything would stay just the same because Marianne was so afraid of abandonment. Since the day her father had left home and hadn't come back, she couldn't tolerate any repetition of those abandonment feelings.

The younger you were as a child when an injury took place, the more blame you will put on yourself. Children are very ego-centered; they see themselves as the cause of everything that takes place in their world. If Marianne's dad left home when she was five or six, her natural tendency would be to think that she was somehow to blame. As a child, Marianne tried to be a better daughter, thinking that would make her daddy come home. As an adult, she was still trying to do everything perfectly, so that those she cared about would not leave her.

The Fear of Being Consumed

Carrie, the girl who grew up with the hovering mother, had the opposite fear. She felt that if she didn't get away from her mother, she would be consumed by her. Because Carrie had not worked through her feelings about her mom, she repeated that relationship with others in her life. Her last boyfriend complained that she was too independent and that she hadn't been that way at the beginning of the relationship. But at the beginning everything is so exciting and easy, especially for people like Carrie. It's what happens later that makes it difficult.

As her relationship continued for several months, Carrie felt more and more crowded. Her boyfriend needed too much from her. He wanted to spend every minute with her. He was too dependent, she thought. The only way Carrie could protect herself from feeling that she was going to be consumed by the relationship was to back off and distance herself from him.

Carrie often found herself getting angry at those who were close to her, particularly her boyfriends, for not understanding her need for personal space. She avoided her mother, who now lived two thousand miles away, by leaving her telephone answering machine on and calling back only when she felt her mother was really getting exasperated with her. But when someone asked about her mother, Carrie spoke about her in glowing terms. "We're really there for each other. She's the most important person in my life probably." She hadn't been able to separate herself emotionally from her mother in a healthy way, so she was still fighting the feeling of being consumed by anyone who cared for her.

When we asked Carrie whether she felt that she would be consumed by her mother if she weren't careful, she thought for a moment and then said, "Yeah, that's exactly how it feels. I guess that's why I moved halfway across the country from her when I finished college." Until Carrie got her mother into a proper perspective, she would always fight against closeness in all her relationships while at the same time seeking it.

The Push-Pull of These Two Fears

Of course, these two fears don't operate in isolation. We will experience both of them. Often, our fear of abandonment causes us to try very hard in a relationship, and when we suddenly find that we are closer than we care to be and feel engulfed, we back off from the other person in an effort to regain some comfortable personal space. But then the fear of abandonment rises up within us again, and we start to move back toward the other person. When you add the fears of the other person to the equation, you can see why closeness and intimacy take a lot of work and require a foundation of trust.

We often are attracted to people who are trying to work through the opposite fear from ours. Those who most fear abandonment like to relate to those who most fear being consumed. On a rational level that doesn't make sense, but fear causes us to operate on the irrational level most of the time.

A lot of marriages represent the push-pull of these competing fears. One fear dominates in one person and the other fear dominates in the other person. Breaking this cycle is not as easy as it looks. For one thing, if I fear abandonment, I will do a lot of things for the other person in order to keep him or her interested in me and liking me. Since I am such a good caretaker, the other person has it made—or so it seems. That person doesn't need to do much to keep the relationship going—just be sure not to stray too far away. But this little system we have set up fails to take into consideration that other person's probable fear is that of being consumed.

In our culture the woman usually struggles with the fear of abandonment and the man struggles with the fear of being consumed. But we've met couples who are the opposite and the problems we will describe are the same.

If one person in a marriage fears being consumed, he will direct his energy outside the marriage. You'll have a very stable, but unsatisfying, situation with one person spending the majority of her energy on building togetherness while the other person is directing his energy outside the marriage to develop *separateness* through his job, friends, or hobbies. One becomes the pursuer, and the other, the pursued.

The wife, fearing abandonment, places a lot of her energy and effort into working on the togetherness in their marriage. She expects them to spend time alone together on the weekends and encourages her husband to leave the office at 5:30, rather than working late. The husband, fearing that he will be consumed, puts a lot of effort into doing things independently, acting very responsibly in his job and hobbies "for the sake of the marriage." He's likely to say, "I work sixty to seventy hours a week for my family." The wife, who feels abandoned, doesn't see it that way.

What needs to take place for this relationship to be more satisfying for each person? Unfortunately, the burden of the work falls on the one who is already doing most of the work. But a different kind of work is required. In fact, the person who pursues the most togetherness is going to have to stop being so responsible for nurturing the relationship, to stop being the pursuer.

It's important how the pursuer handles this change. Often some changes occur when the pursuer gets totally fed up and reacts with cold, hard anger. But when this happens, the person who seeks the most *separateness* begins to pursue *togetherness* until the pursuer cools down and things can get back to normal.

Megan tried to reverse the roles in her marriage during a session in our office. At first we thought she was really going to change her pattern of pursuit. She reacted with quick, hot anger to something her husband, Steve, had just said. As she grabbed a pillow and threw it at him, she announced, "I've had it! I'm through with this marriage!" And then she just sat there and glared at him. He had a silly, embarrassed smile on his face at first, but when she stayed mad, he started to squirm.

"I'm sorry," he began. "I know what I just said was stupid. I can't believe I said it. You're not going to end the marriage over that, are you?"

His question went unanswered.

I didn't want to jump in yet because I wanted to see where Steve, the typical workaholic, would take it. His family was one of the symbols of success he had gathered around himself. Now, it was in jeopardy.

Steve went on for at least twenty minutes, going from apology to promise as he pursued Megan in order to try to win her back. She started to smile, but kept the angry glare in her eyes focused on Steve so that he wouldn't get off the hook. At the end of the session, they were talking together and had made plans to go out to eat in order to keep talking.

The next week, Megan said that Steve really tried for several days, but now they were right back where they had started. When Megan's fears of abandonment had subsided, she had unconsciously gotten back into her role of being responsible for their togetherness. Her fear of abandonment returned, and Steve got back into his role of seeking separateness. It had only been a temporary reversal of the cycle; nothing had really changed.

In order for there to be a real change in the way they related, Megan needed to back off on some of the things she did to keep them together and put more energy into her own life. But she needed to do this graciously and without hostility in order for it to be effective. And she needed to keep on doing it, even after Steve began to work on their togetherness.

For example, after the session in which Megan angrily stated that she was finished with the marriage and Steve began to make some moves toward her, she needed to let go of the anger, but hold on to her resolve to begin to take better care of herself. She could have said to Steve, "I know what I said was in anger, and I apologize for being so angry. I know I've been on your case for a long time. Part of the problem is that you have your work and your friends there, and I only have you and the kids to look after. I know I need to do something about that."

Megan did do something about it after our next session, and Steve didn't quite know how to respond. Now, the ball was in Steve's court. She found a class that she wanted to take and signed up for it. She made arrangements for a sitter so Steve could work as late as he wanted, and kindly told Steve of her plans. Now, Steve was even more confused. Megan made sure that she wasn't cold or angry, but she also made sure that she didn't chase after Steve, either. It wasn't easy, for these changes stirred up a lot of Megan's fears of abandonment.

After several weeks of this, Steve started to get anxious. He tried to pick fights with her, but she stayed in her cordial, but firm, position and refused to enter the battle. Next, Steve started coming home from work earlier, suggesting that they could use the time to do some things together. He started to act more inse-cure, and he became aware of some of his own neediness. Grad-ually, they began to work together on a more balanced relation-ship. For both Steve and Megan to maintain this balance, they would need to redefine their boundaries as a couple.

DEFINING OUR BOUNDARIES

Many marital conflicts are power struggles over the definition of the individual boundaries within the marriage. Boundaries are necessary. My skin is a physical boundary that keeps what is in-side of me separate from what is on the outside.

In marriage, personal and emotional boundaries are always issues that need to be resolved. Who I am, who you are, and who we are together are all boundary issues. When a person's bound-aries are too rigid, they keep other people out. They are probably more afraid of being consumed than of being abandoned. These people feel distant toward other people, and other people see them as hard to get to know. In a marriage, they spend a lot of time working on the separateness issues.

On the other hand, people who have fuzzy boundaries often overidentify with their spouses or friends. The wife finds her identity in her husband; the husband finds his identity in his work or his friends or sports and other activities. Each has fuzzy boundaries.

These people are easy to get to know, sometimes too easy to get to know. Other people may feel these people are too dependent; in the marriage relationship these people will often work very hard on togetherness issues. They have a hard time saying no because of their fear of rejection.

In order to develop our own personal boundaries, we need to work through our fears of abandonment and our fears of being consumed, and the reasons these fears are at work within us. When Megan tried to define the boundaries in their marriage, they were too close for Steve; he was afraid his own personal boundaries would be lost. When Steve tried to define the boundaries, they were too distant for Megan; she was afraid he would slip away from her.

Think about your own life. Your sense of personal boundaries is based on your success in building a solid, emotionally bonded relationship with your mother, and then being able to find some separateness from her through your relationship with your father. When this process is incomplete, you will experience problems with personal boundaries. You will have weak personal boundaries if you have not been able to trust both of your parents.

Are you afraid of abandonment? Or of being consumed? People whose fathers or mothers left home (or died) when they were young, or who were neglected because their parents were absorbed by an addiction, such as alcoholism or workaholism, for instance, often fear abandonment. On the other hand, people whose parents were the overwhelming, hovering kind often fear engulfment.

You will have weak personal boundaries if you have not been able to trust both of your parents.

Your fear is invading the way you interact with your spouse. If you are angry with your spouse because he or she doesn't spend enough time with you, your relationship with one of your parents could possibly be fueling that anger and making it much worse than it otherwise might be. That reaction could be causing you to be overly dependent upon your mate, which then causes him or her to run further away from you.

Or if you are constantly moving away from closeness and intimacy, it could be because you were consumed as a child. This can be very frustrating to a spouse, by the way.

Now think about your spouse. Does he or she seem to fear abandonment or being consumed?

Finally, which of you seeks the most *togetherness* (probably the one who fears abandonment, as Megan did)? Who seeks the most *separateness* (probably the one who fears being consumed, as Steve did)?

How uneven is that distribution? Is it ninety to ten, as in the case of Megan and Steve? Or only sixty to forty, which is fairly even?

Working through our issues with our parents in a way that leads to forgiveness and release is an essential step in establishing healthy boundaries in a marriage. We suggest that our patients consider a five-step process.[1]

FORGIVING YOUR PARENTS

1. Recognize the Injury

Begin by thinking about your mom. Was she a hovering mother, an emotionally absent mother, an uncertain mother? If she was, you have been hurt by your relationship with her, and you have experienced losses in your development. You need to work through these issues and ultimately forgive her before you can fully trust your spouse. Think about your childhood and describe one incident in which you felt hurt by your mom.

Now think about your dad. Was he an absent father, an abusive father, or a strong, silent father? If he was, you have been hurt by your relationship with your dad, and you have experienced losses in your development. Think about one incident in your childhood in which you felt hurt by your dad and describe it.

2. Identify the Emotions Involved

Think about that incident with your mom. Identify the feelings below that are closest to your own and complete the statements:

"I am afraid to look at this because _____."
"I feel guilty about _____."
"I feel ashamed and humiliated by _____."
"I am angry that _____."

Now think about that incident with your dad. Identify the feelings below that are closest to your own and complete the statements:

"I am afraid to look at this because _____."
"I feel guilty about _____."
"I feel ashamed and humiliated by _____."
"I am angry that _____."

3. Express Your Hurt and Anger

We treat this as a separate step because it is so important. It is not enough to simply identify what we are feeling. We also need some way to express our feelings. Imagine that Mom or Dad or both are sitting in the room with you. Tell them how you are feeling. (It is usually unnecessary for you to literally do this with either parent!)

If I could say anything I wanted to say to Mom, I would tell her, "Mom, you hurt me by: _____

_____."

"And I am angry about: _____

_____."

If I could say anything I wanted to Dad, I would tell him, "Dad, you hurt me by: _____

_____."

"And I am angry about: _____

_____."

4. Set Boundaries to Protect Yourself

As we mentioned earlier, a personal boundary is what defines who I am, apart from you. Our boundaries can be too rigid or too fuzzy. Ideally they should be flexible, yet firm.

Think about what you can do if your parents are alive, to set new boundaries with Mom. (For instance, "I will not allow my mother to make me feel guilty about not following her advice." Or "I will not call her every day as she would like me to. I will try to be my own person.") Set two new boundaries and write them on a separate sheet of paper.

Now, think about what you can do to set new boundaries with your dad. (For instance, "I will not allow my dad to control me by shouting at me.")

1. _____
2. _____

You may want to talk to someone you trust about what you have written before moving on to the final step.

5. Cancel the Debt

Once you have worked through the first four steps you are ready to forgive. This involves releasing your parents (or parent) from your own expectations. Cancel the debt they owe you. You do this to set yourself free. Often it helps to make the act of forgiveness take some concrete, tangible form. You may want to write *forgiven* over your description of the incident in Step 1.

Once you have done this work within yourself effectively, you can be in the presence of your parents and feel, on the inside, that you are the age you are. If you still feel, on the inside, like a kid or an adolescent, you still need to do some work in these areas. It takes two grown-ups to experience an intimate marriage.

20

When In-Laws Become Outlaws

*hrough the many years that
my husband, Norman, has
been a pastor, speaker, and author, we have both had the opportunity to hear the frustrations of many an aggravated spouse, driven
nearly "crazy" by domineering, possessive, or just plain nosy in-
laws. The truth is, I had some of those frustrations myself in those
early years of our own marriage. It wasn't until I learned to see my
husband's mother as a person instead of a mother-in-law that I was
able to enjoy her for what she was. Some of these anecdotes are
funny, some poignant.*

*I certainly hope you can identify and find a solution for your
own struggle. Of course, it's quite possible that you have a wonderful relationship with your inlaws, who never intrude or make demands on your time. Then you might want to read this chapter*

"When In-Laws Become Outlaws" is adapted from *Secrets of Staying in Love*, Ruth Stafford Peale (1984).

from Secrets of Staying in Love *anyway, just in case you have a* friend *who does.*

—*Ruth Stafford Peale*
Secrets of Staying in Love

The pretty young wife seemed both apprehensive and angry. "Mrs. Peale," she said, "my husband's mother is coming to visit us next week. She's going to stay ten days—ten whole days! And I can't stand it!"

She had approached me in the aisle of the church following the second Sunday morning church service. She identified herself as a member of the church's Young Adult group. Her problem, she said, was one she couldn't discuss dispassionately with her husband. Could she ask me about it?

"Of course," I said, and she told me about the imminent visit of her mother-in-law. "I just can't stand it!" she repeated, and actually stamped her well-shod little foot.

"What is there about it that you can't stand?" was the question I asked her.

"I can't stand the way she tries to manage everything," she said. "From the moment she comes into our house, she just takes over. She has tremendous energy. She's a very positive sort of person. So the way I prepare the meals isn't right; she always knows a better way. My housekeeping isn't well-organized; she keeps telling me to do it differently. No matter how I handle the children, she always has other ideas. By the time she's been in the house twenty-four hours, I feel as if it were no longer mine, but hers. She's my husband's mother, and I know I'm supposed to love her, but, Mrs. Peale, this woman drives me right up the wall."

Then she continued a little more calmly, "She's a widow, and Jack is her only son, so I can't refuse to have her visit us occasionally. But it causes so much friction between Jack and me that sometimes I think we'll get in the habit of fighting. And that is bad. What on earth can I do?"

I knew that Norman had scheduled a meeting with his officers to discuss some church matters, so I had a few minutes to spare. "Let's sit over here in the corner of this pew and talk about it," I said.

"There *are* some remedies for this problem of yours. You might find it exciting to try some of them."

It's practically universal, this in-law problem. Very few married couples escape it entirely. Norman and I had our share of it too. We were devoted to each other's parents, but we found them trying at times. Norman felt that my mother was rigid and uncompromising, with little tolerance or understanding of people whose views or standards differed from her own. I had to admit that this was true. On the other hand, I felt that his mother, gifted though she was, could be domineering and possessive. And determined to have her own way.

For example, when we were first married, we always had to go to Mother Peale's home for Christmas. "I may not be here next year," she would say plaintively if I suggested going to my parents or making other plans. So we always wound up going there . . . and I always had to control and mask my resentment.

Both of us got along better with our fathers-in-law than we did with our mothers-in-law. This also seems to be the general rule; the sharp-edged jokes about in-laws are seldom directed at men. Perhaps this is because fathers are less inclined than mothers to judge or criticize the person their child chooses to marry. Or perhaps their interests are focused on their jobs and not so much on personal relationships. In any case, fathers-in-law seldom seem to generate the kind of friction that mothers-in-law do.

It's practically universal, this in-law problem.

Norman and I were lucky in that from the start we agreed to discuss our feelings about the other's parents openly and honestly—in private. We agreed not to get angry or defensive when the subject of in-laws came up, but to treat it as a kind of good-humored verbal pillow-fight in which either of us could say anything within reason and not do any damage to the fabric of our own marriage.

And it was amazing how often the appraisal voiced was accurate, but never admitted by either of us to ourselves previously. There is always that fine line of fearing disloyalty. But such openness between Norman and me always brought us closer together and made for a depth of understanding that was a great experience every time it happened.

"Your mother is so narrow-minded," Norman would complain. "Why does she have to object to my father's cigars? When she sees him light one, she acts as if she had found him breaking all the Ten Commandments at once. What business is it of hers? Why don't you tell her to cut it out?"

"What she really objects to," I'd reply with some asperity, "is that sometimes when your father's cigars don't taste right, he spits in the fireplace! Why don't you tell him to cut *that* out?"

Or I might say, "Why is your mother so full of fears and phobias about things? She's always sure that the worst is going to happen. She sees a disaster around every corner. I don't want this kind of timidity to rub off on my children the way it did on your brothers and you!"

"My mother's *not* timid!" Norman would counter. "She has a vivid imagination, that's all. At times she thinks you can be pretty callous. She told me that when she was with you in the park the other day, and John fell off his tricycle, you didn't even pick him up. You let some stranger passing by do it!"

"That's right," I'd say. "I knew he wasn't hurt. I wanted him to pick himself up. Your mother acted as if he had broken both arms and legs. That's just what I'm talking about!"

So we'd say to each other anything that came to mind, and I think it was the best possible form of ventilation. I also think that we each secretly wanted the other to defend his parents with fire and sword. After all, a person who doesn't love his parents isn't likely to have much love-capacity in him for a married partner or anyone else.

In talking with a young couple a few days before their marriage, I happened to mention that one of the greatest arts they would have to learn as man and wife was to talk together about each other's parents with absolute honesty and openness. The bride-to-be seemed startled. "Do you really mean that, Mrs. Peale?" she asked.

"Of course I do," I replied. "In fact, I think it's an absolute necessity for harmony and understanding between any husband and wife."

Sally turned to Jim. She held back as though in doubt and then asked, "Jim, do you think we can do that?"

He hesitated, and in a flash I knew that inadvertently I had stumbled onto the thing that could be their greatest problem. He looked at her thoughtfully. It was a long moment, and I could actually feel the hold his mother had on him. Then he said, "Honey, let's do it! Will you help me?"

Over the years, Norman and I have seen more than one marriage founder under the impact of the in-law problem. We have also seen cases where marriages were prevented by pressures exerted by a possessive parent, usually the mother. In one strange case a young woman who had spent her twenties and early thirties looking after a supposedly invalid mother came to Norman after the old lady died. She explained that she had never married because her mother needed her. But now she was haunted by a terrible fear—fear that her mother had been buried alive.

It was one of those cases where the fear is so irrational and so deep that ordinary religious counseling is of little value. Fortunately the psychiatrists at the Institute of Religion and Health were able to help the young woman. One of these doctors told Norman later that the young woman's irrational dread was actually a disguised fear that her mother might not be really dead, and she might still come back from the grave to dominate and warp and twist her daughter's life. It took long and patient therapy to rid the young woman of her morbid obsession.

There was another instance where a young wife came to Norman and told him that she was going to have to divorce her husband. None of the usual reasons for such an attitude seemed to exist. Finally it came out that her mother had disapproved violently of the marriage. "If you marry that man against my wishes," she said ominously to her daughter, "it will be the death of me!" Sure enough, soon after the wedding—which she refused to attend—the old dragon had a heart attack and died. This set up such profound guilt feelings in the daughter's unconscious mind that she came to feel that she could atone for her mother's death only by divorcing her husband. "My mother may be dead," she sobbed, "but her influence isn't. I can still feel her surrounding me, pressuring me. The only way I'll ever be rid of her condemnation is by divorcing my husband. Then maybe she'll leave me alone!"

Sometimes Norman's instincts tell him that the best way to deal with an emotional problem is to be brusque. He said to his tormented visitor, "Listen to me. You are now a married woman. You are supposed to be a mature person. You must stop acting like a frightened child. Your mother is no longer here. She's gone. She's dead. To get rid of these feelings that are troubling you, you don't have to divorce a perfectly good husband. All you have to do is repeat these words after me: 'Mother, you cannot dominate me any longer. You have no control over me. I am living. You are dead. I hereby *command* you to take your cold, dead hand off my life!'"

"Oh, Dr. Peale," the young woman gasped, "I couldn't say a thing like that!"

"Say it!" Norman insisted. "Say it and be free!"

Finally she said it, and such is the power of suggestion that from that moment she *was* free, and was troubled no longer. It was drastic, but it worked.

Sometimes it takes more than the power of suggestion to control a rampaging maternal instinct. A friend of ours once told us of a conversation he had with a distinguished California jurist, Judge Alton B. Pfaff. Judge Pfaff, who for years presided over a Court of Domestic Relations in Los Angeles, told of a case where a young soldier appealed to him for help. The boy had married a girl who was completely dominated by her mother. She could make no move, no decision without consulting Mom. Everything had to be reported to Mom. Everything had to be approved by Mom.

To a certain type of personality, exercising this sort of power over another person is morbidly satisfying, and Mom had no intention of relinquishing it. At first she insisted that the newlyweds live in her house, where she watched every move with an eagle eye. The son-in-law, naturally, was miserable. Finally he moved himself and his bride into a small apartment, but even there the mother-in-law followed them, appearing uninvited at all hours, sometimes persuading the bride to go back and spend the night with her instead of with her husband.

Finally, to his vast relief, the young soldier was transferred to Arizona. He took his bride with him, and set about starting a new life. But one day he came home to find that his mother-in-law had flown to Arizona, had persuaded her daughter that she was unhappy there, and had actually taken her back to California. It was at this point that the husband, returning to Los Angeles in search of his wife, appealed to Judge Pfaff.

The judge settled the matter by issuing a court order directing the mother-in-law to stop interfering in the marriage and forbidding her to set foot in her son-in-law's house without an invitation issued by him. She was warned that to violate the order would place her in contempt and bring swift and punitive action from the court. So she didn't dare to disobey it. But it took the full power of the judicial system to make her stop wrecking her daughter's life.

In yet another case that we know of, a woman who was a good Christian and a pillar of her church developed a painful limp. No physical cause for it could be discovered; she simply went lame. Her pastor, a wise man, had recently performed the wedding ceremony for this woman's daughter. He knew that she had disapproved of the marriage and deeply resented her new son-in-law.

In a long talk with the woman, the minister told her that he thought her limp might well be the reflection of a twisted condition in her mind. "I'm afraid you're guilty of sin," he said, "the sin of despising another human being. I believe you hate your son-in-law, although he has done nothing to deserve your condemnation. I believe you have this limp because something deep within you knows that you are not walking uprightly in your heart, and so you can't walk uprightly in your everyday life."

The woman's eyes filled with tears. "You may be right," she said. "What can I do?"

"I want you to come to the church with me," the pastor said, "and kneel at the altar. I want you to confess this sin of anger and hatred, and ask for release and forgiveness. I want you to take Communion and resolve to make a fresh start. Then I want you to go to your son-in-law and admit your fault and ask for his forgiveness too. I believe that if you will do the first few things, the last will not be so hard."

Actually, it was very hard, but the woman did it. She went to the nearby town where her daughter and son-in-law lived. She rang the doorbell. When the son-in-law came to the door, she managed a tremulous smile. "I'm your wicked mother-in-law," she said, "come to ask your forgiveness for many things."

He was a perceptive young man. He didn't say a word. He just gave her a hug and drew her into the house. From that point on, they were friends. And the minister must have been right about the limp, because it disappeared.

Norman has a somewhat similar mother-in-law story that he loves to tell about the man whose mother-in-law lived in the same house. The man came to Norman claiming that she was driving him crazy, not because she was interfering or domineering, but because she was ruining his breakfasts. Every morning, he said, he liked to get up and have a cup of coffee alone in the kitchen. But every morning his mother-in-law would come scuffing downstairs in an old bathrobe with curlers in her hair and heelless slippers on her feet which made a horrible dragging sound when she walked. She never said anything worth listening to. She would pour herself a cup of coffee and drink it with loud slurping sounds. Like a horse, the man said. And not only that, but when she sat at the table she would maddeningly scrunch her toast. One more scrunch, the man said, one more slurp, and he was going to commit murder . . . or else leave his own home for good.

"Well," Norman said to him, "I can give you a solution to your problem. But I doubt if you're brave enough to attempt it."

"Try me!" said the man. "I'll do anything. I promise!"

"All right," Norman said. "Tomorrow morning, when you're about to leave for work, turn back from the door and say casually to your mother-in-law, 'Mother So-and-so, how about having lunch with me today downtown, just the two of us?' "

The man stared at Norman as if he had lost his mind. "You must be joking," he said.

"Not at all," Norman replied, "and make it the best restaurant in town. Remember, you promised you'd do anything."

With many misgivings, but because he was a man of his word, the son-in-law took Norman's advice. To his amazement, when his mother-in-law appeared at the restaurant, she was a completely different woman, well-groomed, alert, intelligent, good-humored, a highly agreeable luncheon companion. Why? Because like all of us, she responded to attention, to being treated like a woman instead of like an undesirable piece of furniture. A completely new relationship was established, and it went on for many years.

The moral of the story—and this is probably the best single rule for anyone facing an in-law problem—is this: stop thinking of your marriage partner's relatives as a special breed known as in-laws (a term with faintly unpleasant connotations) and think of them simply as human beings with flaws and imperfections but also lovable qualities. Just discard the in-law label in your mind. Think of them as people. Treat them like people!

Think of [your in-laws] as people. Treat them like people!

This was what I told the young wife who accosted me at church that Sunday. But I said some other things, too. "You tell me that your mother-in-law is full of energy and tends to take over. Instead of resenting this, why don't you turn it to your advantage? Which aspects of housekeeping do you dislike? Ironing? Sewing? Why not plan to have a small mountain of ironing on hand and ask your mother-in-law to do it for you? Do you need curtains made, or slipcovers? Get the material and leave it in her room. And while she does the work, get out of the house and do something with your husband. If she insists on taking over, let her take over tasks that you'd rather avoid anyway!" I said another thing to the girl. "Instead of resenting your mother-in-law, why don't you make a study of her—a calm, thorough, objective analysis of what makes her tick? That's what I did with my mother-in-law. I tried to figure out what made her the way she was. I tried to understand her motives and her actions. In the process I learned an amazing amount about my husband and why *he* was the way he was. After all, Norman's mother had been the strongest influence in his life before I met him. Trying to understand her helped me to understand him.

"Finally," I continued, "you can turn this whole thing into a challenging exercise in controlling your own emotions. You're a member of this church; well, put your faith to work! Learn to forgive your mother-in-law for her intrusive or domineering ways. Remind yourself that she means well. Remember that if you're patient and kind with her, your husband will know it and appreciate it and love you all the more for it. Stop thinking about her visit as ten days of misery. Take it an hour at a time. Stop wringing your hands and stamping your foot and saying 'I can't stand it.' Tell yourself calmly that you can stand it and you will stand it and that you can even profit by it."

She thanked me and said soberly that I had given her some good and much-needed advice, and that she would try to do as I had said.

21

Can You Childproof Your Marriage?

*A*rnold." He grimaced. "They went and named me Arnold. You know, the only way you can go through school as an Arnold is if your last name's Schwarzenegger. Even my name works against me."

In our office, frail, slim, balding Arnold sat in his chair in a knot. Not only were his legs crossed but the toe of one foot wound around behind the other leg—a double cross. His crossed arms tightly guarded his heart. Arnold was not a happy man.

"Tell us about your first wife," we asked.

"What's to tell? We were married nine years. Then things turned against me. I was a pastor. I guess she got tired of playing second fiddle to the entire congregation. She left."

"Children?"

"Can You Childproof Your Marriage?" is adapted and taken from *Passages of Marriage*, Dr. Frank and Mary Alice Minirth, Drs. Brian and Deborah Newman, Dr. Robert and Susan Hemfelt (1992).

"Three. She has custody. Except holidays."

"Let's talk about your chil—"

"And my birthday."

"Beg your pardon?"

"My birthday. The kids get to visit on my birthday. Also on Martin Luther King Day." He shifted in his chair and retied his knots.

We nodded. "How old are your—"

"And Columbus Day. Some schools get out on the Monday when the banks close, and some celebrate the actual day, October 12. No uniformity. So I got it in writing that the kids visit on the legal holiday, whenever that falls. I work in a bank, you see— I had to resign my pastorate during the divorce—and I wanted the guarantee that I have the day off when the kids are here."

"What do you do in the bank?"

"Advise churches and other nonprofit organizations about investments. I'm considered very good at it. Our bank has seen a 27 percent increase in investment accounts in the last year, and nearly all are with nonprofit institutions. Special rules, you know. It's not your usual investment strategy."

"Your experience as a pastor must be invaluable in that line of work."

"Exactly!" And Arnold launched into a detailed explanation of IRS rulings, and the difference between Fanny Maes and Ginny Maes. We drew him back to the subject of his children, learning eventually that they were aged eight, six, and four.

He seemed to loosen a little, and his face sagged, sadder. "There was a lot of financial pressure when I was pastoring. And time pressures. Demands. Kids take so much time. And confusion. The house was always in an uproar, and a pastor lives in a fishbowl. You know that. Appearances. What will the neighbors think? Kids give nosy neighbors a lot to think about."

He grimaced again. "Ironic. It's all against me. Each year the kids get older, they cost more. More money. More time. Now that I'm making a better-than-decent living at an eight-hour-a-day job, I don't have the kids anymore."

Kids—and the lack of kids if they've always been a part of

your dreams for your family—raise the stress level of any marriage. The last task in the Second Passage of marriage is to childproof your marriage.

THE FOURTH TASK: CHILDPROOF YOUR MARRIAGE

"It's a dangerous myth" says Debi Newman, "that having a baby will help save a marriage. They add enormous stress."

Remember our formula:

$$1 \text{ person} + 1 \text{ person} = \text{conflict}.$$

You can see that adding another member promises friction by multiplying the possible combinations. Mom mothers, but at times she also fathers. Dad fathers, but occasionally must assume the mother role. And then there is each adult's individual private life—work, the world outside the home—and their life as a sexually united couple.

Tossing one child into the pot multiplies the opportunities for friction exponentially, and most families have more than one child, all interacting in a multitude of roles. That's more chances to disagree, more power struggles, more differences of taste and preferences, both within and between the generations. Children present many more needs than do adults; needs to be emotionally nurtured on the road to adulthood (and that's not just a pat on the head in passing. Kids have intense needs that must be met immediately).

Kids introduce another hidden negative element, too: From the parents' viewpoint, they provide more opportunity to fail. The woman with low self-esteem, the man who is unsure of himself, not only faces the possibility of being considered a bad spouse but a bad parent as well. And those two occupations are pursuits the world thinks ought to come naturally.

Brian and Debi Newman comment on that. "Over and over in counsel we see parents react out of a fear of failure. But they don't actually acknowledge that fear of failure. Thus they don't realize the grip it has on them."

"We've all felt the pull to give in to our children's temper tantrums in the store, just to keep people from staring and wondering what kind of parents we are," says Debi Newman. "A more extreme example is the mother who was overweight as a teenager. She may now fear that her child will become overweight and experience the same rejection she experienced in childhood. When she sees her three-year-old daughter enjoying food and eating healthily, the mother may panic and try to take away the food, not realizing the power plays or feelings she may be creating in her daughter."

Still More Pressure

This multiplicity of personalities, with all their frictions and quirks, is the least of it. As Arnold realized, children apply financial pressures from conception on. No parent needs to be told the bewildering variety of ways kids cost money, and non-parents don't want to know.

Children do not sit quietly in a corner. They get involved in activities—sports, clubs, myriad activities to crunch the already-busy parents' time and energy.

In the course of these activities, children meet other adults. As a necessary part of growing up, the kids forge strong personal relationships with some of them. When these relationships reach worshipful proportions, and there is a brief, normal period in every child's life when just such a relationship happens, the parents often feel jealous or threatened. Because it sneaks in, unexpected, unprepared-for, the jealousy causes all the more friction and damage.

THE SHIFTING SANDS OF PARENTHOOD

As rapidly as a newborn child changes, the parents change also. And the maturation is quite as predictable and certain in the parent as in the child. The maturation can be broken down into five stages, which obviously do not parallel the marriage passages we're talking about. We will discuss two of these stages—the period of surprise (the first child) and the period of drifting (school-age children) in this chapter. The other three stages—the stage of turmoil (adolescent children), the stage of renewal or death of relationship (the empty nest), and the stage of joy (grandchildren), we discuss in later passages, in *Passages of Marriage.*

THE PERIOD OF SURPRISE—THE FIRST CHILD

The surprise factor, summarized, is the way that third little person multiplies the happiness and the stress of all the family's interrelationships.

Julia Karris gave voice to one element of surprise. "I baby-sat when I was a kid. But then I went home. Even with brothers and sisters, I never realized how a baby ties you down. Every moment it's either with you, or you've arranged for it to be with someone. There's no off-time, no time to walk away from it."

Carl Warden shook his head over the memories of another element of surprise. "I remember our first one. Annie was actually an easy kid as babies go. Still, parenthood was nothing like what I expected. I don't know what I expected, but this sure wasn't it. And I didn't get the worst of it. Annie was two years old when I got home from overseas. Bess took the brunt of it.

"I mean, here's this tiny person all over the house, babbling, insisting you listen to her, play with her, read to her. Tugging on your pants leg. Fussing.

"But the biggest surprise were the power struggles. A child three feet high can't read or write or mow the lawn, and you get into this powerful contest of wills. And Bess and I would get into power struggles, too, over Annie. I don't know how parents ever get past that first one."

Power struggles—that old question, "Who's in control here?" now rephrased to "Who's in control of this child?"—can indeed unravel the marriage fabric, but they also offer the potential to improve intimacy. Power struggles are, in effect, a form of conflict and can be dealt with as the parents would deal with other conflicts. Negotiation between the parents reveals the parents' thoughts and preferences to each other. As the problem is ironed out, each gets to know the other a little better.

One solid principle for keeping kids from damaging the marital bond is for spouses to agree upon their philosophy of child-raising before the fact, not after the kids come along and generate a crisis. The parents should agree in advance on a united front. If that sounds like a war strategy, it is. Kids will divide you if they can, to gain their own ends.

In counseling we again suggest that couples review the parenting they observed in their family of origin. Take a moment to think about how your parents' actions affect your attitudes toward raising children by reading the statements below and considering which may apply to you.

"In my family children were encouraged to voice their opinions concerning family decisions."

"In my family children were given an allowance tied to their chores."

"In my family everyone ate something different at mealtimes."

"In my family sons were treated differently than daughters."

"In my family both my mom and dad would try to attend my sports, school, and church functions."

"My father (or mother) didn't pay much attention to me."

"In my family the father was the person who disciplined the children."

"In my family it was okay to spank the children."

"My parents would get angry and slap the children."

Now consider which of the following may reflect your own beliefs about child raising.

"I believe children need to learn how to manage money as they grow up."

"I believe that it is all right for children to talk back to their parents."

"I believe that both father and mother should be involved in the daily care of the children."

"I believe that it is important for children to be involved in extra activities, like dancing, sports, piano lessons."

"How children behave and their manners are very important to me."

"I believe that both parents should discipline the kids."

"I plan to spank our children as a way of discipline."

"I want our family to hold and hug each other."[1]

Compare your beliefs from the second set of statements with your beliefs from the first set of statements. Which of your attitudes about child rearing has been influenced by your parents? Is that influence good or bad? Now discuss these issues with your spouse. Once you have talked through your thoughts about child rearing and how they have been influenced, for better or for worse, by your parents, we suggest that the two of you enter into a verbal or written covenant concerning child rearing. You can use this second set of statements as a guideline for this covenant.

It is critical that the parents be parents and the children be children.

Remember, however: the family is not a democracy. It is critical that the parents be parents and the children be children. In counsel we find two situations that usually begin right in this first period of parenthood, and either can irreversibly damage both the marriage and the children.

Fear of Rejection

We are constantly amazed and dismayed at how deeply some parents fear their kids will cease to like them. One of our clients, Amy Marchand, tells her story:

"I suppose every mother worries that maybe her kid will turn out hating her. Look at how children scream and holler when you want them to do something they don't want to. Or tell them no.

"When my little Pete yelled 'Mommy, I hate you!' one day, I think that's what really got me. Pete wanted to play in the mud around the storage shed we were building out back. It was nap time and I didn't want him to get dirty. He threw a fit when I tried to drag him inside, and then he said that.

"I'm ashamed to admit it now, but then I guess I was just shocked. I turned him loose and he ran back to the mud hole. It wasn't long before all he had to do was screech once and we'd give in, both my husband and I. And the more we let him have his way, the more we tried to please him, the worse he got."

We asked Amy this question: "If you were to crack down and enforce a reasonable discipline, do you think he'd hate you?"

She replied, "Yes. He's too used to having his own way."

"Does he really love you now?"

"No."

"Then what will you lose?"

Emotional Incest

When children come into a marriage from prior marriages, the conflict shoots up even higher. Joel and Carolyn found that out the hard way.

Carolyn sat in our office on the verge of tears. "Joel is wonderful. I realize a bride who's only been married eight months is going to say that, but he really is. He's so—so mellow. My former husband, Ralph, was verbally abusive. Extremely so. Our daughter Michelle grew up in a constant state of terror."

Even though Carolyn had only been married eight months she was already in the Second Passage of marriage, since this was a second marriage and she and her husband had children from a previous marriage. Her problems were not as unique as she thought.

"How old is Michelle now?" we asked.

"Almost fourteen. I met Joel at Michelle's sixth-grade open house. His Janna was in the same class. Michelle seemed thrilled that Janna's dad and I were getting together. Michelle was our biggest booster."

"But when you married, her attitude changed."

"Did it ever. There's a lot of jealousy. Joel's kids are jealous because they can't live with him, and they make life miserable every time we have them. Okay. I can see that. But Michelle's got it made. Her natural father yelled at her and put her down all the time. Joel doesn't do any of that. She *wanted* us to make a family. And now . . ."

It's a pattern we see so often. "How is she acting out?"

"Big mouth, talking back. Boys. It's the boys that worry me most."

"Other than Michelle, everything's going all right?"

Carolyn brightened. "Before I ever met Joel, I had already worked through most of the issues associated with the first marriage in counseling—both Michelle and I. We pretty much got our heads on straight, finally. And Joel and I appreciate each other more than most couples do because we've both been around the block. We really got a good thing going, with work."

So what could go wrong? We talked to Carolyn's daughter, Michelle. In the years of living alone with her mother, Michelle had learned to depend upon Mom. She thereby felt safe as never before. Mom supported her. Mom wouldn't let her down. Unfortunately, Mom developed almost exactly the same dependency upon her daughter. Mom needed Michelle for affirmation. She needed Michelle to pick up the slack when life and work got too much. Michelle became confidante, a job she was too young and ill-equipped to handle. When the child nurtures the parent, as Michelle nurtured her mom, we call it emotional incest.

We are seeing that emotional incest, the transfer of intimacy from spouse to child, is the single most damaging thing that kids bring to a marriage; and it's not their fault. Kids must be allowed to be kids, without the responsibility and onus of assuming quasi-parental roles.

Kids can also raise the chaos level in a marriage when the couple seems unable to have children.

Pressure When the Nest Stays Empty

Many women have trouble conceiving and carrying a child to term. Some suffer miscarriage for physiological reasons. This puts another kind of stress on the marriage.

Mary Alice Minirth knows that stress too well. "Our first pregnancy and miscarriage, I didn't know happened. Frank was in his third year of medical school," she recalls. "I was teaching in an inner-city ghetto. I thought my period was messed up from the stress. Not long after that Frank was diagnosed with diabetes, and his future has always been uncertain. My father had cancer. It was the lowest I've ever been."

"We tried again. I suffered three miscarriages in two and a half years. I was trying to teach in that stress situation, and I felt hopeless. Everyone else was having kids. After a miscarriage, I'd get on the elevator to go home and see a mother with a baby in her arms. I'd get in the car and just boo-hoo.

"Some doctors and friends advised us to hang it up. Quit trying. They'd say 'Aw, move on. It's over.' But it's a severe loss."

Frank agrees. "Miscarriage is much more of an issue than most people will admit. It's a severe loss, and you have to go through the stages of grief. A husband must be supportive of his wife. He has to try to understand her emotions because he probably has them also. It's an insight into his own feelings. He may not realize how much it's affecting him. It is. Men tend to lack a keen awareness of their own emotions. It's not that they're not emotional; it's just that, in general, men are not as acutely aware of their feelings as women. Also, talk about the losses. Listening and being listened to is the strongest medicine."

Grieving the Loss

A friend of ours miscarried because she didn't understand how certain chemicals could affect the unborn child's health. "I was two months pregnant when it happened," she said. "Dumb old us, we didn't know that some kinds of paint fumes can induce spontaneous abortion. We were refinishing some furniture, and I got sick from it and miscarried." She stared at her hands in her lap. "I always wonder what the baby would have been like."

"When did this happen?" we asked.

Her eyes brimmed with tears. "Twenty-five years ago."

The loss of an unborn child requires a special kind of grieving, because there is that huge dollop of the unknown. What would that child have been like? Who would the little one have become? To the husband even more so than the wife, that little one is nothing more than a theory, a loss described without ever being seen or touched. Parents of unborn children add those other factors in as they work through their grief.

The first step of the grief process, you'll recall, is *shock and denial.* Mary Alice received a particularly hard jolt when she learned that her "abnormal period" and its consequences was the loss of her first pregnancy. The jolt can be even more severe for a couple who learns of the pregnancy, anticipates the new arrival, and then watches the dream shatter, as the Minirths did during the next three pregnancies.

Feelings run deep and are painful. Anger is entirely appropriate. Never let someone try to talk you out of an emotional response with, "It's only a tadpole at that stage," or "It's not the end of the world" (for this moment, it is), or the cruelest of all, "You (will) have other children. It's not so bad." It is so bad! A death is a death.

The second step is *depression.* Mary Alice Minirth recalls, "I felt hopeless about my past, present, and future. I was almost clinically depressed. I wanted to sleep a lot." This step may be complicated by physiological factors. A woman's hormones alter during pregnancy, and with them her emotional state and balance. Should you lose a child, your body's hormones are thrown for a loop. The physical condition can cause depression apart from the depression of the grieving process. If depression becomes exceedingly severe or lingers far too long (months and months), seek medical help. But do expect depression. It's normal.

The third step, *bargaining,* must not be confused with the advice to never give up hope, and certainly not with prayer. "Lord, please give me a child" is not the same as "Lord, if you just give me a child, I'll _____ in return." Bargaining and magical thinking are part of grieving and should be temporary in nature. Guard, though, against letting one of your bargains or magical thoughts turn into a plan of action. Magic won't help you.

The next step is *sadness.* Losing an unborn child is so sad. Again, you may receive sincere but wrong advice, particularly if your sadness shows clearly or persists a while. Besides, you're overcoming the medical effects of the loss, just as would a woman who gave birth. That makes it all the harder. It is natural and necessary to feel great sadness, let no one tell you otherwise.

The final phase of grieving, *forgiveness and resolution,* brings a measure of peace, but they do not close the book or erase memories. Whom would you forgive? In the case of the woman above, she had to forgive her and her husband's ignorance which led to the circumstance. It was not a deliberate act, but it required forgiveness *for the woman's sake.* If a person was instrumental in causing the miscarriage, such as a reckless driver responsible for an accident in which the unborn baby died, that person must be forgiven—again, *for the couple's sake.* Not forgotten. Not let off the hook. But forgiven.

Resolution is the healthy outcome of the grieving process. Part of the resolution to Frank and Mary Alice's losses was developing a plan of action. "Frank knew how sad and depressed I was," Mary Alice says, "so one day he sat me down and said that, with God's help, we would have a child. 'We will do everything we can—including going to an adoption agency—and then we will leave the rest up to God.' "

Six months later, when Mary Alice became pregnant again, they regrouped. "Frank's plan was for me to stay on the sofa all nine months if I had to. I organized drawers to keep busy. I read the whole Living Bible. It's the last time I did any embroidery."

At three months the Minirths were able to hear the baby's heartbeat. The next two months—the times when Mary Alice had miscarried before—went by without incident. At five months Mary Alice was able to buy maternity clothes for the first time. Everything went well until the thirty-second week of pregnancy when the doctor said that Mary Alice was showing signs of premature labor.

Mary Alice Minirth spent the last six weeks of that fourth pregnancy in the hospital. "It was a frightening time, because I imagined that every little pain would lead to stronger labor pains and to a premature baby. And all along, I feared that the baby would not be healthy. After six weeks, the labor pains seemed to stop."[2]

Yet eight and a half months had finally gone by and the baby could arrive any time.

Two weeks later Rachel Marie Minirth was born, a healthy, seven-pound, eleven-ounce, bright-eyed baby. Frank and Mary Alice Minirth had been married seven years. They named their little girl Rachel because of the verse in Genesis that says, "Jacob served seven years for Rachel, and they seemed but a few days to him, because of the love he had for her."[3] Both Frank and Mary Alice felt that God had worked out His plan for their lives in His own way and His own timing.

"We lost one other baby after Rachel," Mary Alice says. "It was right after we moved here. It was excruciating, too, because it went on for three weeks. Lose it or save it? We lost it. But God had given us Rachel, so there was hope. Frank had his career, a new life to look forward to, a new practice. We had a new home and we had company all summer, too, which kept me busy. Old friends. It kept me going after the miscarriage.

"I think I had to fight self-pity most. We had so much, yet I didn't see it. You're blinded to what you have when you're in despair over what you don't have. I kept showing myself I had friends, and I had one child coming into her twos, and we had a worthy goal in life. God was opening up things for Frank.

"By the time our second one was born healthy, my father's cancer was arrested. He lived a full and happy life for many more years."

Today the Minirths have four girls: Rachel, age 16; Renee, age 13; Carrie, age 10; and Alicia, age 1. During this latest pregnancy, as with the others, Mary Alice spent months resting on the couch and Frank suspended any travel outside of Dallas so he could support her and help with the older girls.

Together the Minirths grieved the loss of four unborn babies and together they share the joy of their four lovely daughters, who are now in those years we call, "the period of drifting."

THE PERIOD OF DRIFTING—SCHOOL-AGE KIDS

We call this a period of drifting for several reasons. For one, it seems the family members are each cast adrift, going separate ways, aimlessly. For all the churning activity, you see very little real progress day to day. In fact, with school-age kids, how do you measure progress, if any?

Also, the family itself tends to drift. Pressed severely by all the issues school-age kids dump into the family stew, parents have little time for work, for play, for each other—even for the kids. It just didn't seem this hectic a generation ago.

Schedule Clutter

"Here in Dallas it's achieve, achieve, achieve," observes Mary Alice Minirth. "Overscheduling, both kids and adults."

How do busy parents avoid neglecting the kids' interests?

"Frank is careful about that," says Mary Alice. "The kids' school holidays are already X-ed off his schedule for next year. Renee's school play, for instance. All that. I try to be there all the time, and he's there most of the time. He went with Renee on her wilderness trip, canoeing, and camping. He takes each of them on a trip to Arkansas at least once a year and they get to take another friend and her dad.

"He's a workaholic at play too. He works at playing with the kids, and he loves it. They share hobbies—horseback riding, camping, the outdoors.

"But it's hectic. Last week a policeman called to tell us the horses had gotten out. So Frank was out chasing four horses, with the policeman helping. At the same time a litter of kittens was being born in the barn. Renee came screaming up to the house each time a new one appeared. It was an unusual morning.

"We had no vacation at all for the first seven or eight years. Business or some seminar always involved travel. Then it dawned on Frank that it was time to do something besides work. We vacation regularly now. We still talk about Hawaii—how the flowers smelled, how the pineapple tasted. But mostly we go to Arkansas. The kids like that."

Stability Flutter

What children need most of all, though, at any age but particularly during the school years, is a stable family life. Unfortunately, as the kids get wrapped up in school with all their needs and demands, and the parents struggle with work demands, stability tends to flutter.

Family stability is no stronger, no less fluttery than the stability of the marriage itself. Parents who would give their children the best possible schooling, then, would make the marriage their first priority.

There is a retirement benefit to this. Someday your link to the past, your parents, will pass on. Your link to the future, your children, will fledge. In your house will be you and your mate, your marriage the only commitment designed to last a lifetime. It behooves you to keep it strong now, as insurance toward the future.

Both partners must be involved in this complex process of child-raising. It's not just Mom's duty. A child's concepts of God are shaped by the earthly father. In fact, there are far more Bible verses addressing fathers than mothers.

What children need most of all, . . . is a stable family life.

We've long known that the child blossoms when the father loves the mother. How can the children learn to express love in a family situation? Include them when picking out Mommy's Valentine gift. Might they plan a special Mother's Day or Father's Day dinner . . . and then help buy the groceries? Encourage them to make place cards for Sunday lunch. Let them help choose the Christmas tree. Children learn love and family unity best by being part of the loving family unit.

Raising Positive Kids Is a
Team Effort

There isn't any success in the world equal to the success of raising positive kids. It's a rough world out there. Negativism pounds at our kids from all sides. What's the key factor in producing children that won't succumb to all the negative forces in their world? A team of two—a mom and a dad that are firmly united in their efforts to raise those kids. This is what we have to say from Raising Positive Kids in a Negative World.

—Zig Ziglar
Raising Positive Kids in a Negative World

Much of the music our kids listen to deals with their right "to be free" and "to do their own thing." Evidence is solid, however, that what the kids really want is security. Clinical psychologist Dr. Martin Cohen says this security is provided by parental authority and that

"Raising Positive Kids Is a Team Effort" is adapted and taken from *Raising Positive Kids in a Negative World,* Zig Ziglar (1985).

it's scary for kids when they're not experiencing that authority from their parents. He says that a kid may press the parents harder and harder until they finally have to stop him.

What he's really doing is asking his parents to behave as parents. The child is checking to see if that strength he's always depended on is still there. He's just taking a peek to be sure he wasn't mistaken about his source of security. And parents, you can't disappoint him —you have to remain firm in your place as parents.

Authority, according to the dictionary, is "the power or right to give commands, enforce obedience, take action or make final decisions." One thing kids need—and even demand—is the right to experience the disciplining pressure of parental authority, which keeps them headed in the right direction.

When we deal with our children, we must remember that they *are* children. An old African proverb goes like this: Everybody's been young before, but not everybody has been old before. One of a child's most critical needs is having parents who understand their authoritative place in the dynamic plan for the family. It is to be an example, to lead, guide, direct, correct, and encourage.

Sometimes when our kids give us trouble and reject our authority, we often wonder just what's going on. Remember that though kids will often try us, deep down they want us to win and maintain our place of authority so their security will be complete.

Kids want to know that someone's in charge—they want to know who to follow, who's going to lead, and to whom they must answer. It's a basic fact of life. It's something that's a part of every social unit of society, including the family. And it's something that parents are going to have to grasp if their parenting is going to be a success and, as a result, their kids successful.

MOTHERS AND DADDIES ARE SPECIAL

Recently I saw a thought-provoking bumper sticker: "Anybody can be a father, but it takes someone special to be a daddy." That's right, and anyone can have a baby, but it takes someone special to be a mother.

When you study some of the great, positive, history-making

figures, you will often find they speak of the influence of a parent. Abraham Lincoln is quoted as saying, "All that I am I owe to my angel mother." General Douglas MacArthur said, "My sainted mother taught me devotion to God and a love of country which have ever sustained me. To her I yield anew a son's reverent thanks." The great preacher G. Campbell Morgan had four sons. They all became ministers. At a family reunion a friend asked one of the sons, "Which Morgan is the greatest preacher?" With his eyes beaming with delight, the son looked over to his father and said, "Why, it's Mother!"

Likewise, there is an old saying that goes like this: One father is worth a hundred schoolmasters. It's true that in the hands of parents are the destinies of their children. In that sense, being a parent is really a sacred thing. Committed into the hands of parents is the future of entire nations in that our future resides with our kids and the world they will build. The humbling thing is that the model for the world our kids will build, their vision for tomorrow, largely depends on how they see us as parents and how we raise them today. What an awesome responsibility!

The very fact of who parents are in the structure of the family gives them authoritative power. That power can be used in a positive way to convince kids to make the effort, to win, to succeed, to respect their fellow man, and to be people of honesty and integrity. Parents can choose that route, or they can choose to leave their kids to themselves and the influences of a negative world.

IT TAKES TEAMWORK AND TEAM LEADERSHIP

Raising positive kids is best done as a team effort and since the family is truly a unit, it functions more effectively as a team. Families working together can accomplish more than they can as individuals. When you have a family project and family goals that everyone has chosen (whether it's scheduling a family vacation, conducting study courses, planning a picnic, or building a swimming pool), the results will be better. And working together on projects brings the family closer together. Fortunately, working together as a family helps the kids develop communication and cooperative skills that can be taken directly into the school and business community.

Most people agree that any team must have a captain, a leader, a commander in chief. A football team without a quarterback would not be a team—it would be a disaster. A business without a board chairman or an army without an officer in charge would be inept and would quickly disintegrate. The same situation exists in the family. The family needs a leader, because while it is far *more* than a business, it *is* a business.

With the expected rate of inflation, if husband and wife raise two children and stay together until they're sixty-five years old, they will have invested well over $1 million in raising the kids and providing for their own needs. That's pretty big business.

In the regular business community, the corporate structure has, in most cases, a board chairman, president, vice president, treasurer, and secretary; but as President Harry Truman said, "The buck has to stop somewhere." In the corporate world, that's easy—it's the man in charge. In the family, it's not quite as easy, but it's just as clear *and* just as important. I believe the individual who should be the chairman of the board of the family is the man, the husband, the father.

There are several reasons I say this, but one significant reason is that our society is organized that way. That's not to say that the wife (the corporate vice president) has little to say about decisions affecting the family. She's the second in command (*not* second in importance), so to speak, and very important in the effective working of the family as a unit. Any chief executive officer worth his salt is going to hold conferences regularly with the second in command concerning significant decisions. Additionally, it is critically important that the second in command have full authority when the board chairman is gone.

THE GENTLE, LOVING ONE

Even a two-car parade gets fouled up if you don't decide ahead of time who's going to lead. With this in mind, you'll understand what I mean when I say kids need to understand that if they are going to be led, they need to know who will be leading and what it means to follow.

Author Helen Andelin brings another significant factor into focus when she points out that male leadership also conforms to psychological law. The male has within his makeup the necessary qualities to lead, in that he is more aggressive, decisive, and dominating than the normal female. In the normal male the desire to lead is strong—he will cringe when his position is threatened. When robbed of it altogether, he will feel emasculated.

She elaborates by saying that "Male leadership does not suggest a dominating, high-handed action, based on selfish motives. To be successful in the family the father must have the welfare of each family member at heart and his decisions and plans must be based upon what is best for them. He carefully considers their viewpoint and feelings, especially those of his wife. They try to work things out together. When there are those unresolved differences and the wife cannot support her husband's plans, she can at least support his right of leadership."*

CHAIN OF COMMAND CLEARLY DEFINED

Yes, a clearly established chain of command in our homes, as we have in *all* other *successful* businesses and institutions, is important. On occasion I've had people ask the question, "Suppose the wife is smarter than the husband?" That still doesn't alter the chain of command. In my own family I'm extremely fortunate in that I have a wife who in many ways has insights and wisdom I do not have. Her I.Q. is at least as high as mine, and her grades were certainly better in school. However, when important decisions are to be made in our family, and the Redhead and I, after a thorough discussion, disagree (a truly *rare* event) as to which route to take, she has the complete assurance that she is never going to be burdened with making the decision.

* From the book *All About Raising Children* by Helen Andelin, Pacific Press, Santa Barbara, California (1981).

Naturally, I prayerfully ask for guidance before making any decision of any significance.

THAT MAKES SENSE

I remember an occasion in Rochester, New York, when I spoke at a large high school. After addressing the assembly, I was invited to talk with the student leaders. About twenty of the top students were present for the question-and-answer session. It was interesting, lively, and informative.

I'll never forget one young man who said to me, "You seem to put a lot of reliance on God in your life, in your family, and in your business. I don't believe in God, and I'm puzzled as to why you put so much emphasis on it."

I responded that one of the reasons I did was because I wanted to have my children be as responsible as possible, and I understood the importance of authority.

He quite naturally asked, "Well, what does God have to do with that?"

I said, "It's simple. When my children see me bow in obedience to a Higher Authority, they instantly recognize my respect for authority. And that's not only the authority of God, but the authority of government, law enforcement officials, my employer, judges, the courts. When my children see that I respect authority, they know I am not being hypocritical when I insist that they respect my authority over them. The net result is I have better disciplined, more loving, and obedient children."

The young man was taken aback for a moment, but then he said, "Well, I still don't believe in God, but what you're saying certainly makes sense."

---

*When we deal with our children, we must remember that they **are** children.*

As a practical matter, from a numerical point of view, the family is a small unit, so it's vital that every member of the team

—including the chief executive officer—forget about his "title" when work needs to be done. In a family unit made up of a husband, a wife, and two small children, if the husband acts *only* in the capacity of major decision maker, he will soon lose the love and respect of his wife *and* his children. Realistically, if *four* people *create* work in the home and only a part-time mom *does* the work, an impossible situation exists that is headed for trouble.

THE WINNING TEAM—MOM AND DAD

The solution to the problem is simple, but far from easy. If the family is going to function as a unit, *both* dad and mom must make contributions that go far beyond bringing in a paycheck. For example, dad can look after the children if mom's skills are greater in the kitchen. He can help them with their homework and talk with them, instead of reading the paper and "relaxing" while an already tired mom prepares dinner. After dinner, mom and dad can work together to clean the kitchen. If the kids go to bed immediately after dinner, then mom and dad can alternate between cleaning the kitchen and getting the kids tucked into bed. When bedtime comes, if the kids are still up, dad can participate in the ritual of getting them ready for bed and tucking them in.

The main point I'm making is that to raise positive kids, if both a dad and a mom are in the home, they should both be involved in *all* aspects of raising the children. That's the *only* way mom, dad, and the kids are *all* going to win.

THE ONE-PARENT FAMILY

In a one-parent family, the need for discipline and routine is even more important. The mother (or father) who has to get up early, prepare her children's breakfast, get ready for work, get the children ready to take by the nursery or the baby-sitter, then put in a demanding work day has already had a hectic, ten-hour day. At that point she has to shift gears and pick up the kids on the way home. Then she has to prepare dinner and look after the children, including preparing them for bed, reading bedtime stories, and entertaining them while maintaining a positive mental attitude. The demands are enormous on her physical and emotional resources. It seems to me that the only way for such a parent to survive on a long-term basis is to adopt a rigorous, organized family life-style where discipline and routine are emphasized.

WHEN THE TEAM DOESN'T FUNCTION

In families where mom and dad don't function as a team, it's easy to understand why there is so much difficulty. It's also easier to understand why we see ever-increasing evidences of child neglect and abuse. Further, when dad often takes a spectator's seat in the home, it's also evident why we have more mothers than fathers abandoning their families. They are simply throwing in the towel and walking out on their husbands, their children, and their responsibilities. How tragic and how unfair! How those parents will regret those actions for the rest of their lives. Many a broken family relationship begins with a lack of team effort. I believe thousands of women have left their family responsibilities out of a growing sense of despair at their inability to cope in a situation in which the husband is not pulling his weight at home. Some parents will try to bury the memories of an abandoned family in a passionate romance and a temporarily carefree life-style, but they never quite succeed in doing so. The missing of those little hands and arms around their necks, those calls of "Mommy" or "Daddy," those expressions of infant, toddler, and childhood delights will have been burned indelibly into their minds and will be part of them forever.

At this point I'd like to interject that as a result of the feminist movement, more and more women, in their demand for their rights, are losing a degree of perspective and balance. In some tragic instances reason, judgment, and love drop out of the picture.

To avoid the temptation of even thinking about dissolving the family through divorce or desertion, dad needs to climb down out of his ivory tower, roll up his sleeves, and do his part. Mom and dad, as a team, need to instruct and encourage the children to pitch in and make their contributions for their own good (preparing them for their own possible future roles as husbands and wives), and for the good of the family.

Every member of the family can and must be taught and required to do a part. Even a four year old can pick up toys, clothes, or papers that are lying around on the floor so that mom is relieved of these responsibilities and saved an incredible drain on her energy. The beautiful thing is that the parent is giving excellent instructions in discipline and obedience. These are two superb characteristics that can help children build winning lives in their own futures.

This approach will help the child who needs to grow rich in every aspect of life learn that before he can "cash in" on life, he has to "chip in" a little, too. As he chips in as a family member and sees positive results, he'll understand why he has to chip in at school and then chip in, in the business world. This approach greatly reduces the possibility of raising negative, overindulged, spoiled kids who have only a cash-in mentality and basically believe they should get all they can, while they can, regardless of what it may do to other persons.

Another beautiful thing about having family projects and responsibilities with every member of the family involved is that most of us want—and even need—to belong to some type of unit. It's natural that kids want to belong—and know they belong.

The wonderful thing about a solid family unit is that it teaches cooperation, mutual respect, and love. The acceptance of your child in your family unit with definite responsibilities makes him feel like an important member of the team. This will substantially reduce his likelihood of joining some other close-knit group, perhaps a neighborhood gang, just so he can "be accepted" and "belong." He doesn't "need" that, since his needs are being met at home.

BUILD RESPECT—IT'S A MUST

To build a relationship of love and respect, you must remember that your children respond to you according to the way they feel about you. If those feelings are ones of love and respect, you will receive obedient, loving responses from the children because that is what they want to do. However, if there is no respect, you can rest assured the responses will be rebellious and disrespectful. That's why parents should conduct themselves in a manner that creates respect and builds love. There's no real unity without respect.

The parents who break promises to their kids, scream and shout at each other in private or in public, come home stumbling drunk, and treat each other with contempt and disrespect will destroy any sense of honor and respect the child might have for them. When that happens, obedience and discipline go out the door. In addition, there will be considerable confusion in the child's mind. He undoubtedly loves you as his parents; but without respect, he can't really like you, so he truly is in an emotional dilemma.

What's the solution? Answer: If the preceding paragraph describes you in a reasonably accurate manner, the chances are pretty good you need help. Get it. If your emotions are shot, you can often get help through a local mental health association, or in many cities the pastors and ministers in the churches are excellent sources of help. If you have a drinking or drug problem, you need to demonstrate your maturity and your love for your kids by getting help before your behavior moves into serious addiction, alcoholism, or child abuse that ultimately will destroy both you and the kids.

Actually, one of the best sources of help, especially if your problem is not too severe, is in your hands. I encourage you to read, reread, and apply the principles emphasized in this book. I've shared them with thousands of people in seminars and recordings, and I can tell you that in hundreds and hundreds of cases they are working. You've got nothing to lose by giving them an honest shot, and to paraphrase an old commercial, "The family you save will be your own."

FATHER'S AND MOTHER'S WORK

Raising positive kids is definitely a team effort. It's neither "woman's work" nor "man's work." It's father's and mother's work combined. Many times, however, when husbands and wives both work, far too many men have been conditioned to believe that preparing dinner, cleaning the kitchen, helping the kids with homework, and tucking them into bed are things the wife and mother is supposed to do.

The real problem is brought clearly into focus by Sey Chassler in a January 13, 1985, *Parade* magazine article from which I quote, with permission:

> About 20 years ago, my wife and I were having one of those arguments that grows into fury—the kind that leaves a dreadful pain that lasts for years. Suddenly, unable to stand my complaints any longer, my wife threw something at me and said: *"From now on, you do the shopping, plan the meals, take care of the house, everything. I'm through!"*
>
> I was standing in the kitchen looking at the shelves, the sink, the refrigerator, the cleaning utensils. At my wife.
>
> I was terrified. Tears trickled down my face. No matter what, I knew I could not handle the burden she had flung at me. I could not do my job and be responsible for the entire household as well. I had important things to do. Besides, how could I get through a day dealing with personnel, budgets, manuscripts, management, profit-and-loss figures, and, *at the same time,* plan dinner for that night and the next night and breakfasts and lunches and a dinner party on the weekend and shop for it all and make sure the house was in good shape and that the woman who cleaned for us was there and on time and the laundry done and the children taken care of?
>
> How could *any* one do all that and stay sane? Natalie watched me for a while. Finally she said, "O.K. Don't worry. I'll keep on doing it." She put on her coat and went to her hospital office—to manage dozens of people and more than 100 patients.
>
> Despite her simple statement that she would go on taking care of our home and family, I stood a while telling myself that *no one* could do all of that. Slowly I saw that *she* was doing it.
>
> In the days and weeks that followed, I began to realize that most women carry a double burden: an inside job taking care of

their homes and families, and an outside job, working for wages. Most men, on the other hand, can come home and do little more about their families than help with household chores and with the children. *Helping is useful, but it is not the same as doing;* it leaves the basic responsibility to someone else. In most homes, it leaves the basic responsibility to women: *All the worries, all the headaches, all the planning, all the management, all the DOING is theirs.* How many men understand this without being shocked into it as I was—or by the loss of a wife? How many of us appreciate how invisible to us women are? How many of us really see women or hear them? How often do we go to bed at night feeling the comfort and love of our wives but knowing them so little that we do not recognize the burden they bear?

MOM AND DAD IN AGREEMENT

If you remember, I warned you earlier that there were no really easy steps or methods of raising positive kids, but there are many essential ones. And the most critical of all has to be the relationship between mom and dad. If the child grows up seeing mom and dad showing little respect and kindness toward each other and often engaging in verbal—if not physical—conflict, the child slowly but surely sees that marriage is a battleground and that the family is not something to enjoy but something to tolerate —and leave as soon as possible.

This can be compounded, of course, when one of the parents sides with the child against the other parent. As the child grows older, he becomes an expert at manipulating the parents. Each parent then has a tendency to want to win the child's approval; it will be two against one, with both parents making unwise concessions and overtures to the child; and the stage is set for conflict and disaster.

BLUEPRINT FOR DISASTER

When a child goes to one parent with a request that is denied, only to have the other parent grant the request, the results are disastrous. Whether the second parent knew or did not know that parent number one had turned down the request, the results are still bad. When a child approaches one parent and asks for permission to do something, the first question should be, "Have you asked your mom (or dad) about it?" If the answer is no and there's a question or doubt in your mind about the advisability of it, you can say, "We'll talk about it and let you know." If the child has talked to the other parent and the personal safety or the reputation of the child is at stake, both parents should definitely be involved in the decision.

A strong, unified parental team has the best shot at positively influencing children for good.

I remember one occasion when our son was a junior in high school. He had asked his mom about going with one of his classmates to a Friday night basketball game in a town roughly a hundred miles from Dallas. She told him, "I don't think so, but ask your dad." When he came to me for permission, I said no, and he naturally wanted to know why. I explained that on Friday and Saturday nights one driver out of ten on the road is legally drunk, that the hour at which he would return would be very late, and that I feared they might go to sleep while driving. I further explained that neither he nor his friend had been driving very long and that all of these factors combined indicated to me the dangers were simply too great. My son accepted without argument my explanation of why I did not want him to go.

To this day I believe I saw a half-smile on his face as we terminated the conversation and he gave it that last try, which really wasn't a try, as he said, "So you won't let me go, huh?" And I said, "No, not this time, son. Your day is coming, but not now."

Had circumstances been different, the answer could well have been yes. For example, had his friend's dad been going along to drive, that would have presented an entirely different picture. Had it been a shorter distance and on a night other than

Friday, that, too, would have made a difference. On that occasion in the Ziglar household, the team concept functioned well.

What can ordinary parents do to have a better chance? There is one sure thing that you can go to the bank on—a strong, unified parental team, which practices loving, mutual respect, has the best shot at positively influencing children for good.

God brings unity to our marriage first; then we have the freedom to raise our kids with the oneness God desires.
—Teresa Ferguson
Intimate Moments

Chapter

23

Modeling Your Proper Role

A s parents we are stewards rather than owners. We have been entrusted by God with the lives of our children. We are accountable to Him for our actions toward our children, and we are responsible to ingrain in our children a sense of personal accountability to God.

We are best able to maintain a loving, loyal relationship with our children and impart to them the values we would want them to have if we are modeling our God-assigned roles. This chapter from How to Keep Your Kids on Your Team *explores the importance of modeling our proper roles.*

—Charles Stanley
How to Keep Your Kids on Your Team

"Modeling Your Proper Role" is adapted and taken from *How to Keep Your Kids on Your Team*, Charles Stanley (1986).

The most extreme teenage counseling situations that I have faced as a pastor have come as a direct result of families violating this principle. When children grow up in a home where the parents have ignored divinely assigned roles, they are set up for disaster—morally, emotionally, psychologically, and spiritually. I believe the failure of parents in this area has caused the rapid growth of the homosexual community in this country, and I also believe it is the cause of much of the drug and alcohol abuse among children and teens. I am not alone in this opinion. Counselors across the nation are seeing a trend among their counselees who are suffering from both social and sexual maladjustments. The same family pattern keeps showing up—*a domineering mother and a passive or absent father.*

Paul D. Meier, M.D., part of a team who heads up a clinic in the Dallas area, says he believes "a domineering, smothering mother and a weak father lie at the root of the vast majority of mental illness in children." After seeing thousands of patients and spending hundreds of hours in research, he concludes that role confusion in the home has the potential for producing homosexuals, sociopathic criminals, schizophrenics, anorexic teenagers, and even hyperactive children (*Christian Child-Rearing and Personality Development,* [Grand Rapids: Baker Books, 1977], pp. 89, 49–78). That is not to say that each one of these cases is the result of improper modeling at home. It is to say, however, that disregarding God's order for the home greatly increases children's chances of suffering from one or more of these personality problems.

I believe this so strongly that whenever parents come in for counseling concerning behavioral problems in their children, this is the place I begin my questioning. I sometimes get right to the heart of the problem by asking, "If I asked your son or daughter, 'Who is really in charge at your home?' what do you think their answer would be?"

Time and time again I have seen a mother drop her head and begin to cry as her husband sits silently by and watches. This penetrating question is often the first step to putting a family on the road to recovery, but not always. Many parents run from this question, for it uncovers what many are too proud to admit—a major flaw in the fabric of their homes, a refusal on their parts to assume their God-ordained roles in the home. The result may be denial, and the consequences of such denial are devastating.

FATHER ON THE RUN

I'll never forget one mother who called me about her thirteen-year-old son. She was concerned that he was demonstrating homosexual tendencies. As she described his behavior, I knew she had good cause for concern. After listening for a while, I told her that her son's behavior (especially at his age) was usually a reflection of a deeper problem at home. I went on to tell her that young children with homosexual tendencies characteristically come from homes where the mother is the dominant figure and the father is either absent or passive. There was a pause. And then tears.

She admitted that there was a serious role problem in their home. I suggested that she and her husband should come in for a counseling session. The morning of their appointment, however, a man called and canceled. I imagine it was her husband. I never heard from them again, but I can almost guess what happened.

It is not what you think that influences your children, it is what you communicate.

There is something very threatening to a man when he has to face up to the truth about neglecting his role at home. I imagine that when the father of this home heard from his wife how I diagnosed the problem, he decided not to come. Usually, a father in that situation wants to believe that his *child* has the problem, not *him*. The very thought of being to blame for a son's homosexual tendencies is more than many men can bear. Consequently, they run, and the problem is never handled.

FATHER ON A LEASH

A scene that is all too common to me is Mom leading Dad down the aisle of the sanctuary after the service to talk to me about their wayward child. Usually, the conversation becomes a monologue as Mom pours out her heart and Dad stands by, nodding now and then in agreement. The blame is often placed on some neighbor child who has been a bad influence on their child. Sometimes a bad school system receives the blame. On and on she goes. She assures me that if I could take an hour out of my busy schedule to talk to their child, she is sure everything would be fine.

But I know better. I know that ten hours of counseling with their child would do no good unless Mom and Dad are willing to make some changes. I know that an hour of counseling can be undone in five minutes of family interaction when the roles are confused. And the worst thing of all is that I know unless Dad is willing to get involved in the process, there is little hope for change.

WHY ALL THE CONFUSION

The preceding discussion raises two important questions (1) Why is there such a tendency on the part of husbands to sit back and let their wives dominate the family? and (2) Why is there such a tendency on the part of wives to take control? To answer these questions, we need to look all the way back to the first husband-and-wife relationship.

When God made the first man and woman and put them in the Garden of Eden, they functioned together in perfect unity. What he needed she provided, and what she needed he provided. This is implied by the inclusion of the phrase "a helper comparable to him" in Genesis 2:18 and then again in verse 20. Literally translated this phrase says, "I [God] will make him [Adam] a *corresponding helper*" (Genesis 2:18b) (Allen P. Ross, *The Bible Knowledge Commentary,* [Wheaton, Ill.: Victor Books, 1983], p. 31). The picture painted for us is one of a man and a woman living in perfect harmony under the authority of God.

What is important insofar as our discussion is concerned is that both the man and the woman were completely satisfied as they functioned in their God-ordained roles. Thus, there was no conflict.

After they sinned, however, a change took place not only in their relationship with God but also in their relationship with each other. The result of this change was acted out when God approached Adam and Eve in the Garden. Alienation replaced unity. Adam was quick to turn on Eve when confronted about his disobedience.

God pronounced judgment on all the parties involved, beginning with the serpent:

> Because you have done this,
> You are cursed more than all cattle, . . .
> On your belly you shall go. . . .
> And I will put enmity
> Between you and the woman,
> And between your seed and her Seed.
> —Genesis 3:14–15

From the serpent God moved to Eve,

> I will greatly multiply
>   your sorrow and your conception;
> In pain you shall bring forth children;
> Your desire shall be for your husband,
> And he shall rule over you.
> —Genesis 3:16

I believe verse 16 provides the explanation about why there is a power struggle in many homes today. To get the full impact of this verse, we need to understand the context as well as the author's use of the word *desire*.

The context of this verse is that of judgment. The things pronounced by God did not come as good news to those involved. It was not good news to the serpent that he would be cursed more than any other animal. Nor was it good news that he would have to crawl from then on. It was not good news to Adam that he would have to work the rest of his life; instead of picking fruit provided by God, he would have to grow it himself (see Genesis 3:17–19). Along the same lines, it was not good news to Eve that she would have to suffer in childbirth, and that "cheery" bit of information was followed by two key phrases,

> Your desire shall be for your husband,
> And he shall rule over you.

The context seems to indicate that this was bad news, too. That is, the idea of Adam's ruling over her was clearly viewed as punishment like everything else God had mentioned to that point.

Another clue here supports the idea that this whole passage carries with it a negative tone is the term *desire*. This term appears again in the narrative of Cain and Abel. There we get a clearer idea of its full meaning.

After Cain realized that God was not pleased with his offering, God said to him,

> Why are you angry? And why has your countenance fallen? If you do well, will you not be accepted? And if you do not do well, sin lies at the door. And its *desire* is for you, but you should rule over it.
>
> —Genesis 4:6–7, emphasis added

The latter part of verse 7 is about a struggle for control. Sin, as personified by the author, was struggling for control over Cain, but Cain was expected to overcome sin and "rule over it," or master it. The author used the term *desire* to communicate the idea of mastery or control. I believe the idea of mastery is what the author had in mind when he used the term *desire* in relation to God's pronouncement of judgment on Eve. That is, part of her judgment was that she would naturally desire to master her husband, but he would in fact be expected to rule over her. Thus, from the very beginning there was built-in potential for a power struggle between a husband and a wife. This certainly came as bad news to Eve.

And the Curse Goes on

There is no denying that the curses related to the serpent and to Adam are still in effect today. Anybody who has ever planted a garden knows that. Therefore, it is not unreasonable to assume that the curses related to Eve are still in effect as well. Any woman who has had a baby knows from experience that this is the case. However, I think many men and women have a tendency to overlook the implications of verse 16.

If I have interpreted it correctly, it means that every woman has a certain negative potential that is as real as the pains of childbirth. I believe that as a result of the Fall there is within every wife a natural resistance to the authority of her husband. This is certainly more obviously expressed in some cases than in others. And it has a great deal to do with how well the husband is fulfilling his responsibilities at home, responsibilities he will have a tendency to neglect since, he, too, is cursed.

I am not saying that every wife is consciously trying to control her husband. I am saying that every wife has that potential and needs to be aware of it. I am also saying that when this potential goes unchecked in a woman who is married to a man neglecting his God-given responsibilities, the roles naturally become confused and can get reversed. The result is a domineering wife and a passive husband. The trend we see toward role reversal in our society is simply the playing out of the original curse. Unfortunately, children who come out of these types of homes often suffer the greatest consequences, and it is for their sake that I have gone into such great detail here.

GETTING TO THE BOTTOM OF THINGS

The apostle Paul was certainly aware of the tendency of husbands and wives to confuse their roles. Why else would he begin with the issue of submission when addressing wives in his epistles? Why else would he begin with the issue of love when addressing husbands?

> Wives, submit to your own husbands, as to the Lord. For the husband is head of the wife, as also Christ is the head of the church (Eph. 5:22–23a).

> Husbands, love your wives, just as Christ also loved the church and gave Himself for it (Eph. 5:25).

> Wives, submit to your own husbands, as is fitting in the Lord. Husbands, love your wives, and do not be bitter toward them (Col. 3:18–19).

The Colossians passage is especially interesting in that these two verses are the total of Paul's advice in this epistle to husbands and wives regarding their relationship with each other. Paul knew that the issues of love and submission were really the bottom line. He understood that the tensions that arise in a marriage are usually associated with an abuse of one or both of these maxims. When a husband loves his wife the way he should and his wife submits to him as the head of the home, everything else seems to fall into place. That being the case, Paul went right to the heart of the matter in his discussion (or should I say his mention) of the marriage relationship.

Submission

The idea of submitting to someone usually conjures up negative images in our minds. We tend to think of people bowing and scraping, of slaves, and of all-around abuse, both mentally and physically. But that is not the picture given in Scripture. God set forth the concept of submission in the context of a loving, sacrificial relationship. Only when we isolate the concept of submission do negative images appear. It is then that we think about all the awful things we have seen take place in marriages where a wife tried to submit and suffered for it. In its proper context, however, submission is the logical response of a wife to a husband.

I will never forget a conversation I had one afternoon with a woman journalist. She was raking me over the coals about a Mother's Day sermon she heard me preach. In this sermon I had stressed the responsibility of wives to submit to their husbands. This journalist proceeded to tell me that this submission stuff was "trash" and that if I thought she was going to be a "doormat" for some guy to wipe his feet on, I was crazy.

I assured her that I was not suggesting anything like that. Then I asked her to imagine something with me. I said to her, "Imagine being married to a man who loved you with all his heart. A man who cherished you, took care of you, always placed you before himself. Imagine a man who was sensitive, yet strong. A man who made you proud to be with him."

On and on I went, describing what I think God wants every husband to be for his wife. As I talked, I literally saw this woman's countenance change. The harshness faded. The criticism left her eyes. When I finished, I said, "Now, do you think you would have any trouble submitting to a man like that?"

"With pleasure," she said.

This young woman was suffering from what many people suffer when it comes to the idea of submission—an unbalanced perspective.

Submitting to an Unloving Spouse

If every husband was like the one I just described, there would be no need for this chapter or for this book, for that matter. Submission is usually not a major issue in a home unless a husband neglects his role or a woman has grown up in a home where her father neglected his role and her mother struggled with submission, leaving her daughter a poor example. In both cases, however, a man's refusal to fulfill his role was part of the problem.

In the case of an unloving husband, a wife still has a responsibility to be submissive. Peter made this clear when he wrote,

> Likewise you wives, be submissive to your own husbands, that even if some do not obey the word, they, without a word, may be won

by the conduct of their wives, when they observe your chaste conduct accompanied by fear. (1 Peter 3:1–2.)

I am totally aware of the difficulty in applying this principle. A friend, whom I will call Ray, told me his story. His father died when he was a baby. His mother remarried when he was eleven, and the man she married turned out to be a totally irresponsible human being. He abused him and his mother until Ray was old enough to become a threat to his stepfather physically. Through all of that, however, his mother continued to serve and submit to her husband. Recently, Ray asked her why she put up with what she did those many years. She looked at him as if he had said something disrespectful. Then she answered. "When I married him, I promised to love him for better or for worse."

It is difficult for me to comprehend that kind of love. But as I look around at the children that come out of homes where Mom refuses to fulfill her God-given role, I wonder what would have happened to Ray if his mother had used his stepfather's irresponsibility as an excuse to leave? Mom, I know it can be tough. But for the sake of your children, submit to your husband. Your obedience in this matter may be their only hope for a healthy childhood.

Anytime there is a threat of physical abuse from a husband, I do not hesitate to recommend separation for a time. But I would never recommend that a wife take over the household while her husband is still at home. To do so is to assume a role God never intended for her to fulfill. (For an excellent discussion on submission to unloving husbands, see Darien B. Cooper's book, *We Became Wives of Happy Husbands.*)

Loving a Wife

Although the biblical authors usually addressed the wife first in their discussions on marriage, most of what was said was directed to the husband. There seemed to be little need for an explanation of what it meant to submit to one's husband. However, the idea of loving one's wife needed both explanations and illustrations. The importance of the wife's role was not minimized, but the difference in emphasis may have had something to do with the magnitude of the husband's responsibility.

When the apostle Paul exhorts husbands to love their wives, he certainly has more in mind than a kiss on the cheek on the way out the door each morning. The illustration he chooses makes this painfully clear:

> For the husband is head of the wife, as also Christ is head of the church; and He is the Savior of the body. Therefore, just as the church is subject to Christ, so let the wives be to their own husbands in everything. Husbands, love your wives, just as Christ also loved the church and gave Himself for it, that He might sanctify and cleanse it with the washing of water by the word, that He might present it to Himself a glorious church, not having spot or wrinkle or any such thing, but that it should be holy and without blemish. So husbands ought to love their own wives as their own bodies; he who loves his wife loves himself. For no one ever hated his own flesh, but nourishes and cherishes it, just as the Lord does the church. For we are members of His body, of His flesh and of His bones. (Eph. 5:23–30)

Paul compares the love a husband is to have for his wife to the love Christ has for the church. If that is a fair comparison, a husband has an incredible task ahead of him. He must be the provider, protector, servant, intercessor, motivator, and decision maker. All this and more is associated with the term *love* in the context in which Paul uses it.

There is no allowance for passivity and laziness on the part of the husband. There is no allowance for self-centeredness, either. Christ gave His life for the church. In the same way a husband is to be willing to give his life for his wife. Husband, you are responsible for fulfilling this role in your home. To fail to do so is to pressure your wife into a role God does not intend for her to fill as long as the two of you are together. Second, to ignore your God-ordained role is to set children up for temptations they otherwise could avoid.

A STARVING GENERATION

It grieves me deeply to see children bear the consequences of a father's refusal to take seriously his role in the home. When a father ignores his role, his children starve for the male affection they need to mature both sexually and psychologically. The result is that children from these homes are driven to make up for this lack of male affection in other ways.

Girls from homes where Dad failed to fulfill his role may make up for his affection by finding it through relationships with men. Girls from homes like this are easy prey for guys, especially older ones, with the wrong intentions. Their eyes seem to say, "Take me, I'm available." Since they have never experienced real love from a male, it is almost impossible for them to distinguish between that and lust. Time and time again they will fall in with the wrong type of guy until they get into serious trouble. Anyone who has worked in a crisis pregnancy center knows about the high percentage of girls who have a background similar to the one described here.

I will never forget a fourteen year old in our church whose Dad basically ignored her for the first few years of her life and then finally left home. Whenever our youth group would go anywhere, she would almost always end up meeting some undesirable guys.

After observing this pattern in her for some time, I decided to say something. I pulled her aside after a service one evening and said, "I know this may sound strange, and I hope you are not offended, but I have seen a pattern in you that really concerns me."

She was shocked, to say the least, but she told me to continue.

I said, "I have noticed that guys are very attracted to you. What really concerns me, though, is the type of guy I often see you with." I went on and explained my fear for her and her need to be discerning in that particular area of her life.

Several weeks later she excitedly told me that she had a new boyfriend and that she could hardly wait for me to meet him. She told me how great his family was and how cute he was and that he had even agreed to come with her to church. I smiled and encouraged her to bring him.

The following Wednesday night my heart sank when I met him. He seemed no different from the guys she usually went with. He looked the other way when I reached out to shake his hand. He did not have much to say and only muttered responses to my questions. All the time, however, the young girl was just glowing with pride.

Less than a month later I was sitting in my office with her and her mother, both of them in tears. The young man had pressured her into having sex with him, and for reasons unknown to her, she had given in. "I don't know why I said yes," she said, wiping the tears from her cheeks. "I did not even enjoy it."

I can remember how angry I was that night. Not with the young girl, although she was certainly responsible for her actions. I was angry with her father, even though I had never met him. You see, by abandoning his family, he set his daughter up for what eventually happened. He was too selfish to give her the love and affection she so desperately needed as a young girl growing up. He was too self-centered to make the personal sacrifices necessary to guarantee her a fair chance at growing up sexually and psychologically healthy.

Dad, if you are man enough to bring a little girl into this world, for her sake you better be man enough to assume your role of leadership in the home and provide for her the love and affection she needs. And the same thing can be said about what you should provide for your son. Simply providing for your children financially and educationally is not enough. You owe them a debt of love. If you fail to do that, you set them up for disaster.

THE SAME OLD STORY

I have already mentioned that I believe the growth of the homosexual community is greatly due to a refusal on the part of parents to fulfill their proper roles in the home. I have yet to counsel with a man or a woman who was practicing homosexuality whose parents assumed proper biblical roles in the home. In fact, a friend who often counsels with persons practicing homosexuality told me that when his counselees begin telling him about their background, he often stops them in the middle of the story and finishes it for them! He has heard the same story so many times that he knows what comes next.

Without fail, one or both parents refused to assume biblical roles in the home. As a result, their son did not get the affection he needed from his father and thus grew up with a deficiency. Unaware of the real problem, such young men seek to make up for what they missed through sexual relations with other men.

Don't get me wrong. These men are totally responsible for their behavior. One day they will give an account to God for it. But they are not the only ones who will have to give an account. Their parents are responsible to some degree. Homosexuality is not an inherited disorder. It is a learned behavior rising out of a deep need for affection from the parent of the same sex, which is a need that should have been met at home. Dr. Paul Meier says, "It [homosexuality] will be more of a temptation for those who have not had a strong parent of the same sex to identify with, especially during the first six to ten years of life" (*Christian Child-Rearing and Personality Development,* p. 55).

COUNTING THE COST

Dad, passing off your lack of leadership in the home by kidding about how much more capable your wife is may be good for a laugh with the neighbors, but it is no laughing matter in view of the effects it could have on your children. Mom, running the home because Dad is constantly forgetting to do things or because you are so much more capable may get the bills paid on time, but you may lose your son in the meantime.

God did not assign us roles just to give us something to do. His assignments were made with our children in mind. A submissive wife and a loving husband provide a solid basis for the mental and sexual health of children.

You can drag your children to church every time the doors

are open. You can read the Bible to them every night of their lives. You can send them to all the church camps. But, Dad, if you are not loving and leading your wife, and, Mom, if you are not graciously submitting to your husband, more harm is being done than good.

I've met preachers' sons who were practicing homosexuals, and they could quote the Bible backward and forward. I've done crisis pregnancy counseling with church-going Christians' daughters who had all the "right" biblical answers, but for all the Bible they knew and for all the wisdom they had, they felt driven on the inside to find the love they never received at home. On the other hand, some of the finest, most balanced, and well-adjusted men and women I have met in my life have come from homes where neither parent was a believer, but Dad adored Mom and Mom submitted to and willingly served Dad.

The point is simply this: God gave each of us a role to fulfill in the home. Dad, you are to love your wife as Christ loved the church. Mom, you are to submit to your husband. To ignore these principles, regardless of what else you do to try to compensate for them, is to set your children up for failure. On the other hand, fulfilling your God-ordained role in the home is taking a giant step toward keeping your children on your team.

Chapter

24

Parenting Requires Learning: A Personal Reflection

Parenting your parents when they become too old or un-healthy to care for themselves can take its toll on a marriage. My wife, Carolyn, and I spent several years caring for our aging parents —one who could communicate only as a child and one who could think clearly but was physically unable to get around by himself. We had days we became tired and frustrated, days the emotional weight of watching them change and weaken made our responsi-bilities to them seem more than we could bear.

We learned in those years that the greatest thing we had to offer them was our love. I hope that you will find comfort in these words as you look toward the time when perhaps you, too, will be caring for your parents.

—*John Gillies*
A Guide to Caring for and Coping with Aging Parents

"Parenting Requires Learning: A Personal Reflection" is adapted from *A Guide to Caring for and Coping with Aging Parents,* John Gillies (1981); *Caregiving: When Someone You Love Grows Old* (1988).

Isn't it true that we became better parents through the process of being parents? Our third child had more experienced parents than our first.

We also learn to be parents of our own parents. May I share a few highlights of what I have learned?

THE GIFT OF DIGNITY

I have learned that one of the greatest gifts I can give my parents in their declining years is the gift of dignity. Despite the winding down of body and mind, each is a person with a history, with values, and with needs. I must provide them as much dignity as I can in their ongoing lives and as we prepare for their deaths.

CARETAKING

I have learned that I am a caretaker, not a custodian. Providing care—or enabling someone else to provide care—is a large and gracious responsibility given to me by my Lord.

AVAILABILITY

I have learned that I must be available.

I must regularly and personally visit my parents. No matter how forgetful they become, they must see and touch me and I must see and touch them.

This availability affects my life-style, but I must accept this with grace and joy. I must now plan my trips and vacations with my parents in mind. It is no longer possible to place them "out of sight, out of mind." I've purchased a telephone answering device not only to keep in contact with my editors and clients, but also to keep in touch with both nursing homes, wherever I may be.

I must also be available to my immediate family. I must live my own life with the responsibilities and adventures I share with Carolyn and, to a lesser degree now, with my children. However, I now also have grandchildren who need contact with their grandfather.

COMMUNICATING

Communication has been my livelihood and profession for many years. I have instructed others in it. But I have had to rethink my understanding of communication as I have tried to communicate with my parents. I am still learning.

I have learned to listen, to interpret strange sounds, to go beyond the gibberish to understand what is being conveyed through gesture and mood. To listen in this way means to learn to relax, not to assume too much, and to be content when very little is understood.

I have heard myself speak jargon. We all speak it—that special language or vocabulary we use in our work and daily lives that others may not understand. Much of what we say makes little sense to people who do not share our environments nor our professional interests.

Thus, when I speak to Paul about my work or a book I am reading or a seminar I attended, I must be careful not only that he is actually interested in the subject matter, but that he can understand the language I use to describe it.

Sometimes, just in time, I have become aware that I am merely flaunting my new insights or imposing my new enthusiasms, helpful and good though these may be to me. Sometimes I forget Paul's background and his way of looking at things.

Although I may have opened a few windows for Paul, I know I cannot change the habits of thinking and feeling he has acquired through eight decades of living. And I must be careful not to manipulate this person who cannot verbally challenge me nor argue with me. My parents have not traveled my road of growth and experience; in their day and time, they traveled their own roads. I wish I knew more of their journeys, but in fact, I know as little of theirs as they know of mine.

Thus, I am trying to listen more, to understand, to interpret, to be an occasional catalyst for a new friendship or a new idea, to innovate, to receive information, and sometimes to respond. This, of course, is the stuff of true communication.

I, TOO, AM VULNERABLE

Today's news is frightening. International tensions of every kind threaten peace and equilibrium. I read about a future in which the trust funds of Social Security may be exhausted, about a world in which the building of schools must give way to the building of housing for increasing numbers of the elderly, most of whom may be women.

I realize that I, too, am growing old.

I wonder if my children will have to become parents to me. They have no such obligation, of course. Nevertheless, I want them to know some of my wishes for my own latter days. I do not wish heroic measures to be used to extend my life if it has become a mere existence. They should understand my wishes regarding the time of my death, and how I feel about disability if that should intervene.

I must begin to do some things for myself, looking ahead not only to retirement but also to my own death.

If I had to spend a lot of time in front of a television set (heaven forbid!), I understand enough about sports to enjoy watching them. Hockey is the exception, however, because I don't know the rules. I ought to learn them now.

I want to get my files in order. I don't want someone else to have to wade through reams of carbon copies and boxes of slides and photographic negatives, wondering what to save and what to discard. That's something I must begin to do soon.

I hope Carolyn and I will yet be able to see those places we've read and dreamed about. If God wills it, if savings hold out, and if inflation doesn't devour us all, we will. If this doesn't come to pass, we have already been blessed with an enormous amount of travel, so we'll just relax and remember.

Of course, I must not assume too much. Unless we die together in an accident or a disaster, it's likely that one of us will survive the other. And there is the specter of institutionalization. Neither of us possesses some ironclad guarantee that all will be well and serene.

Within the framework of my own vulnerability, I can only

hope and trust the God I have followed. I hope I will be given the grace to continue to think, to read, and to write. If dependency comes, I hope it will be brief and not a burden to anyone. And in the process of caring for Paul and Anna with Carolyn beside me, as well as in the writing of this book, I hope I have learned something I can apply to my own life.

RETURNING TO THE SOURCE

Our Judeo-Christian tradition commands us to honor father and mother (see Ex. 20:12; Eph. 6:2).

The psalmist cries out, "Do not cast me off in the time of old age" (Ps. 71:9).

How can we deal with the commandment and the cry?

Love is the answer. The apostle Paul affirmed that love is the greatest of virtues, surpassing even faith and hope. I know we cannot will to love; we cannot force the emotion. However, we can determine for ourselves how our love will be lived out and expressed.

"Love is patient and kind," Paul wrote to the Corinthian Christians (1 Cor. 13:4). But it isn't easy to be patient with an invalid or handicapped parent when weeks become months, and months become years.

Frustration builds and sometimes explodes into anger. Horror stories about abuse of parents are beginning to appear more frequently.

Perhaps Carolyn and I have had it easier than most couples facing this responsibility. Each of us has a parent who needs our love and care. We can lean on each other, sharing the burden and not blaming the other for the change this care imposes upon our daily life-style and our marriage.

But I must confess to flashes of irritation and anger. I could not understand why Anna could not find and use the bathroom just outside her door. I still get upset with Paul when he forgets, or sometimes refuses, to use the grab bars I placed so strategically to help him. And sometimes Carolyn is affected in this crossfire of frustration.

Patience can dissipate quickly when almost every visit to Anna includes digging out dirt and excrement from under her fingernails. I can become weary in well-doing when the doing means attaching a catheter to my father-in-law every night.

THE MAGIC OF LOVE

Love is patient and kind.

I have to remember these characteristics and demonstrate them. It was necessary to do this as our children were growing up, two of them in that strange and turbulent decade of the sixties. The words of the art song "Plaisir d'Amour" (Égide Martini, 1741–1816) so often seemed poignantly accurate: "The joys of love endure but for a day, The pains of true loving throughout a lifetime stay." It was easy then to say, "Act your age!" Later I wondered which age I had in mind—child, adolescent, or young adult?

My parents now act in ways that reflect their age. I wish their deterioration were not so severe, but I must be patient as they now act out their real age.

Good parenting has never meant forcing children to be extensions of their parents; rather, it means to model or illustrate the values and insights that will help children become responsible citizens and parents themselves. In the new parenting role we must sometimes assume for our own parents, we should also provide and model the care and security we gave our children. But our parents still must be allowed the privilege of being themselves and be given the honor and respect they still deserve.

I've always considered myself a rather generous person. But I also know I am a perfectionist who feels comfortable with schedules when they are kept and who prefers to solve problems rather than analyze them. It is difficult to be kind when one is rigid and it is almost impossible to be patient.

Reviewing the past six years of my life with Paul and Anna, I hope I have been kind and I think I am becoming more patient. At least I am more flexible.

It would be conveniently pious to say that the changes have

come as I have learned to do the demanding things for my parents "as unto the Lord." Intellectually, I know we perform a service to Christ as we help those in need and in pain; I may even have thought this from time to time. Emotionally, however, I must declare that I do not picture Christ as I comb Anna's hair or adjust Paul's tie.

MY "NEW" PARENTS

I have come to a new perception of Paul and Anna. As we children grow older, we see and understand our parents in new ways. That is part of maturing. The process for me has simply continued longer than I expected.

Ours was a strict, rigid family. We were Eastern European by background, polite, predictable, and not really close. We didn't embrace each other, and we wondered about those who did. We kissed only perfunctorily and rarely.

As an only child, much was expected of me—particularly in "Christian service." After all, my father was a minister and a missionary. At the age of five I memorized Scripture under the threat and use of a belt, usually administered by Anna; I learned a verse for each letter of the alphabet. At age seven I began to play the portable pump organ at street meetings. At age twelve I was pushed into a pulpit as a boy preacher.

That's a sampling of the emotional baggage I have had to discard.

I no longer see my mother as I saw her at age five, seven, or twelve. I see her now as a person who was herself pushed into situations and performances for which she was not prepared and about which she had her own fears and misgivings. I see her now as a person who was denied the affection she needed—first as an orphan and later by her husband and son.

I'm trying now to make up for the lack of affection. I have come to realize the necessity for tactile expression of affection for Anna. I hold her hand. I massage her back. I wash her face and hands, no longer with exasperation but because it is necessary. I kiss her before I leave. I'm not sure how much this means to her.

Sometimes I think that touching may be the only way we communicate anything now. But I know this new dimension has taught me much, and I find I am touching many more of Anna's older friends, and I see how warmly they respond.

And what about Paul?

I've mentioned that I saw my own father more as a grandfather than as a father; he died when I was twenty-four, two weeks shy of his own sixty-eighth birthday. I've known Paul for more than thirty years—longer than I knew my own father. I've shared much with Paul during these three decades. He's become a father to me, and I think I've become the son he never had—often an argumentative, obstreperous son!

Paul has been pretty rigid himself—in theology, missionary strategy, family relationships, and politics. His daughters never challenged him. I did many times before his stroke, and often we found it possible to end such discussions in laughter rather than anger.

Things are different now with his inability to speak and to respond. I don't argue with Paul, but I do become irritated and angry when I feel he has needlessly endangered himself. Sometimes he has tried to walk without assistance. At the nursing home he sometimes forgets or refuses to use the call button for help and was found on the floor twice. At such times I've exploded, then explained, and finally apologized. Paul will often wave his hand, smile his half smile, and say what sounds like, "It's all right." In those moments I have experienced Paul's forgiveness and we can begin again.

I'm sure that in caring for Paul I am caring for my own father, who died too soon and whom I knew so little. I'm sure I'm also doing some of the things I wish I could do for Anna.

In trying to be patient and kind, I do so not so much "as unto the Lord" as I do simply for two people whom I love and who are my parents. In large measure, I do it for myself because I have a need that must be met.

I've written about the "new" parents in my life. There is also a new me.

LOVE MUST BE REAL

The apostle Paul wrote to the Christians in Rome, "Let love be genuine" (Rom. 12:9). Let it be sincere, not artificial. Don't pretend, and don't try to fake it.

Paul Young's mind still works; he understands. Anna's doesn't. But I think they both sense the authenticity of our love.

This business of parenting parents—facing and making decisions for those we love—will be easier if we remember that genuine love is patient, kind, honest, and realistic. Sometimes the expression of this love may not appear to be loving, especially when we must weigh long-term needs against the short term. Hard decisions have to be made for the good of our parents and ourselves.

We do not need to carry a burden of guilt throughout our lives if we remember and practice the criteria of love.

LET THERE BE JOY!

The apostle Paul wrote, "Rejoice in the Lord always. . . . Let all men know your forbearance" (Phil. 4:4,5). He had more than his share of woe, but he believed difficulty and depression could be overcome.

Sister Corita says, "Laughter is a sign of hope. We are saved and we can afford to laugh once in a while."

This business of parenting parents . . . will be easier if we remember that genuine love is patient, kind, honest, and realistic.

I was washing Anna's hands one day when her roommate, Mrs. Williams, a kind and aware person, lent me a towel. In trying to keep Anna calm, I suddenly thought of an old kindergarten song and began to sing: "This is the way we wash our hands!"

Mrs. Williams picked it up, then so did Olga across the hall.

Soon several of us were boisterously singing the old ditty. Anna didn't sing, but she was beaming and playing with the warm water. When we were through, Mrs. Williams said, in all seriousness, "Mr. Gillies, that was nice! How do you remember all those old songs?"

Anna doesn't get the point of jokes anymore, but she'll listen to a story now and then. She likes pictures and color. She likes to watch other people, especially children, and she smiles easily and frequently.

Paul always loved to tell stories, and he still enjoys a good joke. We cut out cartoons and put these on his wall. "Family Circus" is a current favorite, and he enjoys showing these to his friends. It's delightful to hear his deep rumble of laughter.

A sense of humor, the gift of laughter, and an atmosphere of joy make life so much easier for Anna and Paul, and for us. I must not take myself too seriously, and I dare not take Anna and Paul too seriously.

HOW SHOULD WE PRAY?

Jesus encourages us to pray for God's will on earth, for daily bread, for deliverance from evil, and to ask in order to receive.

A great promise is found in Psalm 91:15: "When he calls to me, I will answer him; I will be with him in trouble, I will rescue him and honor him."

The next verse intrigues me: "With long life I will satisfy him, and show him my salvation."

Should I pray for long life for Paul and for Anna? Or should I ask the Lord to take them to be with Him?

Anna is marking time. Life has lost all meaning for her. I do believe she will be happier in a new existence. Paul, on the other hand, is still aware of life. He still has many concerns for family members, for colleagues on mission fields, and for work and ministry yet to be completed. Paul's important ministry today is one of intercessory prayer. Should I pray that it should end, for my own convenience? No, I want God's will for both of them.

Since I do not know, then, how to pray, I am grateful for

Romans 8:26: "Likewise the Spirit helps us in our weakness; for we do not know how to pray as we ought, but the Spirit himself intercedes for us with sighs too deep for words."

I pray for Carolyn and for myself, that we may be given health, patience, wisdom, and the ability to express our love.

I pray for Anna and for Paul, that God's Spirit may so surround them that they will always feel secure in His love.

And I pray for those who care for Anna and for Paul, that they too may be given patience, wisdom, and the ability to express *their* love.

A DAY AND A NIGHT IN THE LIFE OF A "NEW" PARENT

It was Sunday, and we brought Paul into town and church. In the transfer from car seat to wheelchair, Paul did not stand fully erect nor take the usual step backward. I wrenched my back trying to keep Paul's 185 pounds upright while I shoved the wheelchair sideways, closer to Paul, with my foot.

Carolyn and I had been talking about resuming long-term care for Paul in our home. As I nursed my lower back pain, I pondered whether I would still have the physical and emotional stamina to respond lovingly and competently.

Paul was tired that morning, and slept through most of the service. I wondered whether these kinds of efforts really made that much difference to him.

Later that same Sunday, I spent an hour with my mother. She had been restless during the vespers, chattering away to herself and pushing against the brakes of her wheelchair. I had felt she needed the opportunity to listen to the singing and reading, that some structure would be helpful. Now I wondered whether I was placing too great a value upon such reluctant participation. Was the service really helpful to her? I didn't think her presence and chatter were helping the vespers leader. Could we find other ways to better use this time together?

In the meantime, Carolyn had returned Paul to Trinity Home

in Round Rock. She joined me and Anna, and we sat together until it was time to take Anna to the dining room for her supper.

I had brought two felt pens and some paper. I asked Anna to write her name. She smiled and scrawled some squiggly lines. I drew a circle and put in two eyes. She had entertained me this way when I was a toddler. I asked her to put in a mouth—which she did first with a straight line, turning it up on one side, and extending the other side beyond the face. It looked like an enormous smile, and Anna beamed at her work. Then she doodled, drawing what appeared to be borders around the page. Ten minutes had passed, and so had her interest. We proceeded to the dining room.

Most of that night was restless and sleepless for Carolyn and me. Carolyn was ill with severe lower intestinal pain. I was aware of the discomfort of my lower back. Also, the chest pains that always come when I am very tired had returned; they are probably psychosomatic.

Doubts and fears began to crowd into my mind. Could Carolyn and I continue to cope with the needs of our parents? And what if our parents should outlive us?

When sleep finally came, I dreamed about Anna. There had been some sort of picnic, arranged by the nursing home. Carolyn and I were present but were obligated to leave early; the nursing staff assured us everything would be fine. Later, I returned to check on Anna, but she wasn't in the nursing home—and no one knew where she was.

I found her in the picnic area, *standing* in front of her wheelchair. She was swaying slowly as she stood. She looked terribly emaciated and dirty, as though she had fallen and played in the dirt. She did not recognize me. She stood bewildered, staring blankly into space. She looked so forlorn and abandoned.

As I lay awake, I realized that Anna was worrying me more than Paul, although there was very little we could do now for Anna. I glanced at Carolyn, sleeping beside me. We have survived these years in remarkably good fashion, but we both share scars from the experience.

Why do we bother?

Paul is often morose. Anna is detached. We certainly do not struggle to provide loving care for praise or even thanks; we get very little of this from Paul, and none from Anna.

In the quiet of that dark night, it seemed to me that we had been given a gift—the possibility and opportunity to serve two people who need us. Somehow, through all of this, all things will work together for our good (Rom. 8:28).

WE LIVE WITH HOPE

Who shall separate us from the love of Christ? Shall tribulation, or distress, or persecution, or famine, or nakedness, or peril, or sword?

> No, in all these things we are more than conquerors through him who loved us. For I am sure that neither death, nor life, nor angels, nor principalities, nor things present, nor things to come, nor powers, nor height, nor depth, *nor anything else in all creation* [doesn't that include the effects of stroke and senility?], will be able to separate us from the love of God in Christ Jesus our Lord (Rom. 8:35, 37–39, italics mine).

Karl Barth, the great Swiss theologian, was once asked at Princeton Seminary how he would summarize his faith. His reply shocked some of the seminarians: "Jesus loves me, this I know, for the Bible tells me so!"

There's a verse of Anna Warner's old Sunday school song that isn't often sung, but it applies beautifully to our parents who are ill or handicapped.

> Jesus loves me, loves me still,
> Though I'm very weak and ill;
> From His shining throne on high,
> Comes to watch me where I lie.

I need that reassurance, too.

PART FIVE

When Things
Go Wrong

Chapter

What Does God Want Me to Do in a Crisis?

Dear Daughters,

We are in Hong Kong! What a strange and fascinating place! Although I am average height for an American, I feel foreign and big. Standing on the subway, I am taller than all the women and many of the men. Since I'm traveling to China tomorrow, I thought it appropriate to begin this letter with something from this difficult and interesting language. In Chinese, the word for *crisis* is a combination of the symbols for *danger* plus *opportunity.* Applied to our marriages, in crisis there is either danger that we will let the crisis destroy our oneness or opportunity that our oneness will grow deeper and more beautiful through the trial.

As inevitable storms rumble through our lives, it is imperative that we turn to God and to each other, and that we assume personal responsibility for our choices during each crisis.

I'm sure you're tired of hearing your mom talk about choices. I have to keep saying it because our secret choices determine

"What Does God Want Me to Do in a Crisis?" is taken from *How to Really Love Your Man,* Linda Dillow (1993).

where we are headed. At no time is it so difficult to choose to love, to forgive, to encourage, to accept, than during a time of great stress and yet so necessary. The temptation is to withdraw from each other and try to handle our hurts, becoming self-centered. God wants you and me to do the difficult thing, to decide, "I will do my part to help our marriage team pull together during this crisis."

Recently, I talked to Barbara, a young woman who was facing the first big crisis in her marriage. She was down in the dumps and also dumping on her partner because *his* faults were so evident when crisis mode brought high tension to the relationship. Barbara's crisis was the house they were building. Everything had gone wrong, and both she and her husband, Stan, wished they had never decided on the building project. Because of the wrong estimate, they were under great financial stress, and it seemed every time they talked, the topic of conversation was the house, the house, and the house, which just increased the tension.

My first advice to Barbara was that she take personal responsibility for her part of the "dump routine," and make positive choices. The house situation was not good, but her response was making it worse and causing the house crisis to become a marriage crisis.

Second, I shared with Barbara one practical suggestion of what we did during a time of great stress. Several years ago we had a trial, a kid crisis (of course, not anyone you know), and our relationship felt more like a teenage crisis center than a marriage. Every time we opened our mouths, it was, "What do you think we should do? How should we react? What should we say? Do you think this would help, and what about this?" We knew it was unhealthy for our relationship, but no matter what we began talking about, the conversation always came back around to the kid crisis. What is on your hearts will be on your lips. We felt like we didn't have a life, just a problem.

Our solution was to go away for a week alone and put a moratorium on the problem. Neither of us could talk about children; not one word could we utter! It was so refreshing! We were exhausted and too tired to ski on our ski vacation so couch potatoes we became. We watched a video series, vegetated, loved, relaxed, escaped, and it was wonderful!

By day six of our seven-day escape, we were able to look at each other and say, "Okay, now let's pray once again and seek wisdom from our God." We had gained a better perspective and could discuss the issues without the crisis possessing us.

I suggested to Barbara that she and her husband try to get away, at least for one night, to relax and love and forget about the house. The plans, financial stress, questions, and problems would still be there when they returned. Barbara said they felt like they fell in love all over again. Their getaway was so invigorating that they decided to keep the house moratorium in place and only permitted themselves to talk "house talk" for a half hour.

Of course, some problems cannot be forgotten for a day, or for six days, but when possible, try this escape suggestion during your crisis. You will find it gets your eyes off the problem and on to God's working in the midst of the mess.

Love,
Mom

Financial Setbacks

ew things are able to create havoc in a marriage like financial crisis or critical illness. A heart attack, terminal cancer, a business failure or loss of a breadwinner's job can wind up shattering the lives of a normal family. How does a marriage and family survive? These are the times when a couple can truly feel as though they are "together on a tightrope," wondering if there is a net to catch them if they fall. Acting wisely, rather than reacting to crisis situations, can be so difficult when the pain is blinding. The next two chapters were written for Together on a Tightrope *in the hopes that families facing times of trouble can learn to see their way straight to a brighter future.*

—*Rick Fowler and Rita Schweitz*
Together on a Tightrope

"Financial Setbacks" is adapted from *Together on a Tightrope,* Dr. Richard Fowler and Rita Schweitz (1992).

Mike Carlson shook my hand firmly as he entered my office, then set his notebook on the corner of the desk. He said, Dr. Fowler recalls, "There it is," with an eagerness in his voice that suggested he was pleased with the work he and Patti had done. And Patti had a sparkle in her eye when she added excitedly, "Last week when you said that setting goals was an *excellent* communication tool you were up to mischief!"

"Hum? Not me! What makes you say that?" Dr. Fowler teased back, and then asked, "How did it go?" He already had a pretty good idea. It is often clear within the first few minutes of a counseling session how the previous week's assignment has gone, and from all indications their project had been a profitable one.

"Writing out our plan of action forced us to talk things through in specific terms. There were a few tense moments, but working through the conflicts made it clear that money wasn't the real issue," Mike answered. He picked up the notebook and pointed at the goals they had listed. "We wrote it out as you suggested: Long-term perspective/Short-term objective."

LONG-TERM PERSPECTIVE/SHORT-TERM OBJECTIVE

The exercise Mike and Patti completed at the Minirth-Meier Clinic would be helpful to any family who is facing financial problems, whether those problems resulted from unexpected medical bills, loss of a job, or extenuating circumstances. The exercise was not complicated. Mike and Patti looked at the relative importance of the various problems we had identified in our discussions, chose the ones they felt were the most significant, and wrote down what they wanted to see happen in the long run —their flight plan. After listing the long-term perspective in these areas, they broke the goals down into short-term action steps.

From a long-term perspective, the Carlsons listed three goals. First, Mike wanted to secure employment that would provide a comfortable income for his family and utilize his past experience. His first short-term objective under that goal had already been accomplished. At Dr. Fowler's suggestion, Mike had invited five of his friends from different fields to a "brainstorming party" earlier that week. Together they had helped him think of types of jobs he should apply for, and offered input on his résumé rough draft. His second objective was to stay in touch with his friends for encouragement and accountability as well as possible employment leads. Mike's next action step was to get the résumé professionally produced and send out five to ten résumé packets each week. He wanted to become proactive—taking the initiative to solve their problems—rather than behaving reactively with a depressed outlook and victim mentality.

The second long-term goal Mike and Patti listed had to do with Mike's feelings of insecurity based on his childhood experiences. Their goal was to keep Mike's relationships with his father and mother on an adult-to-adult level, and to make the decisions they felt were best regardless of his parents' response. "We both agreed on our long-range goal for the health of our family," Mike said. "But then Patti suggested the first action step should be to refuse to accept any gifts or financial help from my parents regardless of how bad things became. I got defensive and said that her family didn't have enough money to help us out, so there wasn't much choice."

"What did you feel, Patti, when Mike drew your parents into the discussion?" Dr. Fowler asked.

"At first I felt angry at being shut off. Then I realized that we were falling into what you called the *binary trap,* where you focus on the question 'Should we do this or not?' as if saying yes or no is the only alternative. And I realized the real question was 'Where is the best place for us to borrow money if it comes to that?' When I told Mike what I was thinking and put the question that way, we came up with more options to consider—none of which involved either set of parents."

"I'm proud of you, Patti. That was a terrific way to handle things!" Dr. Fowler responded.

"When Patti rephrased the question it made me realize that I had subconsciously been thinking that I was trapped—that I had no choice but to fail without my parents' help," Mike added. "When I could see other options, I agreed that it would be best to leave my mom and dad out of it. Patti's second action point, that

I always talk things through with her before asking my folks for advice, made sense in light of our long-term goal too. But it's not going to be easy for me to do."

For their third long-range goal, Mike and Patti listed getting out of debt and reestablishing a savings cushion that would tide them over if unexpected circumstances ever came up again. Their short-term plan was simply to reduce spending in several small ways they had worked out together and to pay off everything they had purchased on a payment plan or with credit cards, starting with the smallest bill first.

Balancing Your Accounts

The Carlsons were beginning to exhibit many characteristics of strong families—good communication, spiritual unity, appreciation, and commitment to each other. In *The Secrets of Strong Families*, Nick Stinnett and John DeFrain explain that these strengths "serve as a pool of resources that [strong families] draw on when times are difficult—rather like we save money for a 'rainy day.' In contrast, unhealthy families are worn out and depleted on a daily basis by the stress of poor relationships. When a crisis comes along, the unhealthy family must add it to the burden they already struggle with. No wonder the load is sometimes too much."[1]

The analogy between balance in a relationship and balance in a bank account is a helpful one. Words of appreciation, respect, time spent together, and thoughtful actions are all "deposits" into your relational account. They add to the strength and security of the bond. But taking one another for granted, criticizing, or unthoughtfulness deplete the account. For example, Mike's moodiness and emotional detachment from Patti drained their relationship, just as bills and house payments depleted their savings.

In financial terms, we all understand the need for a cash flow margin—having more money coming in than going out. In the same way, keeping a positive margin in a relational ledger *on a daily basis* is a key to building and maintaining balance. Refuse to run in the red for an extended time. If you drain the account with an outburst of anger, then counter the damage by saying you are sorry and asking for forgiveness. Praise each other often. Figure in times of refreshment and restoration.

When the Krajewski family went through a period of financial difficulties, tension began to mount between Mary Ann and her husband. But they took constructive steps to maintain their marriage. In response to our survey, Mary Ann wrote, "Larry and I made a commitment to never blame each other. It was very needed! I could not blame him and he could not blame me—we established a mutual trust fund."

In relationships, all interactions have a cumulative effect. The little things or seemingly insignificant irritations can empty an account. And when either person's needs remain unmet for an extended time, the relationship is at risk. The good news is that it works both ways. Even when you don't have much money, you can still nurture your relationships and fill your love accounts. In the good times you can continue to add to good memories so that you have something to fall back on the next time a situation puts a strain on your friendship or family.

When either person's needs remain unmet for an extended time, the relationship is at risk.

Mike and Patti began to stabilize their love account when they started pulling together, talking things through, and adding the positive feelings of joint accomplishment. Here are some other practical ways to balance the draining effects of adversity and to keep money matters from driving a wedge in your relationship.

Write out your financial goals. Writing out your goals encourages communication, clarifies your thoughts and feelings, and encourages joint effort.

Pull together. Have you ever tried to drive a car with the emergency brake on? That's a good description of the way many families initially work against themselves in the area of finances. One cuts back while another spends. One asks for professional advice while the other refuses to follow it. One makes decisions while another resists them. After a couple learns to keep the crisis in perspective and to work together at problem solving, the brake is released and forward movement is unhampered.

Respond rationally, not emotionally. People who seek counseling for overwhelming financial problems are often paralyzed by panic. They take no action because they are immobilized by the fear of making a mistake or by the conclusion that all effort is pointless. Or they slide into an obsessive/compulsive cycle, where they are obsessed with their money problems at all times and handle it through compulsive behavior, for example, workaholism, stealing, deceitfulness. Rather than setting a deliberate course and following it, they tend to do only what they feel good about or what the circumstances force upon them. They respond to the emotion of the moment and make poor choices. In contrast, when individuals respond rationally to the financial facts, their relationships are more stable and their financial position generally improves.

Seek wise counsel. When your heart is breaking or you are under extreme stress, it is very difficult not to respond emotionally. Therefore it makes good sense to get an objective outside opinion and to avoid hasty decisions. Many churches offer inexpensive or free financial counseling. Hospitals and insurance companies will generally help answer questions and work through possible payment arrangements. Or the advice of a trusted friend, whose judgment you value, may help you make wise choices.

Invite God's help. John MacArthur extensively researched what the Bible had to say about money and then summarized, "16 out of 38 of Christ's parables deal with money; more is said in the New Testament about money than heaven and hell combined; five times more is said about money than prayer; and while there are 500 plus verses on both prayer and faith, there are over 2,000 verses dealing with money and possessions."[2] God repeatedly used practical illustrations with money to illustrate spiritual truth, making it clear His wisdom applies in both the spiritual and practical realms.

Many of us recognize that God has the wisdom and desire to help with our financial problems. But we are like a little boy who ran to his father saying, "This tag on the back of my shirt is bothering me." Then before the father could reach for the scissors, the little boy jerked the tag, tearing it loose from the shirt collar— and ripping a hole in the seam in the process. We say we are asking for help, but instead we are taking matters into our own hands because we are unwilling to wait. Beware of quick, impulsive decisions. They rarely solve financial problems.

Allow others to express their love. One of the ways we express our love and compassion for others when they are faced with adversity is to share our time, possessions, and money. Your community, church community, or friends may step in to shoulder some of your burden. If they do, appreciate their concern and accept their help.

But if no one offers assistance, ask yourself two questions before responding with frustration or bitterness: First, *Have I let my close companions know what my real situation is?* They may not be aware of the seriousness of your situation unless you have shared your concern. Don't assume they can read your mind or your bills.

And second, try to objectively consider: *Am I taking things too personally and unrealistically expecting too much?* Certain problems will always generate more compassionate response than others. For example, people often rally around a family whose house burned down or whose preschooler has cancer and needs expensive treatment. The needs incurred when a loved one is placed in a nursing home, however, will largely go overlooked. Be realistic about how much you expect from others.

Recognize issues under the surface. In our culture, money is tied very closely to issues of power and self-worth. What appears at first glance to be a problem with handling the stress of insufficient funds may really be a struggle with feelings of worthlessness, low self-esteem, or loss of identity through loss of financial status or employment. Tension also arises over financial concerns when one spouse feels an extreme need to control and uses money for leverage. Try to discern whether any of these factors are undermining your relationships.

It is often helpful to ask yourself: *In what ways have money matters complicated or eased my current circumstances? Do my attitudes toward money strengthen or divide my family? Are money problems only a symptom of personal problems that have not been resolved?*

Keep a sense of humor. Regardless of your bank account balance, a healthy dose of humor and a cheerful outlook will improve your relationships. Humor is a great antidote for stress as long as it is not cutting or sarcastic. Laughing together at inside jokes can bring much-needed breaks in the tension and reaffirm that "we're in this together." It is important to treat serious things seriously, but life's load will seem lighter if you can learn to see the humorous side of things too.

When Is Support Beneficial?

Although it is healthy to give and to receive help in times of trouble, not all help is good. There must be guidelines and limits. Here are some marks of beneficial support.

It Is Voluntary

Because of our love for others, we should freely desire to help them out. But if we are shamed into it by manipulation, pressure, or guilt, then it will not have the same positive effect on the relationship. On the receiving end, we must always be allowed the dignity of declining money. As Mike and Patti discerned, it was not in their best interest to accept money from Mike's parents. Don't give or receive money that has strings attached or will have a negative impact on the relationship in the future.

Don't Ask for Help Merely to Be Rescued

Sometimes it is easy to let someone else carry the baton when you are perfectly capable of running yourself. Also, resist the urge to rescue others without considering whether it is truly in their best interest. Don't give money in response to repeated cycles of urgent need because of poor financial planning. Laziness or irresponsible money management do not constitute legitimate reasons for receiving continued financial support. In such cases offer financial training and the encouragement to be responsible.

Marked by Gratitude and Humility

Healthy giving is characterized by an attitude of gratitude, humility, and love. We are to be thankful for the many blessings God has given that enable us to share with others. We are also to receive with gratitude and humility, thankful for God's willingness to meet our needs and the kindness of caring friends. There is no place for arrogant pride in demanding help or in smugly giving it.

Handled Quietly and with Dignity

When support is given in healthy ways, the dignity and respect of both parties involved is taken into consideration. Offering financial support should not call undue attention to either the one giving or the one receiving—neither should feel awkward or embarrassed. And the terms of the agreement, including the time frame for repayment if the money is loaned, should be clearly understood to prevent misunderstandings later.

Money given out of love and concern encourages, supports, and offers relief for people in need. In a truly loving relationship money will never be offered if it enables people to live irresponsibly, to shirk their duty toward their families, to foster a dysfunctional dependency, or to continue in any sinful life-style. Love will achieve the balance between two emotionally costly mistakes —taking too much responsibility for the feelings, behavior, and choices of others, or not taking enough responsibility for *our own.*

*Love will achieve the balance between two emotionally costly mistakes—taking too much responsibility for the feelings, behavior, and choices of others, or not taking enough responsibility for **our own**.*

Concentrating on making the best of a bad financial situation is often the best coping strategy of all. Money was tight when Mike's birthday rolled around, but Patti refused to focus on the lack of presents or spoil the day moping. Instead she and the kids planned a surprise sand volleyball party at an area beach. When she invited close family friends, Patti requested that they bring snacks and soft drinks in place of gifts. Then Patti and the kids browsed through the line of contemporary cards at a local discount store and chose a birthday card for Mike. On the card was a goofy-looking man saying, "It's your birthday! Time to forget about your past—to forget about your future . . .

". . . but most importantly—forget about your present! ('cause this is it!) Happy Birthday."

Chapter

Critical Illness

$\mathcal{E}$rin experienced a series of typical childhood health problems after her heart surgery at age three: chicken pox, ear infections, and recurring strep throat, which led to a tonsillectomy. Her checkups were routine for a child her age except for extra blood work, angiograms, and echocardiograms. When she turned eight, surgery was scheduled to connect her heart to her lungs, artificially replacing the trunk of the pulmonary artery. Arlan and Rita were told there was a chance they could do the procedure in one operation rather than the repair stages they had previously expected.

Rita recalls the day of the surgery, "When the surgeon and his assistant, still dressed in scrubs, stepped up to the door of the cardiac intensive care waiting room, all eyes turned to them. Arlan and I immediately recognized him and moved quickly across

"Critical Illness" is adapted from *Together on a Tightrope*, Dr. Richard Fowler and Rita Schweitz (1992).

326

the room for the first word of how Erin's open-heart surgery had gone. Dr. Puga motioned us into the hall and reported, 'The surgery went well, but we were unable to complete the repair. In three to six months you will need to bring her back, and we'll do the homograft [reconstruction using donor tissue] then.'

"It's been nearly a year since then, and we are still on hold. Although the reports keep changing, at Erin's most recent appointment our cardiologist told us we could expect to wait another year, possibly even two. We're thankful for Erin's good report and for the extended time to regroup before the next surgery. Even so, the news was unexpected and it feels a little like running in a cross-country race where someone keeps changing the route and moving the finish line—just when it appears within reach.

"But in the nine years since Erin's birth, we've learned that the finish line is an illusion," Rita adds. For families who have been touched by a major medical trauma, things never really go back to normal as it was defined before. That's not necessarily such a bad consequence. Suffering gives ample opportunity for character development and personal growth. Some families come out of their trials stronger and more appreciative than ever.

THE ACHE INSIDE

Individuals who have never encountered tragedy on a personal level usually have a general faith in good fortune, a carefree lack of anxiety based on the unspoken assumption *it will never happen to me.* The American Cancer Society reports that cancer will be diagnosed in 1 out of 3 Americans; 3 out of 4 families will have someone stricken by cancer.[1] These sobering facts alone show that *it will* happen to you—you or someone you love. No one is immune from pain or illness.

When a crisis does occur, we are no longer naive. We know that we are not exempt from pain and sorrow. We ache inside over the loss.

Four years ago Elizabeth Berg was diagnosed as having an immune system cancer. In an article entitled "Moments of Ease," she wrote, "You look at photographs of yourself from before, aching. It is as though the essence of you has moved away, leaving behind a fragile shell that waits in vain to be what it used to be. You think you'll never be careless again, that you'll never laugh all the way, or lean back in your chair sighing and smiling, eyes closed, arms loose at your sides, *full of some naive sort of confidence you didn't know you had until you lost it*" (emphasis added).[2]

Even mature people with strong religious convictions can subtly confuse that breezy, "naive sort of confidence" with faith. When they can no longer accept that everything is going to work out right, when they lose their faith in good fortune, then it may appear that they have lost their faith *in God*. Some people confuse God with life—when they become disappointed with life, they become disappointed with God too. When life is not good, they jump to the thought that God is not good.

Although we may feel vulnerable and badly shaken when our sense of security is lost, the loss of our false confidence need not interrupt our relationship with God. God never gave a lifetime guarantee of good health. A mature faith has to rest on a deeper level of loving God for *who He is* and not just for *what He does or does not do* in this particular moment to ease our pain.

Critical illness strips away the veneer that we are in control of our lives. It uncovers our complete dependence upon the Creator of life. During that fragile time of sorting through emotions and working through our questions about God's involvement, many misunderstandings can arise that cause inner pain and a rift in our relationship with God. These misunderstandings may spring from our own misconceptions of God's character. Or the well-meant remarks of friends can touch a very sensitive spiritual nerve.

In a radio interview, Dr. James Dobson commented: "It's been my experience at the hospital that those who are going through suffering and pain, or what's sometimes worse, those whose children are going through life-threatening experiences like that, often already have a tremendous cross to bear. And then Christians—well-meaning Christians who really believe they are doing right—make it worse by saying those kinds of things that give them an emotional burden to carry in addition to what they already have."[3]

For example, a nonsupportive comment may place blame on the sick person or their family, implying, "You wouldn't be going through this if you hadn't displeased God. There must be sin in your life. You need to confess so that God can answer your prayers." But Job's story clearly demonstrates disaster can strike the innocent and give no indication of God's displeasure.

Another misunderstanding is expressed in remarks like this one a friend made to Rita: "Sickness is never God's will. God will heal Erin if you only believe and pray. You have to have faith." It is not necessarily a person's faith that is at fault. God can work miracles, but God also chose *not* to heal Paul: "My grace is sufficient for you, for My strength is made perfect in weakness" (2 Cor. 12:9).

Philip Yancey, author of *Where Is God When It Hurts?*, explained in a radio interview, "Jesus made very clear that He was not setting up a different category of human beings called 'Christians' who would have a different experience in life. In other words, He wasn't saying that from now on germ cells won't attack Christians if you believe in Me. From now on tornadoes will hop over your houses. The tidal wave will mysteriously fold around your homes. We are a part of this world—part of this world that has been stained by the fall of man—and Jesus is saying 'Live out your faith in the midst of this world.' "[4]

When many questions were swirling around in her mind, Rita looked for reassuring verses like, "The Lord is good to those who wait for Him,/To the soul who seeks Him. . . . /Though He causes grief,/Yet He will show compassion/According to the multitude of His mercies./For He does not afflict willingly,/Nor grieve the children of men" (Lam. 3:25, 32–33).

RELATIONSHIPS FREED FROM SUPERFICIAL VALUES

Long after the diagnosis is in or the surgery is over, you will find that a close encounter with critical illness has altered your circumstances and how you relate to one another. Often those changes are a result of personal growth as well as the physical condition. People facing a loss of health may gain insight that leads to changed values and a greater emphasis on relationships.

At age eighteen, playwright Libba Bray was in a car accident that led to thirteen reconstructive surgeries. Her accident prompted her to shed a superficial value system: "I realized that all my life I had been thinking, *If only I can lose those 10 pounds/ grow my hair out/stop chewing my nails—then I'll be perfect.* Finally, my artificial eye allowed me to see that I would never reach that ideal. It was terrifying . . . and very liberating. I was free to step off the Treadmill of the Beautiful and into a wonderful world of mismatched eyes, crooked smiles, and size-8 hips. And I have never looked back."[5]

Like Libba, you will find your relationships enriched if you give up the idea that a person's value or identity is tied to their physical strength, stamina, or beauty. Focus, instead, on the inner person—character, spirit, and heart.

If you or someone you love is suffering from intense medical problems, you will also need to confront and think through common deceptions our culture promotes. Confront performance-based acceptance. (A man's work is not his worth; a woman's productivity does not define her identity.) Confront the quick fix and fast lane society that breeds frustration when we are forced to rest and wait, to be patient and endure. Confront the glorified stress on youth and power that implies that the old or handicapped, bedridden or nonathletic, are somehow second-class citizens. And face off against the imbalanced emphasis our culture places on independence and individualism.

In *You Gotta Keep Dancin'*, Tim Hansel writes about his own journey through intense daily pain: "Perhaps God gives us difficulties in order to give us the opportunity to know who we really are and who we really can be. We live in a world that is sometimes constipated by its own superficiality. But life's difficulties are even a privilege, in that they allow us or force us to break through the superficiality to the deeper life within."[6]

Changing Priorities

Beth Leuder, in her article "Through the Pain," talks candidly about her needs after back injuries that left her in chronic pain: "Difficulties have taught me to admit I need others. For most of my life I have been hesitant to let people into my struggles. Perhaps because of my own pride and fear of rejection. Or perhaps because it's unacceptable with some Christians to express true feelings about tribulations.

"The cloak of denial I was wrapped in tattered when I began to be honest with God and others. I found freedom in admitting I was weak and in need of prayer and encouragement. Time after time, as I've let friends into my world of pain, they have been God's hands to bring me comfort and hope. True, some people will never understand my ongoing bout with pain and discouragement. And I cannot expect them to. But it's still OK for me to practice gut-level honesty with close confidants . . . and with the Lord."[7]

A crisis situation often encourages us, as it did Beth, Arlan, and Rita, to admit our need for people and to put a higher priority on relationships. In healthy relationships increased appreciation and expressions of love help balance the shared pain and fear. The ordeal binds us together. One teenager, whose father suffered a massive heart attack, says, "We appreciate life and each other more, much more than I think other families do. We tell Dad that we love him every day, and he tells us. When I leave home in the morning and when I come back, I'm just glad to see Dad there. I think it's drawn us all closer."

Families that develop strength through crisis also learn to place a higher priority on communication. They talk about their fears. For Beth Leuder there are times when she is "afraid of more tests, more doctors, more pain, more time off work, more bed rest, more debt, more paperwork, more legal complications, more tears, more lonely times, more insurance hassles, more false hope."[8]

There is so much more involved than "Are you feeling better today?"

Talk things through. Suppressed emotions often result in depression, isolation, hopelessness, resentment—or more medical complications such as ulcers and headaches. In family counseling sessions at the clinic patients and family members learn how to better communicate feelings of anger, frustration, and fear—how not to keep everything bottled up inside. This is not to imply, however, that *every* negative feeling you experience should be indiscriminately dumped on those around you. The focus is on more understanding and appropriate sharing of feelings. And skills forged in the crucible of crisis serve the family well long into the future.

Families that develop strength through crisis also learn to place a higher priority on communication.

Fear, regret, and blame often mingle with the medical problems a family faces. A woman might blame herself for not finding her husband sooner after a stroke. A father regrets giving the car keys to his teenage son after an automobile accident. Or the families of cardiac patients may live with the constant fear that they will do or say something that will overexert or upset the patient, bringing on a fatal collapse. The listening ear and reassurance of a pastor, friend, or family member can help those working through overwhelming feelings.

Of course, close families that communicate well beforehand have a distinct advantage. As Pastor Charles Swindoll put it, "We cannot prepare for a crisis *after* that crisis occurs. Preparation must take place *before* we are nose to nose with the issue." Ideally, every family member should be taught good listening skills from an early age. It is essential for adults to learn how to discuss emotional issues. Adults as well as children should be encouraged to use the "I feel" format: "I feel (scared) when (Mom has to go back to the doctor)." Children can be encouraged to use artwork and storytelling to express their feelings.

Families who endure a crisis also place a higher priority on being together. After being diagnosed with cancer, Elizabeth Berg wrote poignantly, "You think you'll never yell at your children again. Everything they do seems so wonderful, so full of meaning, so close to being lost. You spend more time with them in the day, listen to them with all of yourself rather than half."[9]

Ironically, this increased tenderness and desire for togetherness can contribute to the stress of the situation. You may say you will never yell at your children again then the lack of sleep or mounting frustrations make you irritable. Trivial things irk you. Medications alter your moods. The guilt of responding in ways you never wanted to can add an extra burden. Especially now, you must be willing to forgive and to make allowance for each other. There are no perfect patients or caregivers. Be gentle toward one another. Don't be too hard on yourself.

Try to remain flexible when your desire for togetherness conflicts with other responsibilities. Dolores Curran, in her excellent book *Traits of a Healthy Family,* says that lack of time is possibly the most pervasive enemy the healthy family has. The illness of a family member compounds the problem. Insurance paperwork, hospital visits, and work all take time. Each family must arrive at workable compromises that allow for the emotional and physical needs of all family members, not just the needs of the individual facing medical problems.

Living with the Losses

And as the stricken person recovers, he must be eased into carrying his own load again. Don't let your desire to take care of someone degenerate into unhealthy overprotection or foster long-term dependence. There is a place, a noble place, for sacrificial love. But recovery requires allowing a person to regain as much as possible of what was lost—to again assume responsibility for her own schedule, behavior, feelings, and choices. Even though you are together on the tightrope of stress, you must refuse to carry someone who needs to regain emotional and physical strength by standing on her own two feet.

The day she came home from the hospital, Erin wanted not only to stand on her own two feet, but to ride her skateboard and her bike around the farm! Her mother would have preferred that she quietly read every story and poem in the *Childcraft* encyclopedia then go outside to play sometime next year, or at least wait a couple weeks. It took compromise from both sides to avoid overprotection and set reasonable limits on Erin's activities.

Total recovery, however, is not an essential requirement for healthy relationships. Steve, an engineer in his late forties, came into Dr. Fowler's office knowing his wife would never recover. He was concerned about his relationship with his twenty-five-year-old son, who would not come to visit Steve and his wife anymore. The family history revealed that Steve's wife was in a terrible car accident five years earlier. She recovered physically but never regained her preaccident status mentally. She now had a five-minute memory, would forget who her son was, and had to be placed in a day care center while Steve was at work.

Steve's wife could no longer respond to him emotionally, spiritually, or sexually. But he chose to accept what he could not change and to stay true to his vow "for better or worse, in sickness and in health." He expended his energy by running and competed in the Boston Marathon and other major runs. Steve's son, however, chose to deal with his mom by detachment, "out of sight, out of mind." He deserted his family.

When faced with overwhelming circumstances, nearly everyone faces the temptation to take what initially appears to be the easier way out—to run away, emotionally withdraw, or detach. Some, like Steve, will choose to see their loved one through eyes of commitment and unconditional love. They will choose courage.

Relationships deepen as people determine that they will live with unavoidable losses and separations. In *A Path Through Suffering*, Elisabeth Elliot writes insightfully about the separation between health and sickness: "There is a fellowship among those who suffer, for they live in a world separated from the rest of us.

When my husband Addison Leitch was dying of cancer he felt keenly the impossibility of my understanding his experience. 'It's two different worlds we're living in,' he said, 'and there's no commerce between the two.' He could not help feeling that I did not care enough. I cared as much as a wife can care for a husband she adores and cannot bear to lose, but it was not enough. I did not know what Add knew. I had not been there. When we went to the waiting room of the radiation department at the hospital, however, we met others who *knew*—a little boy with red X's on his temples, a man whose lower jaw had been removed."[10]

Recovering and learning to live with permanent losses take time.

As the parent at the bedside of a sick child, you may long, as Rita and Arlan did, to somehow trade places. You ache for the chance to take the pain upon yourself and spare your child. But of course you cannot. Your loved one is caught in a body separate from yours, and you cannot enter their experience to the degree compassion compels. Support from others who have encountered similar circumstances can be of great help at such times, although you may not have the strength to endure the sadness of anyone else's story at first.

With life-threatening or disabling illness you may also lose cherished parts of life—the traditional father figure role, the opportunity to be homemaker, or the carefree childhood most little girls and boys take for granted. Besides this, the patient may lose control over certain aspects of his physical body. After his stroke, award-winning novelist Paul West wrote, "It is as if I am my own laboratory specimen, over which I have no control. Indeed, being a novelist, I now regard my medical self as one of my characters, whose every tremor and twinge I monitor."[11] For relationships to remain strong, family members must adapt to these changes and remain flexible.

There is no superglue for putting your life back together after illness or trauma has intruded, shattering your dreams and security. Recovering and learning to live with permanent losses take time.

Here are ways you can help hurting families endure the day-to-day pains that inevitably come from living in an imperfect world. If you know of someone who currently needs your help, keep them in mind as you read.

Allow family members freedom to work through their own emotions. Both the initial diagnosis and the crisis of hospitalization can prompt a variety of feelings. Ranging from anger, worry, and frustration to tenderness, compassion, and helplessness, these emotions mingle into a blur of stress. Let them handle that stress in the way that works best for them—not what seems best to you.

Encourage exercise. Plan a brisk walk or a chance to climb stairs. Resist the urge to tell a friend, "What you need is a good cry." Maybe what she *really* needs is a good aerobic workout!

Allow plenty of time for emotions to stabilize. Unlike the episodes of daytime TV dramas, real-life emotions seldom resolve within thirty minutes. Expecting a speedy resolution can make family members feel pressured to pretend.

Encourage the patient and family to ask their physician the emotionally charged questions that may be gnawing at their peace of mind. "Can the defect be traced to something in pregnancy?" "What happens next?" "Why do the nurses seem so concerned?" If the family is uneasy with the diagnosis or treatment, the vital question they may be reluctant to ask their doctor is "Who would you recommend for a second opinion?"

Create a supportive home environment. Understandably, more attention is focused on the physical and emotional needs of the patient and those who stay at the hospital with him. But the family members left trying to maintain a normal work routine while inwardly aching also need support. Remain alert to opportunities to help out at home.

Really listen to the patient and family members. Many people avoid visits because they do not know what to say, but often the most helpful thing you can do is listen. Just being there to offer an understanding ear can lessen the lonely ordeal the family faces.

Help the family keep up with responsibilities on a day-to-day basis. Life goes on. Families facing medical problems may also be burdened by finances, keeping up on the job, and the details of staying in the hospital or rehabilitation center, especially if travel is required. It is here that listening friends can be of great help. As you sense a need, you can ask specific questions and offer help: Suggest that you drive them to and from chemotherapy, pick up Grandma at the airport, or get their little girl to a classmate's birthday party. Do whatever the recipients perceive as helpful—not what you think they ought to appreciate. These loving gestures will demonstrate genuine understanding and support. Doing little things can be a big encouragement!

If you are unsure what to do or say, send a personal note. A letter or card is a universally accepted expression of care that can strengthen your relationship and provide encouragement. One that deeply touched Rita was from a little boy named Zachary, a friend of Erin's. When Erin was transferred from intensive care following open-heart surgery in Rochester, three hundred miles from home, Zachary sent her a picture. In the corner he had carefully printed "To Erin" in bright crayon letters. Underneath he had drawn a little blonde-haired girl in a hospital bed—with guardian angels circling above her.

This Thing Called Reconciliation

Maybe it looks like the end to you. After years of trying to keep your marriage together, the pain has just become too acute. How is it possible to forgive when so many wrongs have been done? You're tired of trying and you can't see any way out except divorce, though instead of relief, that option just seems like a route to a different kind of pain. Do you have an ounce left of faith that reconciliation is possible? Consider with us the possibility of the work of putting your marriage back together again. An ounce of faith may be all you need.

—*Jim Talley*
Reconcilable Differences

The credit manager at the department store was very nice. As he talked with you, he checked off one box after another on the credit application. Then he hit a nerve.

"This Thing Called Reconciliation" is adapted and taken from *Reconcilable Differences*, Jim Talley (1985).

"Married?"

You paused for a split second, halting the automatic response built in through five years of marriage.

"No," you said, but the mental parade wouldn't stop. You remembered the day you looked into that special person's eyes and said, "I love you," for the first time. You were sure you meant those words, but today the slightest thought of your marriage to that person rekindles bitter feelings. Even hearing the word *married* is enough to set you off and get your stomach acid flowing.

Now suppose I mention the word *reconciliation*. How do you respond? Do you panic, tune me out, or become angry? You are perfectly normal if those are your reactions. I see them all the time. Some people I counsel are so angry they think they could cheerfully kill their ex, and when I suggest a workshop on reconciliation, they immediately (and sometimes explosively) reject the idea.

You see, they think reconciliation means remarriage. Yet to be reconciled is not necessarily inviting a former spouse into the house again. At first it may only mean reducing the danger level when children are exchanged for visits.

A California couple, for example, tired of beating each other about the head verbally and physically each time they exchanged their children, now meet on the steps of the city's police station. They find they can be more civil to each other when they are away from the old battlefield of the home. They are not smiling at each other yet, but they have taken the first step toward reconciliation.

Others have a tougher time overcoming the hostility in a broken relationship. For example, after the divorce, Dick remarried and moved three hundred miles away. When he wants to find out about his three sons, he has to use the telephone. He has been doing this for five years now, but he still becomes unsettled every time he calls his children.

"I just know that before the conversation with my sons' mother is over, I am going to get angry—and I hate it," he confesses. "I pay my child support on time, and she still finds ways to get to me."

Yet reconciliation is possible in this situation too. And things would be much smoother for everyone concerned if it were effected. Life is difficult enough without people inflicting needless pain on each other.

The primary goal of reconciliation, . . . is . . . to be friendly again and bring back harmony.

The need for reconciliation does not occur only after years of marriage. Reconciliation may be necessary very early in a marriage. In one of my groups, a couple who had been married only three days separated. He filed for divorce. I began working with him so he would at least begin to be civil to her.

Sometimes the first reconciliation has to be to geography; that is, the people involved have to be able to remain in the same room or location for a period of time. In this particular case, as part of therapy, I met the woman at a large social function and said, "Okay, there are a lot of people in there. Let's go in."

"Is he in there?" she asked.

"Yes," I said as I opened the door and pushed her in.

I stood in the hallway, watching the four doors, and sure enough, one of them popped open and he came out just like a jack-in-the-box. I could see I still had a long way to go before I effected reconciliation for them.

I have used the word *reconciliation* several times so far, and I have also touched on the need for it. So what is reconciliation all about? The primary goal of reconciliation, as I will discuss it in this book, is to enable those of you who are angry, bitter, and hostile to be friendly again and bring back harmony, whether you are separated, divorced, or remarried. I will try to do this by helping you better understand yourself and your ex, by developing ways you may cope with potential areas of conflict, and by sharing steps you can take to defuse your anger.

SOME TERMS YOU NEED TO KNOW

Let me explain certain words I will use to describe stages that people go through as they relate to each other.

1. Friendship

I define *friendship* as "a deep and enduring affection built on mutual respect and esteem." It is genderless, which means you do the same things with either sex. It is nonexclusive, which indicates you may have many friends of both sexes. The support provided by a strong circle of friends makes you a better candidate for the next level of a relationship.

Unfortunately, many people say they do not want friends because that level of commitment is too low. They want a genuine relationship. Yet none of us is ready to handle the demands of a relationship until we have established the fact that we can operate at the friendship level with both males and females.

2. Relationship

When friends develop an intimate reliance upon each other, they have entered into a *relationship*. There are many kinds of relationships, but the relationship I refer to here is gender oriented—focused on the opposite sex—and mutually exclusive. That is, you can have only one at a time.

Many a seventeen-year-old, and a surprising number of older singles, attempt to cycle through three or four relationships at a time. Determined to find the best possible combination through an A, B, or C process of evaluation, these people can get into deep trouble.

How do you know when you have moved from friendship to a relationship? The clearest indicator is when you start doing things with the opposite sex you would not do comfortably with someone of the same sex. Once that happens, you have crossed the line from being a friend to entering into a relationship. All the rules change at that point, and you'd better know when that happens.

3. Marriage

I use the term *marriage* to describe "the union of two people in an emotional, moral, and legal convenantal agreement." Be aware of the dynamics of all three facets of marriage: emotional, moral, *and* legal.

4. Divorce

A *divorce* represents "the severing of the marital covenant by a legal decree and the sundering of the relationship." The legal aspect is eventually finalized when the decree is issued, but recognizing such a finality of the moral and emotional parts is much less easy to accomplish.

To describe what a divorce does to the emotional part of marriage, I used the word *sundering*. There is a ragged, rough tearing apart of a relationship. That is why it is so difficult to put back together again.

People make their biggest mistake when they feel they can deal with the moral and emotional parts simply by walking out and saying they are not in love anymore. Or they will walk out on a Friday night and feel free—free to date and do what they want, although they have not dealt with the legal aspects of marriage. Sooner or later their miscalculation catches up with them.

5. Reconciliation

In *reconciliation* people begin to deal with the moral and emotional parts, for the goal is to be friendly again and to bring back harmony. (Notice that the word *marriage* does not enter into the discussion here.)

A quick look at the British legal system may help. A conciliator works for the divorce court as a sort of family counselor. This person's goal is to conciliate the differences between the parties in the divorce and to reduce the hostility level so they can be friends again.

I say that reconciliation has been accomplished when both of you can carry on normal human communication. This is a goal to achieve at whatever your legal, moral, or emotional level. Your stomach does not knot up, your blood pressure does not rise anymore, and your voice does not rise in verbal communication. You are able to communicate with each other as you would with any person in your circle of acquaintances.

A GOAL WORTH TACKLING

Is that a goal worth tackling? Is it worth spending a few hours reading a book and many more in special effort? I think it is, and many people I have counseled agree that it is.

John and Judy were nineteen years old when they first met. They were in the air force at the time. John drove a truck, and Judy was a medic.

"Our barracks were not far apart, and one day I saw her walking toward her barracks. I decided I wanted to get to know her," recalls John.

They met at poolside.

"I swim like a rock, so we did a lot of sunbathing," he says. "I thought she was the most beautiful thing I had ever seen."

"And I thought he was so tall and good looking! I am five nine and love to wear high heels, so I get to be nearly six feet tall. And it was great to be able to look up to someone," says Judy.

They were married in the chapel at the base one year after first meeting. Greg came along quickly to cement the relationship as a family, and Dean was born four years later.

Once he got out of the service, John became a long-distance truck driver.

"I used to worry about his safety on his long trips. He would drive up to three days without sleeping. But I really didn't worry about anything else," Judy says.

John, on the other hand, found that there were a lot of eligible relationships on the road.

"I was not really serious about keeping our marriage together. I didn't really recognize the value of marriage, so I felt that the grass was always greener outside of my marriage," John says.

A vague dissatisfaction became a conviction that he should opt out of marriage.

"I can't really tell you why that dissatisfaction grew. Maybe it was because Judy began gaining weight after Greg was born, but I can't really put my finger on it," he recalls.

Judy never lost her love for John. As far as she was concerned, he was the best thing that had happened to her. Since she had grown up on a farm and developed self-sufficiency, she did not really mind coping with having her own job, doing all the work at home, and raising two boys while John was on the road.

"When he came home, he had a big home-cooked meal and poured out everything that had happened, all the frustrations and hassles. Then about eight-and-one-half years into our marriage I began to notice that he was not doing the sharing anymore. He came home angry, ate, and went to bed. And he would soon be off and on the road again," she reports.

One day John announced that he was leaving and wanted a divorce.

"I didn't do it nicely. I just blurted it out," he says.

Judy was stunned and angry. She was unable to really recognize why John wanted out of the marriage.

"He insisted that if I did not file for divorce, he would. We lived in Florida at the time, so we got our divorce in twenty-one days," Judy says.

Judy was the first to recognize her need for a personal faith in Jesus Christ. After that, "He wanted to come back again, so I let him live with me for a year. But I felt more and more guilty about it, so I asked him to leave," Judy says. They were divorced for six years, although they actually lived together off and on for the first three-and-a-half years.

Two years after that, John had a motorcycle accident in which he was injured, although he did not need hospitalization.

"I finally realized how bankrupt I really was. Then I remembered the little booklet, 'The Four Spiritual Laws,' that Judy had given me when she asked me to leave. I never kept anything, but for some reason I had kept this booklet. I found it and read it, praying the prayer of commitment," he says.

The next Sunday morning Judy could not believe her eyes when she saw John walk the aisle to the front of the church as a public confirmation of his commitment to Jesus Christ.

"I thought immediately that everything would be all right now, that we could get back together again. But his coming to faith in Christ didn't instantly solve everything," she says.

Gradually John realized that God was asking him to return to the relationship with Judy that he had abandoned.

"Through Scripture and as I thought about it, the Lord impressed me that we needed to be together again," he says.

The start was dinner at Judy's house, and the conclusion was a quick ceremony of remarriage before a justice of the peace in Reno in 1979.

How are they doing now?

"There were times after we remarried I wondered what I had done. I wasn't really that committed to him, but John's commitment to me was so deep. I could see how committed he was in the way he was determined to work out our problems—and that increased my commitment to him," Judy reports.

John says, "Jesus committed Himself to me when He died on the cross for me. Out of that commitment flows my commitment to His will for my life, and His will clearly is that I be married to Judy. That then becomes the basis of my commitment to Judy."

What John says points to a vital step in reconciliation. The apostle Paul described the process as follows, "Now all these things are from God, who reconciled us to Himself through Christ, and gave us the ministry of reconciliation, namely, that God was in Christ reconciling the world to Himself, not counting their trespasses against them, and He has committed to us the word of reconciliation" (2 Cor. 5:18–19). Once John had become reconciled to God through personal faith in Jesus and His death on the cross for us, he realized that he needed to be reconciled to Judy. Personal peace with God meant he could shift his efforts to achieving peace with his ex-wife.

That doesn't mean that absolute peace descended on his relationship with Judy. It took a year of effort for true reconciliation to take place and then daily effort to maintain the new relationship.

Even the great apostle Paul experienced a damaging rupture in a relationship at a time when he was ecstatic over the results of his first missionary trip. He and Barnabas enjoyed a marvelous reception as they reported on what God had done. But the time came for a second tour of the newly formed churches, and Paul sat down with Barnabas to discuss the travel arrangements.

"Paul, I think we ought to take John Mark along again as an intern. I know he abandoned us midway through the first trip, but I think he has learned his lesson. He will not be a quitter again," said Barnabas.

"Can't stand quitters. Never have and never will. He's not going along. We can do without him," Paul seems to have responded hotly. The historian Luke reported, "And there arose such a sharp disagreement that they separated from one another" (Acts 15:39).

Barnabas left with John Mark on his own tour, and Paul set out with Silas. Years went by. In his last letter, written while he was in prison in Rome, Paul charged Timothy, "Pick up Mark and bring him with you, for he is useful to me for service" (2 Tim. 4:11). Clearly, there had been a reconciliation!

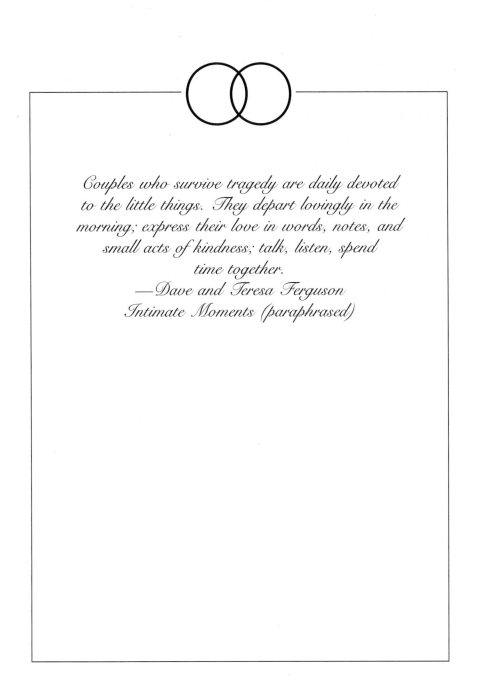

Couples who survive tragedy are daily devoted to the little things. They depart lovingly in the morning; express their love in words, notes, and small acts of kindness; talk, listen, spend time together.
—Dave and Teresa Ferguson
Intimate Moments (paraphrased)

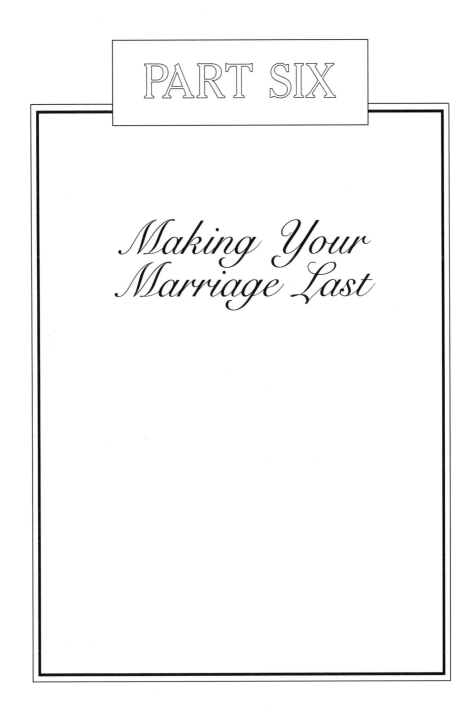

PART SIX

*Making Your
Marriage Last*

29

Building a Christian Marriage

*J*ust pray this prayer, commit your marriage to God, and everything will work out." The words of the Bible study leader were still ringing in Jill's and Sam's ears as they drove home. They had prayed again at the meeting, as they had in the past, that God would heal their marriage, but their communication was as bad as ever. Why didn't God answer their prayers? Shouldn't being a Christian make a difference in the quality of their marriage relationship?

Yes, it should. But it doesn't happen automatically by just praying a prayer any more than a marriage ceremony assures us of a great sexual relationship. Please don't misunderstand us. Having a deep, abiding personal faith in God has greatly benefited our marriage relationship. But to be honest, a few times our Christian walk actually caused friction.

"Building a Christian Marriage" is adapted from *The Marriage Track*, Dave and Claudia Arp (1992).

It wasn't until after we had children of our own that Christianity became a reality in our lives. As wonderful as our newfound faith was, it was not a panacea for all our problems. We remember stressful situations both before and after we discovered a vital faith in Jesus Christ. In other words, having Christ in our lives doesn't mean we automatically know and apply biblical principles to our marriage. It doesn't mean we will have a stress-free marriage—but the potential for improvement is there!

In the first years of our marriage, we had a great relationship even though our Christian faith was quite dormant. Relating to each other was easy for us. We were so "in love" that we felt secure. Sure, we had the usual disagreements, but we didn't experience any serious stress until our first son was born. Then reality began to hit us.

Just three weeks before our first child arrived we completed a move from Germany to Washington State (at the request of Uncle Sam). Stress was building even in our naturally wonderful marriage. A difficult birth and the added trauma of a baby who didn't breathe at first motivated Claudia to pray sincerely, "Please let this baby live, and we will do all we can to raise him in a Christian home!" God answered. He lived and is now a happily married attorney at law, but the in-between part, "raising him in a Christian home," just wasn't that simple.

After four years of marriage, we were used to our freedom and flexibility. Both came to an abrupt end when the first child arrived! Not only were our wings clipped, but we were totally exhausted. We had never really understood the ramifications of that little word *colic*. We got a quick education and had the bloodshot eyes to prove it!

For the first time we began to snap at each other. We weren't getting a very good start in establishing a Christian home. It seemed the harder we tried, the worse things got. Once in sheer desperation, Claudia left the apartment, got in the car, and drove around aimlessly for several hours. (You will appreciate that when you know that on Claudia's list of things she likes to do, driving is next to taking out the garbage or cleaning the bathroom!)

During this time, we were trying our best to stay on track in our marriage. Many long conversations brought us to the same basic conclusion—we were committed to each other and to our son, and we did desire to raise him in a Christian home. We just didn't know how.

Fast-forward with us a couple of years. Living in Atlanta, Georgia, and expecting our second child, we were still committed to having a Christian home, so we got involved in a church. We also renewed friendships with dear friends from our college days, and we began to piece together the elements of building a truly Christian home.

Seeds planted in our childhood began to take root. We both came to a new understanding of who Christ is, why He came to this earth, and what He personally did for us when He died on the cross. We accepted His offer of forgiveness for the past, eternal life for the future, and His daily personal involvement in our lives. As God began to be more real to us in our own personal lives, we began to experience His presence in our home.

Initially this was an "up" time in our lives and in our marriage —as if we had been plugged into a new power source. Finding our security and significance as individuals in our relationship with a living, loving, and caring God freed us to love and accept each other.

From this point it was smooth sailing. Right? Wrong! We sailed right into another time of incredible stress. Two children were even more confining than one. Dave's job as a marketing representative with IBM required quite a bit of travel, and our new faith, though wonderful, wasn't helping our communication. Claudia filled her free time with Bible studies, new Christian friends, and other activities. Dave, who had little discretionary time, resented her enthusiasm for all these "Christian" activities and felt ignored. To be honest, trying to live out our Christianity was complicating our lives, and things were getting worse, not better!

Consider two other couples. Dick and Sally, a Christian couple, were active in the church and appeared to have a deep abiding faith in the Lord. Dick was a deacon and worked with the youth group. Sally was involved in the women's program. Most people assumed they had a great marriage. But, without a word, Dick left his wife and family.

How could a couple love God with all their hearts, base their lives on their Christian faith, yet experience marriage derailment? Christian marriages should be the most stable marriages around. Knowing Christ personally should make a difference!

The second couple, Jim and Sherry, had little interest in spiritual matters, but had a great marriage relationship. We met this couple in Vienna, Austria, where Jim held a high position in his country's embassy. Sherry was a freelance writer and active in the community. They were both involved with each other and with their children. Although in a high-pressure environment, Jim and Sherry made their marriage and family a high priority. God really didn't play an active role in their daily lives. But their marriage seemed to be alive and growing; their children, happy and well adjusted. They were fun to be around and could have written the script for the "Cosby" show.

Wait. Didn't someone mess up the script or juggle the couples? Shouldn't Dick and Sally have the growing marriage and Jim and Sherry be the statistic? For years we have puzzled over marriages that function great outside the church and marriages that barely hang on within the church. But as we looked closer, we began to understand. A marriage of two Christians doesn't automatically make a Christian marriage.

We don't have to look very deeply today to see statistics that Christian marriages are breaking up in great numbers, and sadly those numbers include Christian leaders and pastors. In some churches divorce seems epidemic. Recently a pastor commented to us that he spends most of his time counseling couples and trying to help keep their marriages intact.

Biblical principles for building positive relationships work! But only if you use them and apply them to your marriage. Jim and Sherry unknowingly were tapping into solid, healthy, biblical principles for building positive relationships, so they built an alive, functioning, growing marriage. Dick and Sally, although they loved God and were trying to serve and honor Him, were not applying those biblical principles.

Let's go back to our situation in Atlanta as we struggled to integrate our newfound faith into our marriage. We had become so involved in our Christian activities (or at least Claudia had) that our time for each other was sketchy and shallow, but we were determined to do something about it. We wanted to get back on track. We wanted to have a Christian marriage. But just what made a marriage uniquely Christian?

What Is a "Christian" Marriage?

A Christian marriage involves three—the husband, the wife, and God. As we grew individually in our relationship with God, we also grew closer together. First, we realized that we were each responsible to God for our individual relationship with Him. But as we grew closer to God, our tracks moved closer together and gave us a common focus in life.

A Christian marriage involves three—the husband, the wife, and God.

An enriched, healthy, Christian marriage team involves three. A cord of three strands is much stronger than a two-cord strand. A relationship with God strengthens a Christian marriage. Personally we discovered that "a cord of three strands is not easily broken."

Christian Marriage—A New Way of Communicating

Another unique resource in a Christian marriage is prayer. God delights in the praise and prayers of His people and tells us if we lack wisdom to ask and He will give it liberally to us (James 1:5).

We began the habit of praying together, which we have continued over the years. Sometimes it's easy. Other times it's hard. When our relationship with each other is not running smoothly, it's difficult, if not impossible, for us to pray together. Sometimes we could only pray, "Lord, help us to get back on track so we can pray together!" Amazingly, He answered that prayer.

Another hindrance to praying together was that one of us was more verbal than the other and could "out pray" the other. We discovered if we first made a list of things we wanted to pray about and took turns praying, we concentrated on communicating with God, not trying to impress one another.

Are you in the habit of praying together? Maybe like us, you are hesitant, shy, or reserved. Or maybe you'd like to pray together but just don't know how to get started. Why not take a few minutes right now and make a start? You may want to list things you'd like to commit to the Lord in prayer. For instance, maybe you are struggling with finances or dealing with a strong-willed child. Perhaps you've been hesitant to share with your mate how you really feel about things. Whatever concerns you, pray about it together.

A word of caution: Don't use prayer for attacking your mate. If you're just beginning to pray together, don't start with the most tense situation, like the mate who prayed, "Lord, please help my mate to understand and meet my sexual needs."

A Christian Marriage Follows the Teachings of Christ

When we began to establish a prayer life together, we also began to study the Scriptures to learn what Jesus taught about relationships. Apart from the principles of leaving, cleaving, and becoming one flesh, Jesus had little to say directly about the husband-wife relationship, but He did lay down principles for living that may be applied to all human relationships.

When asked what was the greatest commandment of all, Jesus replied, "Love the LORD your God with all your heart, with all your soul, with all your mind, and with all your strength. . . . Love your neighbor as yourself. There is no commandment greater than these" (Mark 12:30–31).

At the human level, the key word is *neighbor.* In the Old Testament, *neighbor* can mean fellow countryman, dweller, friend, or inhabitant. But in the New Testament, *neighbor* means the person closest to you. And for any married person that is the marriage partner, the one chosen to share life at its deepest and most intimate level. If we love our marriage partner as we love ourselves, we will have his or her best interests at heart, we will want to serve, not be served, and we will resist the urge to manipulate or pull power plays. We will have a relationship based on love and trust. We will also fulfill the original promise in Genesis 2—that God gave Adam and Eve to each other because each needed, above all else, a companion.

Not only did Jesus have much to say about building positive relationships, but He also modeled those principles. His life on this planet demonstrated love in action. So many times marital conflict would be resolved if we followed the example of Christ. Too often we are "me" centered and want things to work out "my" way. Christ taught just the opposite approach. Consider some of the ways Jesus modeled the essence of positive relationships.

Christian Marriage—A New Way of Serving

Jesus said that the first shall be last and the last shall be first, that we should choose to give rather than to receive. Our marriage relationships would be revolutionized if we approached marriage as servants. Jesus washed the disciples' feet. We just want someone to wash the dishes.

It's hard to learn to serve each other, especially in the closeness of a marriage relationship. We never have functioned very well in our marriage when one or the other has to travel. It was especially hard when our children were small and Dave traveled a lot. He would come home exhausted and tired of people. One such time still stands out in our memory. He was selling data processing services to small-to-medium-sized companies and had worked for months with one particular company. At the last minute, when the company was actually supposed to sign the contract, it reneged, and Dave came home empty-handed—all ready to jump into his shell and hibernate.

Claudia, on the other hand, had been at home with two preschoolers. The older had just shared the chicken pox with the younger, and Claudia was "itching" to get out of the house and have some adult conversation.

We were both so caught up in our own miseries that we didn't serve one another. We had to regroup, apologize, and start over again. To be honest, years later, we still get caught in the web of "my needs" and "your needs." Knowing the principle doesn't mean we always apply it. But that is our goal, and sometimes we remember!

Why not make a list of ways you can serve your mate today (like being sensitive to your mate's mood)? If Claudia had not crowded Dave when he came home discouraged from his business trip, things could have gone differently. Or maybe you could give up what you want to do for your mate. For example, Dave could have gone the extra "servant mile" and taken Claudia out for a couple of hours before withdrawing into his shell.

Christian Marriage—A New Way of Loving

In a Christian marriage not only are we to serve one another, but we are to love one another unconditionally. Christ loves us not "if" or "because" we do or don't do certain things. He loves us "in spite of" what we do or don't do. We should love our mate the same way!

If you want to see if you are loving your mate unconditionally, read through 1 Corinthians 13 and substitute your name for "love." Here are several verses to get you started: "_____ is patient, _____ is kind. _____ does not envy; _____ does not boast, is not proud. _____ is not rude, _____ is not self-seeking, _____ is not easily angered, _____ keeps no record of wrongs. _____ does not delight in evil but rejoices with the truth. _____ always protects, _____ always trusts, _____ always hopes, _____ always perseveres" (NIV).

How did you do? Not so well? You may be thinking that you just can't do that. And you're right. Jesus models a supernatural kind of love. He alone can give us the power to love our mates in this way. On the other hand, we need to realize that love is a choice we can make. Too often, if we don't feel loving, we think that love has died. A German doctor, Dr. Arne Hoffman, told us that the biochemical phase of love is sometimes over in as little as three months after the ceremony. Unconditional love is much more than a romantic, tingly feeling. Tingles come and go, but real love manifests itself in the trenches of life.

Sometimes we give each other unconditional love in the hard times—when Dave's migraine headache just wouldn't go away and we had to cancel our dinner out with friends and Claudia resisted the urge to complain, or when Claudia had a root canal and the dentist said, "Take a couple of aspirin when you get home and you'll be just fine." Who was he kidding? Not Claudia, whose tolerance level for pain is slightly above zero. Through the throbbing pain that night she appreciated Dave's ice packs, Jell-O®, and gentleness. In other times and other situations, our unconditional love hasn't been that unconditional, but sometimes we do follow the example of Christ. Let us challenge you to let Jesus be your model and help you put love into action.

Christian Marriage—A Deeper Acceptance

Jesus is our model of how we are to accept each other. Picture this scenario. Jesus, the Son of God, is about to be baptized. Whom does He choose for this great honor? A weird-looking character named John the Baptist. If we had been Jesus, we would have requested that John get some decent clothes for the occasion and visit the local hairdresser. Unlike us, Jesus had the ability to look at the heart, not the appearance.

Are we accepting our mates? Do we often react to surface issues? Claudia will never forget one summer when she decided to get her hair cut—we're talking really cut. It was even shorter than Claudia had expected, and Dave's nonaccepting comment, "It makes you look older, doesn't it?" definitely made Claudia look more angry!

It's not always easy to accept that extra ten pounds you wish your mate would lose or having to live on a restrictive budget or the little irritating habit that won't go away. A starting point to deeper acceptance might be to list ways you know deep down inside you need to accept your mate.

359

Being a Christian doesn't give you instant marital success. As Christ demonstrated, relationships take time and work. Let's go back to our two couples. Maybe you, like Dick and Sally, really love God and desire to serve and honor Him, but your marriage relationship is a struggle. Or maybe you identify with Jim and Sherry. You have a workable, growing marriage relationship, but you wonder if there isn't more.

After we moved back to the States, we kept up with Jim and Sherry for several years. While their marriage remained intact, their situation changed drastically. Jim was part of the fallout of reshuffling at his country's embassy, and he spent almost two years job hunting. At this time the "good life" was not so good to them. When we lived in Vienna, we talked several times with Jim and Sherry about our faith in Christ, and while interest was not too high at that point, we have often wondered if perhaps circumstances have increased their interest in spiritual things. There are no atheists in foxholes.

Being a Christian doesn't give you instant marital success.

Where do you turn when you are in the foxholes of your marriage? This is the place that our Christian faith has really made a difference.

One Foxhole Experience

The day started no differently from any other day, but our lives would never quite be the same again. Dave called to say that he would be a couple of hours late, but gave no explanation. Claudia assumed another big project had come up at work, but Dave's story was something completely different!

Claudia knew he had been frustrated in his job but wasn't prepared for his announcement, "Honey, I quit!"

"But how are we going to live?" was Claudia's immediate response. We had two sons, a house payment, and a meager savings account.

"I'm really not sure," Dave responded. "But you know I've been dissatisfied at work. Well, I prayed about it. I prayed that the company would let me transfer to another division, but it didn't work out, so I assumed God was leading me to another job somewhere else."

"Did you ever consider," Claudia interjected, "that He might want you to keep your present job while you looked for another one?"

If you have ever gone through a job change (by choice or otherwise) you know that fear in the pit of your stomach, which privately tells you, "I might starve to death." If our Christian faith could really make a difference in our marriage and lives, here was the acid test!

Here are the differences as we remember them many years later. First we were able to commit our situation to God and pray about it. That third cord in our three strands held firm and steady even though our two cords were wobbly. When we became fearful about the unknown future, we acknowledged that God was with us in this adventure and would continue to lead and care for us.

Secondly, we found our identity and significance as individuals in who we were in Christ. This gave us a real sense of security. Claudia was not just "the wife of an unemployed husband," and Dave wasn't just "the husband of an insecure, somewhat frightened wife"! We were both children of God, and we sensed He had a purpose for our lives. Finding our security in our relationship with the Lord, we were able to accept each other and pull together and not apart. With God's help we tried to support one another.

Another job did come along—one much better suited to Dave's talents and abilities and one that eventually led us to our work together in marriage and family enrichment. This wasn't an easy time in our lives; we would not like to repeat it. But in thinking about this situation twenty-something years later, we're able to see how our Christian faith allowed us to stretch and take the risk, to step out of our comfort zone and to do it together.

Does knowing Christ make a difference? In *The Sacred Fire* Drs. David and Vera Mace say: "What the New Testament makes possible for a man, a woman, or a married couple is an encounter with Jesus of Nazareth. Therefore, it is only those who have encountered the ever-living Christ and have surrendered their lives to Him who will surely know how to make their marriages truly Christian."[1]

Christ demonstrated how to live, and He will empower us to express love, to be sensitive to the needs of another, to be open and honest, to act considerately and unselfishly, to deal with anger and conflict, to forgive and be reconciled, and to reflect God's love in our love for each other. When we incorporate these qualities into our lives, they will make our marriages truly Christian!

HAVING AN INTENTIONAL MARRIAGE

Let us encourage you to take some time right now to reflect on where you are in your marriage and in your spiritual pilgrimage and in which direction you want to move. Discovering where you are and where you want to go in your marriage relationship can be exciting.

To pull it all together, we suggest writing out your very own Declaration of Intention, a general statement of the goals you want to achieve as a couple. Businesses and organizations spend immense amounts of time to come up with a mission statement —the essence of what they want to accomplish. Your Declaration of Intention is the mission statement for your marriage.

You can make it as simple or elaborate as you want. The key is that you both agree with your final statement. In our Marriage Alive Workshop, couples write out their Declaration of Intention for their marriage as a contract of what they both want to see happen. Usually we don't see what the couples come up with, but recently a couple shared theirs with us. It was so creative that we asked permission to share it with you. Since commitment is so central to the marriage relationship, they wrote an acrostic using the word *commitment.*

OUR DECLARATION OF INTENTION

C—Christ-centered relationship

O—Openness in our communication

M—Maintain awareness of the state of our relationship

M—Mount full-scale war against the one who would tear us apart—not each other

I —Intentional in the application of skills learned

T—Team work is our goal—both of us are necessary, therefore both have valuable input

M—Model for our children and others the teaching of Christ

E—Encourage each other in maintaining an eternal perspective

N—Nurture each other, spiritually, physically, emotionally

T—Train for the road before us, trust one another, train up our children in the way they should go

Personally Applied

One of the great benefits of our work in marriage enrichment over the years is that it has motivated us to continue to work at having our own "intentional marriage." As you can glean from the pages of *The Marriage Track,* our marriage is in process, hopefully in the direction of growth. The argument we had after completing the chapter on communication was not intentional! But we continue to work at the task of building a positive, healthy Christian marriage—to work at keeping our marriage on track.

We keep our own personal Marriage Declaration of Intention in a somewhat fluid state, ever looking for better ways to express the intentions of our marriage. As of our last edit, here is our Declaration of Intention. We hope it will encourage you to dig deep to find your own unique statement of your marriage.

DECLARATION OF INTENTION

As a couple we are committed to the pursuit of the following goals for our marriage team:

· A commitment to growth by regularly setting goals and objectives for our marriage
· A commitment to communicate our true feelings, to build up and encourage each other, and to process and work through anger and conflict situations
· A commitment to find space in our togetherness and unity in our diversity and to continue to grow as individuals
· A commitment to strive to be a model for our own children and for others of the outworking of the teachings of Christ about creative love in close relationships

Writing Our Declaration of Intention

Now write out your Declaration of Intention. Take plenty of time and work together until you are both satisfied with the wording and content.

DECLARATION OF INTENTION

_____

_____

_____

_____

_____

_____

Signed: _____   _____

Date: _____

Have Fun Along the Way!

Our marriage has been enriched by our ability to laugh and play together. Laughter dispels tension and is physically healthy for the body! It's also like a vitamin for the soul!

We asked a friend what he remembered about his parents— what special heritage they passed down to him that had enriched his marriage and family life. He thought for a moment and said, "There are two things that stand out in my mind. At first they didn't seem to be related, but the more I think about it, they really are. One—I remember my parents praying together. Whatever hard situations we were facing in our family, we prayed about it. The second thing I remember is hearing my parents roaring with laughter. They made sure that they had fun together as a couple and with us as a family."

We hope this chapter has encouraged you to pray together and make your marriage truly a Christian marriage. We also want to encourage you to have dates, to talk, to play, and to laugh. To help you do this, we have designed fifty-two dates for mates, which you can read about in our book *52 Dates for You and Your Mate* (Nashville: Nelson, 1992). These dates will help you to have fun tracking on your own.

An enriched, fun-loving Christian marriage can make a difference in our quality of life. We can stay on track and leave the heritage of a positive marriage track for our offspring and their spouses to follow. Take the advice of many who returned from the Gulf War. In their foxholes, they had the time to evaluate their lives and make some decisions about what is really of value. They said, "I'm going to spend time with my wife/husband/family. . . . My faith in God has been strengthened. . . . I'm going to work harder on my marriage. . . . Relationships are what is really important. . . . I just want to be with those I love."

How about you? You don't have to wait until another war or until a crisis. Now is the time to build the relationship with your mate. Now is the time to establish a truly Christian marriage. Now is the time to get your marriage on track!

Chapter

30

Realize Who You Are

Laura, at thirty-nine, was a very attractive woman. Her reddish hair and brown eyes and smooth olive skin were set against the despair on her face. She sat in Tim's office, softly weeping like a child.

"I feel like I've lost *me*," she lamented. "I'm the frame who holds everyone else together. They have their dreams, hopes, and lives; but when I try to do something for me, it gets sandwiched in between their needs. When I sit down to eat a sundae, everybody comes along and wants a bite. By the time they have all had their bite, I don't even feel like eating it. I can't even read the paper without constantly getting interrupted. I feel like I have to be everything to everybody—if I don't it will fall apart. And when I do something for myself, I feel selfish!"

Laura looked at Tim. "I adapt to everyone," she said. "I take

"Realize Who You Are" is adapted from *That Man!* William and Nancie Carmichael and Dr. Timothy Boyd (1988).

on their hurts. If they have a wound, I feel the pain. If they are depressed, I get down. I've found out that I've been so busy adapting that I have lost my sense of who I am. My husband says I'm the Hercules of Guilt. I take responsibility for everyone on my shoulders."

Laura went on to describe another aspect of her dilemma. She feared quitting her job as a realtor because many of her feelings of self-esteem were tied up in her job success. What at home could compare to the strokes she got at work? She felt guilty, however, because she wasn't at home with her children, and she also had a desire to be a full-time mother. She vacillated back and forth between guilt and despair.

"I have a heritage of despair!" Laura sarcastically said. Laura came from a family where there was a great gulf between her mother and father. So she found it hard to determine how much of her hopelessness about her marriage came from the pain and feelings of emptiness that she had brought into the relationship and how much was the result of the problems of her marriage.

WHAT IS IDENTITY?

Laura experienced a sense of confusion in regard to who she was. The name for that inner sense of who we are is *identity*. We are not born with a sense of self—it develops over time. Women's development of opinions, goals, ideas, dreams, and values can be impeded by the cultural insistence that they adapt to what others need them to be. Just as a plant can become pot-bound, with its growth stifled in a too-small pot, we can become culture-bound, locked into roles that stifle the development of our identity.

In *The Screwtape Letters*, C. S. Lewis described how God wants us to be in His image but does not try to take away our will. In the words of a senior demon to a junior demon, Lewis wrote:

> "I know that the Enemy also wants to detach men from themselves, but in a different way. Remember always, that He

really likes the little vermin, and sets an absurd value on the distinctness of every one of them. When He talks of their losing their selves, He only means abandoning the clamour of self-will; once they have done that, He really gives them back all of their personality, and boasts (I am afraid, sincerely) that when they are wholly His they will be themselves more than ever. Hence, while He is delighted to see them sacrificing even their innocent wills to His, he hates to see them drifting away from their own nature for any other reason. And we should always encourage them to do so. The deepest likings and impulses of any man are the raw material, the starting point, with which the Enemy has furnished him. To get him away from those is therefore always a point gained; even in things indifferent, it is always desirable to substitute the standards of the World, or convention, or fashion, for a human's own real likings and dislikings."[1]

What Lewis described as our "own nature" or our "deepest likings and impulses" is our identity. God desires to develop our sense of self, but the world system wants our conformity. Appearance, performance, and status are all goals that are achieved by works. Identity is achieved by the development of the innate personality given to us by God. King David described the way God formed our inward parts and wove us together in our mother's womb, implying that each of us had a unique potential self even before birth (Ps. 139:13).

Taking Inventory

The next step in your being transformed is to take an inventory of your current sense of self. It is important to assess your identity thoroughly. Consider your strengths and weaknesses, your resources, your belief system, your motivation, your level of hope, your goals, and your dreams.

Sit down, take out a piece of paper, and describe yourself to yourself.

1. Who are you?
2. What is it that makes you *you?*
3. How do you feel about your future?
4. Do you look forward to facing a new day?

5. Do you like challenges, or do you shy away from taking risks?

After you've finished, ask yourself what you've discovered. Do you now have a clear self-description which makes you feel good, or do you have a sense of confusion? Perhaps you, like others we've talked to, have only a blank piece of paper. If so, you will no doubt benefit from what we have to say in the remainder of this chapter.

We've found that a woman often becomes angry because "he seems to get to do whatever he wants to do" and she feels *she* has to do what he wants to do also. Rather than trying to get him to stop his activities, she needs to develop her own activities and accomplishments.

If you do not know yourself well enough to have a clear sense of your tasks, options, feelings, insights (the components of any identity), how can you communicate to your partner a clear, concise message? When he asks where you would like to go for supper, "I feel like eating Chinese food tonight, but I am open to your preference," is much more productive than "I don't know. Where do you want to go?"

Taking Control

When we do not have a secure identity, we often live our lives out of control. Being out of control means that we start at tasks from a position of helplessness and feel at a loss to achieve mastery. When we are out of control, our inner hunger is so strong that we have difficulty delaying gratification long enough to get near our goal. This generates a vicious cycle that progresses in a downward spiral. I'm weak—I have a task; I'm overwhelmed—I can't complete my tasks; I feel even weaker—I try again; I fail—and on and on.

Usually there are specific symptoms of being out of control. Eating habits (overeating or crash diets), negative attitudes (being sarcastic, criticizing, nagging, complaining), overwhelming emotions (tearfulness, temper, fears), compulsive spending (credit card buying beyond our means), and our excessive fantasy lives are all examples.

---

*When we do not have a secure identity,
we often live our lives out of control.*

One could also call these *compulsive behaviors* addictions. Behavioral scientists are now finding striking similarities among all types of addictions, be they drugs, alcohol, overeating, sex, or whatever.

Sandra Simpson LeSourd, in *The Compulsive Woman*, tells us the compulsive woman is:

· The woman who volunteers for everything, who can't say no.
· The woman whose TV is on all day long or who lives her life around soap operas.
· The woman whose life revolves around food. She eats too much—or too little. Sweets are often her downfall.
· The woman who is an exercise nut, jogging miles every day, rain or shine.
· The woman who, when she needs a high, shops while debts pile up.
· The woman who is a chain-smoker or a closet alcoholic; hooked on prescription drugs or sex or dependent on male approval for her sense of worth.
· The woman who is easy prey for psychics, spiritualists, cults.
· The perfectionist who never lives up to her own expectations. Her natural drive and energy have become distorted; her motor is running wild. She has an irrational need to do something over and over to the point where she has lost control.[2]

Compulsive behaviors are often misguided attempts to take control of our lives. It's as if we are saying, "Look, I've got everything under control."

Dependent on Others

When we lack identity, we often blame others for our emptiness and frustration. Women frequently blame their husbands for
their unhappiness. "It's all his fault that I'm so miserable. I'd be
happy if he would just _____ (you fill in the blank)."

Women who devote themselves to trying to meet their husbands' every need typically become frustrated: angry at their
mates because it's "never enough" and guilty because *they* aren't
enough. In addition, their husbands usually become bored with
them. Most of the wives' energy goes into "pleasing" behaviors,
which leaves little energy for personal growth and development.

Women have an unfortunate tendency to submerge their identities within their husbands' or children's identities. Scott Peck, in
The Road Less Traveled, said:

> There is nothing wrong with needing each other; we are
> created with a basic need for relationships. It is when we center
> our lives around another—when we are so busy trying to get them
> to notice us—to value us—to meet our needs—that we lose our
> sense of self. We become dependent in an unhealthy way. People
> with this disorder, passive dependent people, are so busy seeking
> to be loved that they have no energy left to love.[3]

Martha was an example of this type of person. She looked to
her husband to demonstrate God's love for her. As a result, she
kept him at the *center* of her emotional life. Her husband rein-
forced this by insisting that she devote herself to his needs. "He
wanted me to worship him," Martha commented. When she was
able to move God into the center of her life, she grew in inward
security.

Maybe you are not at this extreme, but you can identify with
the tendency. Perhaps a man in your life desires to have you
center your life around him. Guard against making him the
source of your own identity.

Peck said:

One of the aspects of dependency is that it is unconcerned with spiritual growth. Dependent people are interested in their own nourishment, but no more; they desire filling, they desire to be happy; they don't desire to grow, nor are they willing to tolerate the unhappiness, the loneliness and suffering involved in growth. Neither do dependent people care about the spiritual growth of the other, the object of their dependency; they care only that the other is there to satisfy them.[4]

In our research we discovered that many women experience a deep inner sense of despair, an empty space at the center of their beings. They may experience the depth of this when the youngest child leaves home or when the husband forms a relationship with his secretary, but the loneliness lurks even in the best of times. This emptiness seems to be related to a hunger for meaning, for a sense of self that is rooted and draws up nourishment from the ground of their beings.

This vacuum cannot be filled by centering your identity on any human relationship, an unfortunate tendency of many. When something disrupts the role of wife or mother, those women who have centered their life on those identities will feel bereft of meaning. They feel more like a function than a person, more hollow than solid. If being "me" means "what I do for them," I will be bankrupt when "they" no longer need me or their need changes.

It is difficult to assess your own needs clearly when you feel you are emotionally starving. It's like going grocery shopping right before supper when you've had no lunch. One woman said, "I'm getting hungrier, and I despise my neediness."

In *Unfinished Business,* Maggie Scarf stated:

> Women are so very powerfully invested in their affectional relationships—and derive such a sense of self from these vital emotional connections—that their very inner selves become intertwined with other selves, the selves to which they've become so powerfully attached. And women feel powerless, humiliated, and helpless to correct the situation. It is in women's willingness to put or ante up so much of her "self" into relationships that she places herself at so much greater risk. For these bonds are so much

a part of herself, and are experienced so powerfully, that she often responds to their loss or disruption or disintegration with a full range of depressive symptomatology.[5]

When our goal is to be loved, we will continually be disappointed. We need to change our focus to being the kind of a person who is loving, rather than to figuring out how we can hook others into loving us. When we seek at all costs to preserve our relationships, we lose our sense of self. We become so absorbed in trying to pick up on all the cues from our partner that we tend to lose touch with our own self.

MARTYRDOM/SELF-CENTEREDNESS: TWO SIDES OF THE SAME COIN

In chapter 8 of *That Man!* we considered our value as individuals, and discussed the fact that Christian women often find themselves confused over how to act sacrificially in meeting the needs of others, yet assertively in meeting their own needs. They reject the message from the world system that says, "Take care of Number One." But often, instead of developing a healthy self-esteem, they go to the extreme of becoming martyrs, who think in patterns such as, "It doesn't matter if you walk all over me; I'll give you whatever you want." Women who play the martyr role for any length of time generally become bitter and resentful. Although they often deny this resentment, it manifests itself in distorted ways, such as psychosomatic illnesses, alcohol dependence, eating disorders.

When we seek at all costs to preserve our realtionships, we lose our sense of self.

In contrast, other women reach the point of exasperation in pouring themselves out for their men. In turning 180 degrees, they become self-centered. They withdraw from relationships by shutting down their feelings of warmth, by getting into emotional or physical affairs, or even by initiating a divorce. Some women vacillate between self-denial and self-centeredness, trying to get their needs met. These options are neither healthy nor biblical, and rarely do any of them work toward the desired result. The following diagram outlines these two destructive extremes:

Self-centered ← *(Extremes)* → *Martyred*
(I am oriented to get (I give up *all* my needs—
what I want in my others' needs are more
relationships.) important than mine.)

Let's take a closer look at these two no-win extremes. As we have already stated, self-centeredness is not the same as self-love.

Selfishness is a form of greed. Greed is insatiable, like a bottomless pit. Selfish people are always concerned with self and fear not getting the best for themselves. Selfish people rarely are fond of themselves. This type of narcissism stems basically from a lack of self-love.

A martyr, on the other hand, has the goal of eliciting a certain kind of response from others. One man complained about his wife's martyr-type behavior this way:

> She's always waiting on us at dinner time, jumping up from the table to get something for the kids, who could just as easily get up and get it themselves. Later she'll complain about it, but she'll never just say, "I'm tired, please get it yourself." She'll harp about how the kids don't obey her, but she rarely takes the necessary disciplinary action to correct the situation. She often complains about feeling sick but puts off making an appointment to visit the doctor. It makes me angry that she gripes about her situation, but always winds up with the "never-mind-I'll-do-it-myself" or the "It's-OK-I'll-tough-it-out" attitude.

This woman is manipulating her situation, trying to gain affirmation and self-esteem by doing everything for everyone. She has somehow believed the false message that performance will win love and respect. While the martyr role may seem to produce the desired results for a time, ultimately the martyr's effectiveness in manipulating those around her will break down. It's a destructive "give-to-get" cycle that will eventually leave her exhausted and resentful.

THE SACRIFICIAL MODEL

An alternative model to the martyrdom versus selfishness dilemma, and one that integrates with Scripture, is the example of a sacrificial Christ. Christ was certainly not self-centered but gave of Himself sacrificially. His acts of self-sacrifice were never done out of feelings of guilt or obligation but were done on the basis of wise choices (based on what He knew were His resources and the other person's legitimate need). Christ used discernment when others expressed to Him their needs. He looked deep into people's hearts to determine what they *really* needed. And He acted according to what He knew to be most loving for the other person.

In addition, Christ acted according to His awareness of His available resources. In more than one instance recorded in the Scriptures He walked away from people with needs. In Luke 5:15–16, we are told that "great multitudes came together to hear, and to be healed by Him of their infirmities. So He Himself often withdrew into the wilderness and prayed." He knew He needed renewal, or He would be operating on an empty tank (a setup for trouble).

As we attempt to follow Christ, we need His insight and discernment: insight into our own needs and discernment with regard to others' needs. As we understand the importance of nurturing ourselves, as we give sacrificially to others, we will be able to strike a balance. Looking to the continuum, we will be somewhere between self-needs and others' needs.

Meeting My   →   *(Balance)*   ←   *Meeting the Needs*
Own Needs   ↓   *of Others*

Healthy Self-nurturance and Other-Sacrifice

Remember Laura who felt sandwiched between everybody else's needs? She decided to start working on learning how to say no. Soon she was confronted with a difficult situation. A teacher from her son's school called her and asked her to switch the day she was going to help in her son's class. The teacher said that no other mother was willing to switch. Laura had, on previous occasions, accommodated her schedule, but on this occasion she had made plans to meet with friends. Her first impulse was to say yes, and she wondered what the teacher would think of her if she said no. She then took a deep breath and said, "I'm sorry. I know how hard you've been working to set this up. I usually don't say no. In fact, I have a hard time doing that. But it is important that I keep my other plans." The teacher was miffed, but backed off, and was able to make other arrangements.

When Laura got off the phone, she felt guilty about saying no, but she also sensed a growing confidence. It was her first step toward a balanced self-nurturance.

One who sacrifices in a healthy way has transcendent goals that are related to the values they hold. They choose to give of themselves out of inner motivations. Our model of this kind of sacrifice is Jesus, "the author and finisher of our faith, who for the joy that was set before Him endured the cross, despising the shame" (Heb. 12:2). We are told to keep our eyes on Him when we are giving ourselves sacrificially in order that we may not "become weary and discouraged in [our] souls" (Heb. 12:3).

If you are in a difficult relationship and are choosing to "hang in there," remember why you are doing what you are doing. You can continue giving and investing yourself if you look to the potential reward. Perhaps that reward will be a transformed relationship in which you can one day be intimate with your husband. In the short range you can take encouragement in the knowledge that you are modeling Christ.

THE WORK OF LOVE

Following Christ's model moves us toward healthy, Christ-like *love*. Love is not a putting down of myself—it expresses my self-hood. I choose to love. I want to love.

Love is work, the expenditure of emotional energy. It is not measurable by how many dollars are made on a given day as is true of the work of an executive secretary or company manager, but it is hard work nonetheless. Women are often doing the work of love in their families, but they have difficulty measuring the achievement. All of the activities that we do with our children—listening patiently to elephant jokes, playing "Go Fish" for the umpteenth time, or chauffeuring the kids to the baseball game—are forms of attention. They require work and can be acts of love depending on our attitude. We can rob ourselves of the self-re-plenishing nature of love when we do these things out of a sense of obligation (which leads to feelings of resentment). *The acts require the same expenditure of energy, but we experience very different internal results.*

In the *Equal Rights Monitor,* a not-so-funny comic strip showed one woman telling another, "If I spend my days cleaning bathtubs and toilets, my status as a female is equal to a groveling worm. . . . But if I go to work for the sewer company, I'll make headlines as a feminist star. . . . What makes the same job an insult if you do it at home, but an honor if you make it a career?" The answer, "Money."[6]

Paul addressed our tendency to devalue what we see as less honorable. In 1 Corinthians 12, he said that "those members of the body which seem to be weaker are necessary" (v. 22), and are deserving of "greater honor" (v. 23).

When you are doing boring, routine, or menial work, it is helpful to keep Paul's words in Colossians 3:23–24 in mind. They will help you to enlarge your focus to the meaning behind your labor. "Whatever you do, do it heartily, as to the Lord and not to men, knowing that from the Lord you will receive the reward of the inheritance; for you serve the Lord Christ."

Giving away genuine love renews us rather than depletes us.

We are renewed because our sense of personal worth and self-hood is built up when we give unconditionally. Jesus said, "He who finds his life will lose it, and he who loses his life for My sake will find it" (Matt. 10:39).

When we break out of our old patterns of seeking to be loved and learn how to love others, we help the others develop their own identity—to become all that God created them to be. Dietrich Bonhoeffer said,

> Human love constructs its own image of the other person, of what he is and what he should become. It takes the life of the other person into its own hands. Spiritual love recognizes the true image of the other person which he has received from Jesus Christ; the image that Jesus Christ Himself embodied and would stamp on all of me.[7]

True love is a commitment to the development, security, and well-being of the one being loved. If I love you, I will be committed to fulfilling your needs. However, a fine line separates needs from wants. We are not called to fulfill selfish wants. Rather, we must constantly read the needs of those we love, since their needs will continue to change. As John Powell said: "I must be asking: What do you need me to be today, this morning, tonight? Are you discouraged and in need of my strength? Have you experienced some success and are you inviting me to rejoice, to celebrate with you? Or are you lonely and need only my hand softly in your?"[8]

This is why we say that love is hard work. We must be truly listening, looking, learning, and adapting to needs if we are going to be effective lovers. This will give us the necessary insights to discern between needs and wants. It may be that what is wanted is not what is needed. It may be that the need at that moment is to tell another the truth, which they may not *want* to hear.

The person giving out love must choose what real love is at that moment. Of course we will make mistakes sometimes, but as John Powell emphasized, "More important than the rightness or the wrongness of my judgments will always be the fact that I did what I did because I loved you."[9]

In the end, love is a challenge to the one being loved to mature, to develop, to produce fruit on his own. Love is two people in the give-and-take demands of life, committed to each other's ultimate success and well-being.

31

Four Biblical Principles of Money Management

It's said that money and sex are the two areas of married life that give couples the most trouble. Since the book you are holding in your hand covers the latter subject quite thoroughly, I'll stick to the first one! I've included the next two chapters from Master Your Money *because I believe that few things are as important to a healthy marriage as a wise use of financial resources. Understanding the financial principles outlined in Scripture is the beginning of financial wisdom, and putting together a financial plan for your marriage and family can save much heartache in the future. To be sure, no two individuals are going to have the same ideas or habits when it comes to money. That's why handling money was probably so much easier when you were single! I trust these chapters will be a help to you in the handling of your family finances.*

—*Ron Blue*
Master Your Money

"Four Biblical Principles" is adapted and taken from *Master Your Money*, Ron Blue (1986).

An acquaintance of mine, William H. Cook, wrote a book called *Success, Motivation and the Scriptures,* in which he defined success as "the continuing achievement of being the person God wants you to be, and the continuing achievement of established goals God helps you set." I once asked my oldest child how her friends would define success, and she gave me the best worldly definition of success I have ever heard: "To have whatever you want whenever you want it."

One perspective is eternal (long-term) and the other is exceedingly short-term: "I want what I want when I want it." Not only do I want what I want when I want it, but I have a right to it.

Both the Christian and the non-Christian are concerned with success, but in each case success is always relative to goals. The difference is in perspective. One view sees only the here and now; the other sees the unseen. What one's perspective is (or to put it another way, what one believes) will determine attitudes and actions. That is why the Christian, in managing his or her money, is different.

Individually, God has called us to be: salt and light (see Matt. 5:13–16), servants (see Mark 10:45), and stewards (see Matt. 25:14–30).

The idea of being salt and light says that God wants me to be *not* better than, *but* different from. The Christian, therefore, may or may not have more than his neighbor, but that does not distinguish him. What does distinguish the Christian from the world is the absence of any anxiety, which might have come as a result of the loss of something he has managed or even God's denial of something he wants. Why? Because the Christian's treasure is not on earth. The world and its temporal toys do not possess him. He is prayerful, but not the least bit anxious about the tremendous uncertainty facing our national and world economy.

Obviously that attitude is not "normal" but rather "different," and it comes from having an entirely different perspective. The Christian's perspective is eternal, the attitude is one of holding possessions lightly, and the lifestyle is free from worry and anxiety. Truly that is different!

Not only have I been called to be salt and light, but I, and all other Christians, have been called to be a *servant.* "For even the Son of Man did not come to be served, but to serve, and to give His life a ransom for many," says Mark 10:45. Money is one of the most significant resources with which American Christians can serve others. It is not the only resource—time and talents are two others, but it is certainly in greater abundance among American Christians than among non-Americans.

The Christian's perspective is eternal, the attitude is one of holding possessions lightly, and the lifestyle is free from worry and anxiety.

By contrast, the world, one way or another, says that you need to serve yourself: "I want what I want when I want it." God says, "Let them do good, that they be rich in good works, ready to give, willing to share" (1 Tim. 6:18).

Americans are known as generous people. But exactly how generous are we?

• According to the IRS, 1.7% of adjusted gross income is the average charitable deduction taken on Form 1040, whereas the property tax and interest deduction (as indicators of the possessions that the bank and I own) is equal to 18% of adjusted gross income.

• Sam Erickson of the Christian Legal Society once did a personal study of average charitable giving. His conclusion was that all Americans gave, on the average, 25¢ a day or $91 per year, and evangelical Christians gave an average of $1 a day or $365 per year.

• J. Robertson McQuilkin, president of Columbia Bible College, pointed out in a speech that if members of the Southern Baptist denomination alone would give an average of $100 per year to foreign missions, over $1.4 billion per year would be given. They are nowhere near that level now. If they were, the fulfillment of the Great Commission could probably be financed rather easily in this generation by one denomination!

On the other hand, I personally know hundreds of Christians who are serving others by literally giving fortunes away. They have answered the question, Why am I here? One reason you are here is to serve others and if God has entrusted financial resources to you, you must be used to serve others.

Ultimately, financial planning is the predetermined use of financial resources in order to accomplish certain goals and objectives. The difference in financial planning between the Christian and the non-Christian is the source of the goals and objectives.

John MacArthur, pastor of Grace Community Church, Panorama City, California, in his tape series "Mastery of Materialism," said that "16 out of 38 of Christ's parables deal with money; more is said in the New Testament about money than heaven and hell combined; five times more is said about money than prayer; and while there are 500 plus verses on both prayer and faith, there are over 2,000 verses dealing with money and possessions." Obviously, the Bible has much to say about money management.

Financial planning is the predetermined use of financial resources in order to accomplish certain goals and objectives.

THE FOUR BIBLICAL PRINCIPLES OF MONEY MANAGEMENT

Even though the parable of the talents found in Matthew 25:14–36 deals primarily with Christ's return, it has shown me four basic biblical principles of money management that really summarize much of what the Bible has to say regarding money and money management.

1. God Owns It All

> Matthew 25:14—"For the kingdom of heaven is like a man traveling to a far country, who called his own servants and delivered his goods to them."

Very few Christians would argue with the principle that God owns it all, and yet if we follow that principle to its natural conclusion, there are three revolutionary implications. First of all, God has the right to whatever He wants whenever He wants it. It is all His, because an owner has *rights*, and I, as a steward, have only *responsibilities*.

When my oldest child reached driving age, she was very eager to use my car and, as her father, I entrusted my car to her. There was never any question that I could take back my car at any time for any reason. She had only responsibilities while I maintained all the rights. In the same way, every single possession that I have comes from someone else—God. I literally possess much but own nothing.

If you own your own home, take a walk around your property to get a feel for the reality of this principle. Reflect on how long that dirt has been there and how long it will continue to be there; then ask yourself if you really own it or whether you merely possess it. You may have the title to it, but that title reflects your right to possess it temporarily, not forever. Only God literally owns it forever.

If I really believe that God owns it all then when I lose any possession, for whatever reason, my emotions may cry out, but my mind and spirit have not the slightest question as to the right of God to take whatever He wants whenever He wants it. Really believing this also frees me to give generously of God's resources to God's purposes and His people. All that I have belongs to Him.

The second implication of God's owning it all is that not only is my giving decision a spiritual decision, but *every spending decision is a spiritual decision*. There is nothing more spiritual than buying a car, taking a vacation, buying food, paying off debt, paying taxes, and so on. These are all uses of His resources. He owns all that I have.

Think about the freedom of knowing that if God owns it all—and He does—He must have some thoughts about how He wants me to use His property. The Bible reveals many specific guidelines as to how the Owner wants His property used. As a steward, I have a great deal of latitude, but I am still responsible to the Owner. Some day I will give an accounting of how I used His property.

The third implication of the truth that God owns it all is that *you can't fake stewardship.* Your checkbook reveals all that you really believe about stewardship. A life story could be written from a checkbook. It reflects your goals, priorities, convictions, relationships, and even the use of your time. A person who has been a Christian for even a short while can fake prayer, Bible study, evangelism, and going to church, but he can't fake what his checkbook reveals. Maybe that is why so many of us are so secretive about our personal finances.

2. We Are in a Growth Process

> Matthew 25:21—"His lord said to him, 'Well done, good and faithful servant; you were faithful over a few things, I will make you ruler over many things. Enter into the joy of your lord.' "

In reading the Scriptures, knowing that our time on earth is temporary and is to be used by our Lord as a training time is inescapable. The whole parable emphasizes this. I would observe that God uses money and material possessions in your earthly life during this growth process as *a tool, a test,* and *a testimony.* As Paul said in Philippians 4:11–12:

> Not that I speak in regard to need, for I have learned in whatever state I am, to be content: I know how to be abased, and I know how to abound. Everywhere and in all things I have learned both to be full and to be hungry, both to abound and to suffer need.

Money and material possessions are a very effective tool that God uses to grow you up. Therefore, you need always to ask, God, what do You want me to learn? Not, God, why are You doing this to me? My role as a counselor is to help people discover what God would have them learn, either from the situation of their abundance, or from the situation of their apparent lack of financial resources. God is not trying to frustrate us. He is trying to get our attention, and money is a great attention-getter.

Money is not only a tool, but also a test.

> Therefore if you have not been faithful in the unrighteous mammon, who will commit to your trust the true riches? And if you have not been faithful in what is another man's, who will give you what is your own? (Luke 16:11–12).

I don't understand it, but I do know that somehow my eternal position and reward are determined irrevocably by my faithfulness in handling property that has been entrusted to me by God.

We have already looked at the fact that we are called to be salt and light in Matthew 5:13–16. I believe we can say that God can use my use of His resources as a testimony to the world. My attitude as a Christian toward wealth becomes the testimony.

3. The Amount Is Not Important

> Matthew 25:23—"His lord said to him, 'Well done, good and faithful servant; you have been faithful over a few things, I will make you ruler over many things. Enter into the joy of your lord.'"

When you look back to verse 21 and compare it word for word with verse 23, you will see that the same words were spoken to the slave with five talents and the one with two talents. Both were reminded that they had been faithful with a few things and both were promised something in heaven. You can draw the conclusion that the amount you have is unimportant, but how you handle what you have been entrusted with is very important.

There is much controversy today about whether an American Christian is more spiritual on one hand by accumulating much or on the other hand by giving it all away. I believe that both are extremes and not reflective of what God says. He never condemns wealth and commends poverty, or vice versa. The principle found in Scripture is that He owns it all. Therefore, whatever He chooses to entrust you with, hold with an open hand, allowing Him to entrust you with more if He so chooses, or allowing Him to take whatever He wants. It is all His. That is the attitude He wants you to develop, and whatever you have, little or much, your attitude should remain the same.

4. Faith Requires Action

Matthew 25:24–30—"Then he who had received the one talent came and said, 'Lord, I knew you to be a hard man, reaping where you have not sown, and gathering where you have not scattered seed. And I was afraid, and went and hid your talent in the ground. Look, there you have what is yours.' But his lord answered and said to him, 'You wicked and lazy servant, you knew that I reap where I have not sown, and gather where I have not scattered seed. Therefore you ought to have deposited my money with the bankers, and at my coming I would have received back my own with interest. Therefore take the talent from him, and give it to him who has ten talents. For to everyone who has, more will be given, and he will have abundance; but from him who does not have, even what he has will be taken away. And cast the unprofitable servant into the outer darkness. There will be weeping and gnashing of teeth.' "

The wicked slave knew, *but* he did nothing. Many of us know what we ought to do, but we disobey or delay. We have emotional faith and/or intellectual faith, but not volitional faith. We know *but. . . .*

We may know deep down what God would have us do, but we are so bombarded with worldly input, which seems to be acceptable, that we are paralyzed. We take no action because of the fear of making a mistake biblically, financially. Or we are frustrated and confused. We do only what we feel good about. Living by our feelings rather than "the truth" (John 14:6) can be very dangerous.

THE PRACTICALITY OF STEWARDSHIP

Master Your Money gives you principles, technical guidance, tools, and techniques for working out *by faith* the unique financial plan that God has for you and your family, so that when you stand before Him you will have confidence and expect Him to say, "Well done, good and faithful servant." Is that hope unrealistic? Not at all. It is God's desire and His intention. He wants it more than you do.

Two points before we begin. First, a working definition of stewardship:

Stewardship is the use of God-given resources for the accomplishment of God-given goals.

This definition is active, not theoretical. It says "use of." Remember that faith requires action. The definition also acknowledges God's ownership over my possessions and His direction of my use of these resources.

Second, on a separate sheet of paper, I would like for you to list anything that you now possess, about which until now you would have said, "This is mine." Then return the ownership of it to its rightful Owner by a simple prayer of commitment. Sign the page, as you would a deed, and date it.

You now own nothing and are prepared to be a steward.

Chapter

32

A Financial Planning
Overview

E ach year for Christmas I give my children two sheets of paper as a gift. On them I list several things I can do with them during the next year. Some of the options are: going out for breakfast or lunch; going to a professional baseball, basketball, or football game; or going with me on one of my speaking trips. My objective is to let them pick how they would really like to spend time with me.

It's been interesting to observe the difficulty they have in choosing which activity they really want. One that seems to be chosen frequently is "spending four hours with me and having $25 to spend in any way you choose." The first year we began this tradition my third daughter, who was nine years old at the time, picked this option and carefully planned our time together. We were to start at a large shopping mall on a Saturday morning

"A Financial Planning Overview" is adapted and taken from *Master Your Money*, Ron Blue (1986).

and end with lunch. She was filled with anticipation and excitement when the day arrived.

Picture in your mind a nine-year-old child with $25 in her hand, entering a mall with tens of millions of dollars worth of goods available to buy. The dilemma she faced is exactly the same dilemma that you and I face—there is *never* enough money to do or buy everything that you want. There are always more ways to spend money than there is money available. You may respond as she did.

After shopping for just a little while, we went in a store with overpriced notions, such as crazy pens, note paper, and so on, and she selected several items—despite my caution that tomorrow they would not be nearly as attractive. I said to her, "Karen, remember that good decision making requires a long-term perspective." She assured me that she would use and love these items "forever and forever." When the bill was totaled, she had spent her $25 and we still had three hours left and lunch to buy. We ended up going home early so that she could play with her purchases.

The very next day everything she had purchased was either used up, broken, or uninteresting. I will never forget her confessing to me that she had, in effect, responded to the emotion of the moment and, in retrospect, made a poor choice. The problem was that her money and time were both irretrievably lost.

What was not lost, however, was the experience and what it taught her. Now when I am getting ready to buy something she frequently says to me, "Daddy, don't forget that the longer term your perspective, the better your decision is likely to be." Sometimes I wish that I hadn't taught her that!

This story illustrates four truths:

1. All of us have limited resources.
2. Consequently, there are more alternative uses of money available than money available.
3. Today's decisions determine destiny. (A dollar spent is gone forever and can never be used in the future for anything else.)

4. The longer the term of perspective, the better is the decision making.

I can summarize these four points by saying that most of us are responders rather than planners. We respond to friends, advertising, and our emotions rather than plan our spending.

Financial planning is allocating limited financial resources among various unlimited alternatives.

When we know for certain what financial resources we have and plan to use them to accomplish various goals and objectives, our lives take on the contentment of having made order out of chaos. Our frustration in having to choose among the overwhelming multiplicity of alternatives disappears. We are freed from the pressures of the short-term, self-gratifying society around us. We are free to be different.

The financial planning framework that I am going to help you develop will do several things for you: give you a process of managing money; summarize the almost infinite alternative uses of money into just a manageable few; integrate short-range and long-range planning and clearly demonstrate the trade-offs; give you a sense of order and thereby remove some of the guilt or at least the questions that come in using money.

OBJECTIVES OF FINANCIAL PLANNING

One thing I have been implying all along but have never actually stated is that accumulating financial resources should never be an end in itself. They are accumulated solely for the reason of using them to accomplish some purpose, goal, or objective. For example, you do not take a vacation or buy a car just to spend money, but rather to provide something else such as recreation and transportation. Many people ask me how to spend money and I always make it a practice to ask, "What are you really trying to accomplish?" This question helps to focus the decision on real objectives.

In the short range, there are basically only five spending objectives; and, in the long range, only six. Every spending decision or use of money accomplishes one of these eleven objectives.

Short-range Objectives

There are *only* five short-term alternative uses for all income coming into a household. It can be

1. given away,
2. spent to support a lifestyle,
3. used for the repayment of debt,
4. used to meet tax obligations,
5. accumulated or saved (cash flow margin).

Every spending decision, in the short term, will fit into one of these five categories.

How the money is allocated among the five alternatives is a function of just two factors: the *commitments* I already have and my *priorities*. For example, with my wife and five children, I have certain lifestyle commitments that others do not have. Debt repayment, taxes, and giving are all commitments I must maintain. Certain lifestyle expenses such as utilities, food, insurance, and so on are also commitments. A commitment must always be top priority.

Ultimately, my priorities will dictate the allocation of the balance of the limited resources. Giving and accumulation are usually stated as priorities, but in reality, they wind up at the bottom of the priority ladder. I have observed that most American Christians have lifestyle as their top priority and second, because of their lifestyle, debt repayment. Taxes would be a third priority because they have no choice; fourth would be accumulation; and finally, giving. The line of reasoning goes this way: *I am already committed to a certain lifestyle and debt schedule, which God surely wouldn't want me to change. I would gladly give up paying my taxes, but I can't. I am giving and would give more if it weren't for the taxes I have to pay and the money I need to set aside for the future because that is good stewardship.*

Of the five short-range uses, three are consumptive in nature and two are productive. Lifestyle expenditures, debt repayment, and taxes are all consumptive in nature; when the money is spent, it is gone forever. Both accumulation and giving are productive uses of money. Money that is put into accumulation is much like planting a crop—later on, much more than what was planted comes up and can be used again for either consumption or production.

The Bible gives us many principles and guidelines about each one of these five areas, but very little in the way of direct commandment. To determine what God would have us do in balancing our priorities requires the discipline of spending time with Him. No one other person, including your financial planner, can tell you how to prioritize you spending. Why? God has not entrusted the resources you possess (but do not own) to someone else; only *you* are accountable for managing the use of God's resources entrusted to you.

To determine what God would have us do in balancing our priorities requires the discipline of spending time with Him.

Long-term Objectives

As we accumulate from our cash flow margin, we grow our net worth, and we grow our net worth for the purpose of meeting one or more of the six long-term objectives:

1. financial independence,
2. college education for children,
3. paying off debt,
4. major lifestyle desires,
5. major charitable giving,
6. owning your own business.

To be financially independent means that the resources accumulated will generate enough income to fund all of the short-range objectives, with the exception of savings. (Savings are no longer needed if "enough" has been accumulated.) When a couple knows what their short-range objectives are, they can easily calculate how large an investment fund is necessary to accumulate what they need in order to be financially independent.

In addition to accumulating for financial independence, couples with children will need to accumulate in order to meet the major expense of college education. That expense can easily be $10,000 or $12,000 per year for each child.

Many couples also have a major long-term goal of being completely out of debt, including the debt on their home. I believe it is a worthwhile long-term objective to be totally debt free.

The long-range objective of major lifestyle desires is the area that makes each family unique. The objective could be another home, a second home, a new car, a particular vacation, redecorating or remodeling the home. This type of goal finishes the statement: I want to improve my lifestyle by. . . .

One of the first clients whom I worked with at my firm was a man who indicated that the most important long-term goal he could think of was to be able to give away at least one million dollars toward the fulfillment of the Great Commission. This was the first time I had ever considered that people may desire to accumulate over the long-term in order to meet a substantial giving goal. This man not only wanted to give the one million dollars before retirement, but he wanted to continue to give at approximately 15 percent of his total income during the time period that he would be accumulating wealth.

Lastly, you may want to accumulate in order to start your own business, and that is also a legitimate long-range goal.

If you can define and quantify these long-term goals, then you will have answered the question, How much is enough? You know now what your "finish lines" are. It is much like a runner who runs the race until he breaks the tape. Very few runners continue after they have broken the tape. Yet in our financial lives, many of us never stop running because we do not know where the finish line is. We have never quantified where we are headed, and therefore we do not know when we have arrived.

My challenge to you is to determine where you are going, both in the short-term and in the long-term.

INTEGRATED PLANNING

The following outline puts together the short-term and long-term objectives to create a four-step process of financial planning:

Step 1: Summarize your present situation
Step 2: Establish your financial goals
Step 3: Plan to increase your cash flow margin
Step 4: Control your cash flow

If you know where you are, where you are going, and the steps to get there, then you will have made a major step toward being a planner rather than a responder.

As you review the diagram, there are three very important implications. The first is that there are no independent financial decisions. If you make a decision to use financial resources in any one area, by definition, you have chosen not to use those same resources in the other areas. This means that if you choose to set aside money for college education or financial independence, you no longer have that money available to spend on giving, lifestyle desires, debt repayment, and the like. By the same token, if you decide to spend money on lifestyle desires, you no longer have those same resources available for any other short-term or long-term goals.

The second implication, when looking at that diagram, is that the longer the term of your perspective, the better the possibility of your making a good current financial decision. A friend and close confidant once defined financial maturity as "being able to give up today's desires for future benefits." If I choose to give up something today in order to accumulate or save for tomorrow, I have probably made a wise financial decision. The most dramatic example I can think of is the person who chooses a husband or wife. Taking a long-term perspective in that decision makes for a better choice than simply satisfying a short-term need. The same principle holds true in financial decisions.

The third implication of this diagram is the lifetime nature of financial decisions. I mentioned earlier that three of the uses of money in the short-term are consumptive and two are productive. Any time money is used consumptively, it is gone forever and can never be used for anything in the future. I like to remind those with whom I counsel that *decisions determine destiny*. Once I make a decision either to save or spend, I have determined, to some extent, my destiny.

You, of course, have to accept the truth of this implication—you can't have everything you want when you want it. Success is knowing where you are going in life and knowing how to arrive there.

These goal areas, however, are not what we are really trying to accomplish in life, but rather reflect the real desires of our hearts:

- Security
- Properly trained children
- Peace
- Contentment
- Flexibility
- Comfort
- Personal growth

- Obedience to God
- Transportation
- Rest and relaxation
- Self-worth
- Acceptance
- Sense of belonging
- Other goals

Money, then, is one of the resources you use to accomplish the desires you have. Success is knowing what God would have you to be and do and how to achieve that, so that when you stand before Him, you will hear Him say, "Well done, good and faithful servant." When money becomes your focus, you are doomed to disappointment, because it is merely a resource and was never intended by the Creator to be anything more than that.

You can learn the things you need to know to be a great economic partner. Having your finances in order will help your home be in order.

—Patrick and Connie Lawrence
Your 30-Day Journey to Being a Great Wife

Chapter

33

Fun Is Where You Make It

$\mathcal{I}$t's astonishing, in this age of wonders, how often people —even young people—come up to me and complain that they're bored. Life is monotonous, they say. It's dull. It has lost its flavor. Nothing is much fun any more.

Now I know that a share of unhappiness comes to everyone in this life, and it's true that some people have valid cause to be downhearted. But when the average person complains that he's bored, nine times out of ten it's because he isn't making much effort to be anything else. He isn't putting any fun into life, and that's why he isn't getting any out.

It seems to me that all important areas of life should be flavored with fun—marriage, job, housework, friendships, even religion. I've always liked the story of the little boy on his first trip to New York whose parents brought him to a Sunday service at Mar-

---

"Fun Is Where You Make It" has been adapted and taken from *Secrets of Staying in Love,* Ruth Stafford Peale (1984).

ble Collegiate Church. The family sat in the gallery where they had a fine view of everything. Norman was in rare form that morning, and his sermon was full of stories taken from everyday life, some of which had their humorous side. The little boy looked down in wonderment at all the happy faces, then turned to his parents. "This can't be a church," he whispered, "everybody's having *fun!*"

Well, why not? Laughter is one of God's most special gifts to man. "Rejoice!" the Bible says over and over. And "A merry heart does good like medicine." One Thanksgiving years ago Norman preached on this topic. The very next Sunday one lively young couple responded to his exhortation to let religion be fun by putting a well-dried turkey wishbone in the collection plate!

One of the chief ingredients of fun is a sense of humor, and most good senses of humor include a sense of the ridiculous. Norman and I still laugh over an episode that happened early in our marriage. Norman was the young minister in charge of the staid and impressive University Church in Syracuse. Somewhat in awe of the dignified deans and erudite professors who were in his congregation, he took pains never to say or do anything unconventionial or bizarre. He was always very proper indeed.

One summer afternoon, coming home from the church, he passed by the house of an elderly spinster named Miss Foote, who was also a member of his congregation. Miss Foote was in her front yard looking distractedly for her favorite cat, which apparently had run away.

Norman says that I was forever lecturing him on the importance of always helping his parishioners, no matter what their problem might be. So he offered to help Miss Foote find her cat. "Where did you see it last?" Norman wanted to know. "Right over there," cried Miss Foote. "I think it went through that hole in the hedge!"

The hole was a small one, but Norman gallantly got down on his hands and knees and started crawling through it. Twigs and leaves rained down upon him, brambles pulled his glasses askew, but he kept going until suddenly his head emerged on the far side of the hedge about eighteen inches above a sidewalk. There was no sight of the cat, but on the sidewalk was a pair of feet belonging to a pedestrian who had halted in amazement. Looking up, Norman saw the austere countenance of Professor Perley O. Place, the most imperious and forbidding member of the entire faculty. The gaze of incredulity and disapproval that the professor bestowed upon his spiritual guide and counselor was so paralyzing that Norman couldn't even attempt an explanation. All he could say was, "Good evening, Professor!"

"Extraordinary!" murmured the learned pedagogue frostily. "Most extraordinary!" And he stalked away.

One way to have fun in your life is to associate with "fun" people. Some people carry an indefinable air of gaiety around with them, and they're well worth cultivating, because often that gaiety will rub off on you. We have a friend like that named Millard Bennett. Millard is a jovial soul who often gives lectures at business conventions on the psychology of selling. For a while he and Norman went around giving talks together. Norman always insisted on speaking first, because he claimed that Millard was so good that any speaker who followed him was bound to be an anticlimax.

Millard's favorite topic was persuasion. Anyone, he used to say, could persuade anyone else to walk the road of agreement if only he would use the right approach. "A man," he would tell his audience, "can talk to his wife in two ways. He can say, 'Dear, your face would stop a clock,' and she would be humiliated and hurt. Or he can say, lovingly, 'Darling, when I look at you, time stands still.' " The idea was the same, Millard said, but the way it was phrased made quite a difference!

Millard had one story that went on for at least fifteen minutes about how he persuaded his wife one night, under the most adverse circumstances, to fetch him a glass of water. As he told it, the unsuspecting wife was sorting out some beads on the divan where she was sitting. She had them all classified as to size and color, and the last thing she wanted to do was disturb them, as she would have to do if she stood up. But, ever the psychologist, Millard set himself the problem of persuading her to bring him a glass of water, which he really didn't want at all.

First he told her how pleasant it was to be alone with her on a winter evening with the fire crackling on the hearth. Next he observed that marrying her was probably the smartest move of his life. Then he began to praise her homemaking ability. No one, he assured her, could cook the way she did.

All this time he had been thumbing through a magazine.

"Now, here's an advertisement about a ham," he said. "It looks pretty good, but it couldn't hold a candle to the ones you bake." He sighed plaintively. "By the way, is that ham you cooked yesterday still in the kitchen? A ham sandwich certainly would taste good right now."

Up jumped the proud and happy wife, scattering her beads in all directions, and went into the kitchen to fix the sandwich. Whereupon Millard called out that he had changed his mind. "Don't bother about the sandwich, dear," he said. "But while you're up, would you just bring me a glass of water?"

My telling of the story doesn't do justice to it, but Millard always had his audience in stitches. He was a fun speaker and a fun man.

I've been lucky to be married to a very "fun" man. Norman's sense of the dramatic, his interest in everything, and above all his imagination make him a marvelous companion for people of all ages. When our children were small, for example, Norman spent hours telling them stories that he made up on the spur of the moment, right out of his head. This generally took place at the dinner table and the children could hardly wait. I remember one whole series that went on for months about three imaginary characters named Larry, Harry, and Parry. These remarkable young people had a magic airplane that they kept in their pocket until they needed it. If they wanted to go anyplace they would take the airplane, blow on it and, like magic, it became large enough for them to climb aboard and take off. They would soar away to investigate a big, billowy cloud, or to fight with giants, or to live in the forest in the treetops, or to rescue princesses in distant lands. The magic airplane was a very real and exciting phenomenon to our children.

There was another series of stories about a faintly sinister individual named Jake the Snake, who had an even more malevolent brother known as Hake the Snake. The children would listen, spellbound, to the dreadful deeds of the Snake brothers—and to tell the truth, so would I.

Not everyone, to be sure, has the kind of inventiveness and creativity that can lead so effortlessly to spontaneous fun. But I'm convinced that anyone who will work at it can increase his fun capacity. It doesn't require time or money so much as imagination and the willingness to try something new. Any mother can make a meal more interesting by attempting some exotic or unusual dish. Any father, faced with Sunday afternoon with the children, can think up something interesting or appealing if he'll just put his mind to it. I heard of one busy father who keeps what he calls a "why not?" notebook on his desk at the office. In it he jots down all sorts of offbeat ideas that occur to him during the week. Why not take the children to a farm and try to milk a cow? He says he has only one criterion for such ideas: they have to be fun —or hold the promise of fun.

One winter in New York I took our children on a once-a-week sightseeing or investigating tour—those things you always put off doing. Among other things we went to the New York City bus terminal, the largest in the world with the fastest escalator at that time. We went to the Statue of Liberty and to the Empire State Building. And there were lots of out-of-the-way places. We had a great time.

Sometimes youngsters can get a bit carried away by the spirit of fun. I remember vividly one summer afternoon when our Margaret and John were about ten and eight respectively. I was having a rather serious meeting of churchwomen in our apartment on Fifth Avenue. Suddenly the doorbell buzzed, and there was one of the doormen of the building looking very grave. "Mrs. Peale," he said, "there's a policeman downstairs. He has a complaint. Someone is dropping bombs from your apartment windows into the street."

"Bombs?" I echoed incredulously.

"Water bombs," said the doorman. "Paper bags filled with water—and enough sand to make them fall on people's heads."

"People's *heads?*" In the sudden hush behind me I could sense all my churchwomen listening intently.

"Well," said the doorman, "the bombs missed this lady. But it was a near miss. Her clothes are all splashed, and she is very angry. She complained to the policeman. And he is downstairs right now . . ."

"You mean," I cried, "that our children are dropping these— these things on passersby? How do you know our children are the culprits?" Behind me I could almost *feel* the craning of necks and the raised eyebrows.

"Because, Mrs. Peale," the doorman said resignedly, "your children have been practicing their—er—bombing techniques in the air shaft on the inside of the building. The bottom of the shaft is full of water and sand and paper bags. I'm afraid Margaret and John are the guilty ones. There's no doubt about it."

Well, I had to summon the guilty ones, send them in disgrace to their rooms, go downstairs, placate the policeman, apologize to the irate lady, arrange to pay for having her clothes cleaned, and assure the doorman that such an aerial assault would never happen again.

I had to tell Norman, of course. We spoke to the children sternly, telling them that their prank might have hurt someone or caused a lawsuit. We made them go down to the bottom of the air shaft and clean up the debris. We made them pay out of their allowance for the irate lady's cleaning bill. I forget, now, what other penalties we imposed. But I must confess, one reaction that both Norman and I had, carefully concealed behind our stern parental exteriors, was a feeling of relief and gratitude that our youngsters did have a sense of fun—even if a bit misguided. We were glad that they weren't meek and mild goody-goodies, that they were a pair of high-spirited, fun-loving youngsters, even if they were "preacher's kids."

In too many American homes, I think, parents offer all kinds of excuses and rationalization for the inertia that is the deadly enemy of fun. They can't be bothered to change the routine, they can't afford to, they can't find the time, it's easier to turn on the television set . . . and so on.

But all it takes is a tiny spark of originality. For example, one young couple we know, living on a very tight budget, manages to put aside a few dollars a week for what they call their mini-honeymoon fund. When it reaches a certain level, they park their children with friends or relatives, take an inexpensive motel room on the edge of town, dress up a bit, have a carefree dinner, and spend the night together away from all the routine and familiarity of daily living. The wife says that these "mini-honeymoons," which happen three or four times a year, give her such a lift that she wouldn't exchange them for anything.

There are endless ways to break up a pattern of living that has become monotonous. Ask someone you don't know very well to lunch or dinner. Strike up a conversation with a stranger on a bus or a train or a plane (he may learn something, and you certainly will). Try your hand at bowling. Or at wallpapering a room. Fly a kite with a small child. Work as a hospital volunteer. Go and sign up for a course in some subject that has always interested you. Try anything that's new or different.

Of course, breaking out of the prison of routine takes some effort. But there's a wonderful world outside. And sawing through the bars is half the fun and another adventure in being a you-can't-tell-what-will-come-next wife.

The present is all we really have to enjoy!
—Teresa and David Ferguson
Intimate Moments

Arp, Claudia. *Beating the Winter Blues*. Nashville: Thomas Nelson, 1991.

and Dave Arp. *52 Dates for You and Your Mate*. Nashville: Thomas Nelson, 1993.

Sixty-One Minute Family Builders. Brentwood, TN: Wolgemuth & Hyatt, 1989.

Sixty-One Minute Marriage Builders. Brentwood, TN: Wolgemuth & Hyatt, 1989.

Sixty-One Minute Memory Builders. Brentwood, TN: Wolgemuth & Hyatt, 1989.

The Marriage Track: How to Keep Your Relationship Headed in the Right Direction. Nashville: Thomas Nelson, 1992.

Blue, Ron. *Managing Your Money*. Dallas: Word, Inc., 1990.

Master Your Money. Nashville: Thomas Nelson, 1991.

Master Your Money Workbook. Nashville: Thomas Nelson, 1992.

The Debt Squeeze: How Your Family Can Become Financially Free. Colorado Springs: Focus on the Family, 1989.

and Judy Blue. *Money Matters for Parents and Their Kids*. Nashville: Oliver-Nelson, 1988.

Raising Money-Smart Kids. Nashville: Thomas Nelson, 1992.

Woman's Guide to Financial Peace of Mind. Colorado Springs: Focus on the Family, 1991.

Boyd, Dr. Timothy. See Carmichael, Bill and Nancie.

Buhler, Rich. *Love: No Strings Attached.* Nashville: Thomas Nelson, 1990.

New Choices New Boundaries. Nashville: Thomas Nelson, 1991.

Pain and Pretending, Expanded Edition with Study Guide. Nashville: Thomas Nelson, 1991.

and Dr. Gaylen Larson. *The First Book of Self-Help Tests.* Nashville: Thomas Nelson, 1992.

Carmichael, Bill and Nancie Carmichael. *In God's Word.* Eugene, OR: Harvest House, 1989.

and Dr. Timothy Boyd. *That Man!.* Nashville: Thomas Nelson, 1988.

Carter, Les. *Broken Vows.* Nashville: Thomas Nelson, 1991.

Good 'n' Angry. Grand Rapids: Baker Books, 1983.

Imperative People. Nashville: Thomas Nelson, 1991.

Mind Over Emotions. Grand Rapids: Baker Books, 1985.

The Missing Peace: Finding Emotional Balance. Chicago: Moody Press, 1987.

The Push-Pull Marraige. Grand Rapids: Baker Books, 1984.

Will the Defense Please Rest? A Guide to Marital Harmony. Grand Rapids: Baker Books, 1986.

and Dr. Frank Minirth. *The Anger Workbook.* Nashville: Thomas Nelson, 1992.

et al. *Why Be Lonely? A Guide to Meaningful Relationships*. Grand Rapids: Baker Books, 1983.

Cole, Edwin L. *Communication, Sex, & Money*. Tulsa: Harrison House, 1991.

Courage: A Book for Champions. Tulsa: Honor Books OK, 1991.

Maximized Manhood. Springdale, PA: Whitaker House, 1982.

The Potential Principle. Springdale, PA: Whitaker House, 1984.

Real Man. Nashville: Nelson Communications, 1992.

The Sacredness of Sex. Tulsa: Harrison House, 1988.

and Nancy Cole. *The Unique Woman*. Tulsa: Honor Books OK, 1989.

Dalbey, Gordon. *Father and Son*. Nashville: Thomas Nelson, 1992.

Healing the Masculine Soul. Dallas: Word, 1991.

Dillow, Linda. *Creative Counterpart*. Nashville: Thomas Nelson, 1977.

Priority Planner. Nashville: Thomas Nelson, 1977.

and Claudia Arp. *Sanity In the Summertime*. Nashville: Thomas Nelson, 1991.

Ells, Alfred. *A New Beginning*. Nashville: Thomas Nelson, 1992.

One-Way Relationships. Nashville: Thomas Nelson, 1990.

One-Way Relationships Workbook. Nashville: Thomas Nelson, 1992.

Restoring Innocence. Nashville: Oliver-Nelson, 1991.

Fowler, Dr. Richard, Jerilyn Fowler, Brian Newman, Deborah Newman: *Day By Day Love Is a Choice*. Nashville: Thomas Nelson, 1991.

and Frank Minirth, Brian Newman. *Steps To a New Beginning.* Nashville: Thomas Nelson, 1993.

and Rita Schweitz. *Together On a Tightrope.* Nashville: Thomas Nelson, 1991.

and Dr. Robert Hemfelt, Dr. Frank Minirth, Dr. Paul Meier. *Path to Serenity.* Nashville: Thomas Nelson, 1991.

Gillies, John. *Senor Alcaldo: A Biography of Henry Cisneros.* Dillon Press: Minneapolis, 1988.

The New Russia. New York: Macmillan/Dillow, 1993.

Graham, Ruth Bell. *Prodigals and Those Who Love Them.* Colorado Springs: Focus on the Family, 1991.

Hemfelt, Dr. Robert, and Dr. Paul Warren. *Kids Who Carry Our Pain.* Nashville: Thomas Nelson, 1990.

Hemfelt, Susan. See Minirth, Frank B., *Passages of Marriage.*

Minirth, Frank B. *Beating the Odds: Overcoming Life's Trials.* Grand Rapids: Baker Books, 1987.

Happy Holidays: How to Beat the Holiday Blues. Grand Rapids: Baker Books, 1990.

Taking Control: New Hope for Substance Abusers & Their Families. Grand Rapids: Baker Books, 1988.

The Healthy Christian Life. Grand Rapids: Baker Books, 1988.

You Can Manage Your Mental Health. Grand Rapids: Baker Books, 1980.

and Betty Blaylock, Cynthia Spell Humbert. *One Step at a Time.* Nashville: Thomas Nelson, 1991.

and Dr. Les Carter. *The Anger Workbook.* Nashville: Thomas Nelson, 1993.

and Richard Fowler, Brian Newman. *Steps to a New Beginning*. Nashville: Thomas Nelson, 1993.

and Dr. Robert Hemfelt, Dr. Paul Meier, Sharon Sneed. *Love Hunger: Recovery for Food Addiction*. Nashville: Thomas Nelson, 1990.

Love Hunger Weight-Loss Workbook. Nashville: Thomas Nelson, 1991.

and Dr. Robert Hemfelt, Dr. Richard Fowler, Dr. Paul Meier. *The Path to Serenity*. Nashville: Thomas Nelson, 1991.

and Dr. Robert Hemfelt, Dr. Paul Meier, Don Hawkins. *Love Is a Choice*. Nashville: Thomas Nelson, 1989.

Love Is a Choice Workbook. Nashville: Thomas Nelson, 1991.

and Paul D. Meier. *Counseling and the Nature of Man*. Grand Rapids: Baker Books, 1989.

Happiness Is a Choice: Overcoming Depression. Grand Rapids: Baker Books, 1978.

Free to Forgive. Nashville: Thomas Nelson, 1989.

and Dr. Paul Meier, Don Hawkins. *Worry-Free Living*. Nashville: Thomas Nelson, 1989.

and Dr. Paul Meier, Dr. David Congo, Janet Congo. *A Walk with the Serenity Prayer*. Nashville: Thomas Nelson, 1991.

and Mary Minirth, Dr. Robert Hemfelt, Susan Hemfelt, Dr. Brian Newman, Dr. Deborah Newman. *Passages of Marriage*. Nashville: Thomas Nelson, 1989.

New Love. Nashville: Thomas Nelson, 1993.

New Love Study Guide. Nashville: Thomas Nelson, 1993.

Realistic Love. Nashville: Thomas Nelson, 1993.

Realistic Love Study Guide. Nashville: Thomas Nelson, 1993.

Renewing Love. Nashville: Thomas Nelson, 1993.

Renewing Love Study Guide. Nashville: Thomas Nelson, 1993.

Steadfast Love. Nashville: Thomas Nelson, 1993.

Steadfast Love Study Guide. Nashville: Thomas Nelson, 1993.

Transcendent Love. Nashville: Thomas Nelson, 1993.

Transcendent Love Study Guide. Nashville: Thomas Nelson, 1993.

and Pam Vredevelt, Dr. Deborah Newman, Harry Beverly. *The Thin Disguise, Overcoming and Understanding Anorexia and Bulimia.* Nashville: Thomas Nelson, 1992.

and Dr. Paul Warren. *Things That Go Bump in the Night.* Nashville: Thomas Nelson, 1992.

et al. *Ask the Doctor: Questions & Answers about Your Mental Health.* Grand Rapids: Baker Books, 1991.

Beating the Clock: A Guide to Maturing. Grand Rapids: Baker Books, 1986.

How to Beat Burnout. Chicago: Moody Press, 1986.

One Hundred Ways to Live a Happy and Successful Life: Overcoming Depression. Grand Rapids: Baker Books, 1986.

The Workaholic and His Family; An Inside Look. Grand Rapids: Baker Books, 1981.

Minirth, Mary Alice. See Minirth, Frank B., *Passages of Marriage.*

Newman, Dr. Brian, and Dr. Frank B. Minirth, Dr. Paul Warren. *The Father Book.* Nashville: Thomas Nelson, 1992.

and Dr. Frank B. Minirth, Dr. Paul Meier, Dr. Richard Meier, Dr. Allen Doran, Dr. David Congo. *What They Didn't Teach You in Seminary.* Nashville: Thomas Nelson, 1993.

See Fowler, Dr. Richard, *Day by Day, Love Is a Choice.*

See Minirth, Frank B., *Love Is a Choice Workbook.*

See Minirth, Frank B., *Passages of Marriage.*

Newman, Dr. Deborah. See Fowler, Dr. Richard, *Day by Day, Love Is a Choice.*

See Minirth, Frank B., *Love Is a Choice Workbook.*

See Minirth, Frank B., *Passages of Marriage.*

Schweitz, Rita. *Mary In a Martha's World: Quiet Times for Busy Mothers.* Minneapolis: Augsburg Fortress, 1989.

Together On a Tightrope. Nashville: Thomas Nelson, 1990.

and Randy L. Carlson. *In My Father's Image: The Father Memories Workbook.* Chicago: Moody Press, 1993.

and Dr. Norman Wright, Dr. Gary Jackson Oliver. *Women Facing Life's Demands: A Workbook for Handling the Pressure Points in Your Life.* Chicago: Moody Press, 1993.

Stanley, Charles. *A Man's Touch.* Wheaton, IL: SP Publishers, 1992.

A Touch of His Wisdom. Grand Rapids: Zondervan, 1992.

Eternal Security. Nashville: Thomas Nelson, 1990.

Forgiveness. Nashville: Oliver-Nelson, 1987.

Handle with Prayer. Wheaton, IL: SP Publishers, 1992.

How to Handle Adversity. Nashville: Oliver-Nelson, 1989.

How to Keep Your Kids on Your Team. Nashville: Oliver-Nelson, 1986.

How to Listen to God. Nashville: Oliver-Nelson, 1985.

Temptation. Nashville: Oliver-Nelson, 1988.

The Wonderful Spirit-Filled Life. Nashville: Thomas Nelson, 1992.

Thoughts on Listening to God. Nashville: Thomas Nelson, 1993.

Winning the War Within. Nashville: Thomas Nelson, 1988.

Stoop, David. *Forgiving Our Parents, Forgiving Ourselves: Healing Adult Children of Dysfunctional Families*. Ann Arbor: Servant, 1992.

Hope for the Perfectionist. Nashville: Thomas Nelson, 1987.

Self Talk. Tarrytown, NY: Revell, 1981.

and Stephen Arterburn. *The War Is Over but Children Still Have Questions*. Wheaton: Tyndale, 1991.

The Angry Man. Dallas: Word, 1991.

and James Masteller. *Forgiving Our Parents, Forgiving Ourselves*. Ann Arbor: Servant, 1991.

and Jan Stoop. *The Intimacy Factor*. Nashville: Thomas Nelson, 1993.

Wangerin, Jr., Walter. *A Miniature Cathedral and Other Poems*. New York: Harper & Row, 1987.

As For Me and My House: Crafting a Marriage to Last. Nashville: Thomas Nelson, 1987.

Elisabeth and the Water-Troll. New York: HarperCollins Children's Books, 1991.

In the Beginning There Was No Sky. Nashville: Thomas Nelson, 1986.

Miz Lil and the Chronicles of Grace. New York: Harper & Row, 1988.

Mourning Into Dancing. Grand Rapids: Zondervan, 1992.

My First Book About Jesus. New York: Macmillan, 1983.

Potter. Elgin, IL: David C. Cook, 1985.

Ragman and Other Cries of Faith. New York: Harper & Row, 1984.

Reliving the Passion. Grand Rapids: Zondervan, 1992.

The Bible for Children. New York: Macmillan, 1983.

The Book of Sorrows. New York: Harper & Row, 1985.

The Book of the Dun Cow. New York: Harper & Row, 1978.

The Manger is Empty. New York: Harper & Row, 1989.

The Orphean Passage. New York: Harper & Row, 1986.

Thistle. New York: Harper & Row, 1983.

Wirt, Sherwood E. *A Thirst for God.* San Diego: Horizon, 1989.

For the Love of Mike. San Diego: Horizon, 1984.

I Don't Know What Old Is, But Old Is Older Than Me. Nashville: Thomas Nelson, 1991.

Jesus, Man of Joy. Nashville: Thomas Nelson, 1991.

Spiritual Power. Wheaton: Crossways Books, 1989.

Topical Encyclopedia of Living Quotations. Minneapolis: Bethany House, 1982.

Your Mighty Fortress. Nashville: Thomas Nelson, 1991.

Ziglar, Zig. *Confessions of a Happy Christian.* Gretna, LA: Pelican Publishing, 1982.

Courtship After Marriage. Nashville: Oliver-Nelson, 1992.

Dear Family. Gretna, LA: Pelican Publishing, 1986.

Raising Postive Kids in a Negative World. Nashville: Oliver-Nelson, 1989.

See You at the Top. Gretna, LA: Pelican Publishing, 1984.

Steps To the Top. Gretna, LA: Pelican Publishing, 1985.

Top Performance. Old Tappan, NJ: Fleming H. Revell Company, 1987.

Ziglar on Selling. Nashville: Thomas Nelson, 1991.

Zig Ziglar's Secrets of Closing the Sale. Old Tappan, NJ: Fleming H. Revell Company, 1987.

About the Authors

Dave and Claudia Arp have been married more than thirty years and are parents of three adult sons and two daughters-in-law, and grandparents to five kittens.

Together the Arps founded and now direct Marriage Alive International, a marriage and family enrichment ministry. The Marriage Alive Workshop is popular across the United States and in Europe. They also founded the MOM'S and DAD'S Support Groups, family enrichment resource programs located throughout the United States and Europe, which have curriculae for churches and schools.

Ron Blue is the founder and managing partner of Ronald Blue & Co., which offers personal financial planning services from a Christian perspective to more than 1000 clients nationwide. A best-selling author, Blue is also featured in a six-part video series, "Master Your Money," a curriculum used in more than 2100 churches across the country. He has appeared on numerous radio and television shows, including "Focus on the Family," the "700 Club," and "Prime Time America," and is a regular columnist for *Moody Monthly, Physician,* and *Marriage Partnership.*

Ron and his wife, Judy, co-author with Ron of *Raising Money-Smart Kids,* live in Atlanta and have five children.

Dr. Timothy Boyd, co-author of *That Man!,* is a practicing psychologist and has counseled from a Christian perspective for more than fifteen years. He received his master of social work from the University of Chicago and earned his doctorate in psychology from

Biola University. He and his wife, Anita, have been married for six-teen years and have two children.

Rich Buhler hosts the nationally syndicated, daily radio talk program, "Talk From the Heart," which is broadcast live across the United States. He is also the host of two award-winning films, *Fractured Families* and *They Lied to Us*.

Rich's varied background includes nearly twenty years of ministry and professional broadcast experience. A graduate of Biola University in California, Rich has served in several pastoral positions in churches, including more than six years as senior pastor in Long Beach, California.

Rich and his wife, Linda, who is a musician and popular women's speaker, live with their seven children in Westminister, California.

For more than fifteen years **William** and **Nancie Carmichael** have co-published the Christian woman's magazine *Virtue*. They are also the authors of *Answers to the Questions Christian Women Are Asking*. The Carmichaels have been married twenty-two years and are the parents of five children.

Dr. Les Carter is a nationally known expert in the field of Christian counseling with more than fifteen years in private practice. He is a psychotherapist with the Minirth-Meier Clinic and is a weekly guest on the clinic's popular radio program, "The Minirth-Meier Clinic," heard daily on radio stations across the nation including the Moody Broadcasting Network. Dr. Carter is the author of seven other books, including *Imperative People* and *Broken Vows*. A popular speaker, he leads seminars in cities across the United States.

Carter earned his B.A. from Baylor University and his M.Ed. and Ph.D. from North Texas State Univerity.

Edwin Louis Cole, founder and president of the Christian Men's Network, speaks with a prophetic voice to the men of this generation. His message that "Manhood and Christlikeness are synonymous" declares a standard for manhood that has changed hundreds of thousands of lives. He is an internationally acclaimed speaker, television personality, best-selling author, and motivational lecturer. Cole travels extensively, showing men how to realize their dreams of real manhood by looking to Jesus Christ as their role model.

Gordon Dalbey received his M.Div. from Harvard, an M.A. in journalism from Stanford, and a B.A. in mathematics from Duke. He has been a news reporter (North Carolina), Peace Corps Volunteer (Nigeria), high school teacher (Northern California, Chicago), and pastor (Los Angeles).

A popular speaker at churches and conferences around the country, Rev. Dalbey has spoken at Bill Gaither's Praise Gatherings, Florence Littauer's women's conferences, Promise Keeper's Men's Gathering, and at numerous Christian men's retreats. He has appeared on "Focus on the Family," "The 700 Club" (CBN-TV), "Joy" (TBN-TV), "The Minirth-Meier Clinic Program," and many other TV and radio shows. His articles have appeared in a wide variety of publications, including *Reader's Digest, The Christian Century, Los Angeles Times Op-Ed, Catholic Digest, Preaching, Leadership,* and *Christian Herald.*

Gordon lives in Los Angeles with his wife Dr. Mary Andrews-Dalbey, a Christian counselor, and their son John-Miguel.

Reverend Dalbey can be reached by writing:

REV. GORDON DALBEY
Box 24496
Los Angeles, CA 90024

Linda Dillow describes herself first as a wife and a mother, and second, as a speaker, author, and marriage seminar leader on being a creative wife. She and her husband, Joseph, lived in Vienna, Austria, for fourteen years, training Christian leaders throughout Europe. They recently moved to the Orient to continue their work.

Alfred Ells is the founder of Samaritan Counseling Serivces in Scottsdale, Arizona; Clinical Director of LifeGate Treatment Center for Adolescents; and a consultant to Remuda Ranch Center for Anorexia and Bulimia, Wickenburg, Arizona. Ells' clients come from corporate, religious, and private life. His background in counseling and healing has led him to devote much of his life to developing Christ-centered treatment programs for all types of individuals in need. He has a B.S. from the University of Arizona and a Master's in Counseling from Arizona State University.

The author of numerous publications and a much-in-demand speaker and educator, Al and his wife, Susan, have four children: Melissa, Matt, Andrew, and Katie.

Richard Fowler, Ed.D., is a licensed professional counselor with the Texas State Board of Examiners and is the director of clinical services for the Minirth-Meier Clinic of Dallas and Longview, Texas. His doctoral degree is in the field of social psychology.

Dr. Fowler has served as professor at three different colleges in the last eighteen years and has acted as a consultant and a management trainer and seminar leader for a wide variety of corporations.

A co-author with Rita Schweitz of *Together on a Tightrope,* Dr. Fowler is a frequent guest on the national radio call-in program, "The Minirth-Meier Clinic," and ACTS television program, "COPE." He represents the clinics nationally, as a speaker and teacher.

Richard Fowler and Rita Schweitz are available for seminars across the country on maintaining healthy and balanced relationships during tough times. You can reach them by calling the Minirth-Meier Clinics' Speakers' Bureau (214) 669-1733 or by calling Laughter and Joy Bookstore in Oakland, Nebraska, (800) 676-6761.

John Gillies is the author of ten books and a former communications consultant. Now retired, his background includes radio and television, Church World Service, the Texas Department of Human Serivces, and the Presbyterian Children's Home and Service Agency.

John and his wife, Carolyn, served as Presbyterian lay missionaries in Brazil. And as a "commissioned lay pastor," John continues occasional mission volunteer work in Lithuania.

John and Carolyn have three children and four grandchildren, and live in Austin, Texas. Anna and Paul died in the mid-80s.

Ruth Bell Graham is the wife of evangelist Billy Graham, the daughter of missionaries in China, mother to five, grandmother to eighteen, and now a great-grandmother. Ruth and Billy have lived for more than thirty years at Little Piney Cove, their mountaintop log cabin home near Montreat, North Carolina.

Co-author with Dianne C. Sloan, **Jerry D. Hardin** is a marriage and family therapist and director of the Family Life Counseling Center at Central Community Church in Wichita, Kansas. He also serves as president and CEO of Personnel Services, Inc., in Wichita. Jerry has a master of science in clinical marriage and family therapy and a bachelor of science in religion and philosophy from Friends University, in Wichita, Kansas, and is a member of the American Association of Marriage and Family Therapists. Jerry and his wife, Marilynn, have been married more than twenty-five years and have three sons, Steve, Scott, and Paul.

Dr. Robert Hemfelt is a psychologist with the Minirth-Meier Clinic who specializes in the treatment of chemical dependencies and compulsivity disorders.

Susan Hemfelt is a homemaker and the mother of three children.

Dr. Frank Minirth is a diplomate of the American Board of Psychiatry and Neurology. Along with Dr. Paul Meier, he founded the Minirth-Meier Clinic in Dallas, Texas, one of the largest psychiatric clinics in the United States.

Mary Alice Minirth is a homemaker and the mother of four children.

Dr. Brian Newman is the clinical director of inpatient services at the Minirth-Meier Clinic in Richardson, Texas. He received his M.A. in counseling from Grace Theological Seminary and his Doctorate of Philosophy from Oxford Graduate School.

Dr. Deborah Newman is a psychotherapist with the Minirth-Meier Clinic. She received her M.A. in counseling from Grace Theological Seminary and her Doctorate of Philosophy from Oxford Graduate School.

For general information about the Minirth-Meier Clinic branch offices, counseling services, educational resources, and hospital programs, call toll-free 1-800-545-1819. National Headquarters: (214) 669-1733, (800) 229-3000.

Currently general secretary and editor-in-chief of *Guideposts* magazine, **Ruth Stafford Peale** is the recipient of numerous national awards and honors. She and her husband, Norman Vincent Peale, live in New York, where he is pastor of the Marble Collegiate Church.

Rita Schweitz is a freelance writer and co-author with Dr. Richard Fowler, songwriter, and a former teacher and coach of junior and senior high school students. Author of the book *Mary in Martha's World*, her articles have been published in magazines such as *Moody Monthly, Decision, Christian Living*, and *Today's Child*.

Rita graduated Phi Beta Kappa from University of Nebraska. She lives with her husband and children in Oakland, Nebraska.

Richard Fowler and Rita Schweitz are available for seminars across the country on maintaining healthy and balanced relationships during tough times. You can reach them by calling the Minirth-Meier Clinics' Speakers' Bureau (214) 669-1733 or by calling Laughter and Joy Bookstore in Oakland, Nebraska, (800) 676-6761.

Dianne C. Sloan, co-author with Jerry Hardin, is director of the Center on Family Living at Friends University in Wichita, Kansas. Dianne received her Master of Science degree in Family Studies and Clinical Marriage and Family Therapy from Friends University. Dianne has done extensive work in the area of premarital counseling and leads workshops and classes in marriage enrichment and parenting. She has a private practice as a marriage and family therapist and is a clinical member of the American Association for Marriage and Family Therapy.

Dianne and her husband Jim were married in 1968 and have one son, Jason.

Twice elected president of the Southern Baptist Convention, **Charles Stanley** is senior pastor of the 10,000-member First Baptist Church, Atlanta and is a popular broadcast teacher on *In Touch,* a national TV and radio program. Stanley received his bachelor of arts degree from the University of Richmond, bachelor of divinity degree from Southwestern Theological Seminary, and master's and doctor's degrees of theology from Luther Rice Seminary.

Dr. David Stoop is a clinical psychologist in private practice in Newport Beach, California, and is clinical director for the Minirth-Meier Clinic West, a psychiatric treatment program. He is a graduate of Fuller Theological Seminary and received his Ph.D. from the University of Southern California.

Jan Stoop is a graduate of Fuller Theological Seminary and is a doctoral candidate in clinical psychology. She has worked with her husband Dave in his writing, and together they have led seminars and retreats across the country and in France and Australia.

Dr. Jim Talley has served more than twenty years in the ministry and built an internationally recognized singles ministry that has trained leaders from more than ten countries. Director of the National Singles Conference and a long-time member of the National Association of Singles Adult Leadership, Dr. Talley has counseled more than 10,000 individuals. He is also a lecturer and founder of Creative Seminars. Dr. Talley has written numerous books and is a counselor and the minister of singles at Northwest Baptist Church in Oklahoma City, Oklahoma.

You may reach Dr. Talley by writing
2200 N. Drexel Blvd.
Oklahoma City, OK 73107
or calling (405) 949-2227. Fax (405) 943-3630.

Walter Wangerin, Jr., is a writer-in-residence at Valparaiso University in Valparaiso, Indiana, a columnist for the monthly, *The Lutheran,* and an adjunct professor of theology and literature at The Lutheran School of Theology at Chicago. A frequent lecturer at universities and professional conferences, Wangerin has his B.A. from Concordia Senior College in Fort Wayne, Indiana; his M.A. in English literature from Miami University, Oxford, Ohio; and his M.Div. from Christ Seminary-Seminex in Saint Louis, Missouri. He has received numerous awards for his writing, particularly the New York Times' Best Children's Book of the Year for *The Book of the Dun Cow* and the Gold Medallion Award for *Ragman and Other Cries of Faith* (1985), *Potter* (1986), and *As for Me and My House* (1988).

Reared the eldest of seven children, Wangerin has lived in Washington, Illinois, North Dakota, and Canada. He is married and has four children.

Sherwood Wirt, editor emeritus of *Decision* Magazine, author, world traveler, and mountain climber, is an active visionary who enjoys life and all it has to offer.

Founder of the San Diego County Christian Writers' Guild, Wirt is the author of twenty-four books; winner of the George Washington medal, Freedoms Foundation of Valley Forge; former president, Evanglical Press Association and San Diego Gilbert & Sullivan Society.

Zig Ziglar is an internationally-known authority on high-level performance. He is chairman of the Zig Ziglar Corporation, which is committed to helping people more fully utilize their physical, mental, and spiritual resources. Hundreds of corporations worldwide use his books, videos, audiotapes, and courses to train their employees.

Ziglar became a full-time public speaker in 1970 and was soon one of the most sought-after speakers in the country. Today he travels the world over, delivering his messages of humor, hope, and enthusiasm to audiences of all kinds and sizes. He has appeared on the platform with such outstanding Americans as President Ronald Reagan, Dr. Norman Vincent Peale, Paul Harvey, Art Linkletter, Dr. Robert Schuller, as well as many U.S. congressmen and governors.

CHAPTER 2

1. Joyce Brothers, *What Every Woman Should Know about Men* (NY: Ballantine, 1987), 15.
2. Ibid., 13.
3. Ibid., 19.
4. Ibid.
5. "A User's Guide to Hormones," *Newsweek,* Jan. 12, 1987, 50.
6. Brothers, 53.
7. Joyce Brothers, *The Brothers System for Liberated Love and Marriage* (New York: Avon, 1973), 192.
8. Helen Block Lewis, *Psychic War in Men and Women* (New York: University Press, 1976), 47.
9. Walter Trobisch, *The Misunderstood Man* (Downer's Grove, Ill.: InterVarsity, 1983), 31.
10. Brothers, *The Brothers System,* 22.
11. Ibid.
12. Ibid., 23.
13. Ibid., 22.
14. Ibid., 25.
15. Ibid., 24.
16. Ibid., 31.
17. Ibid.
18. Doreen Kimura, "Male Brain, Female Brain: The Hidden Difference," *Psychology Today,* Nov. 1985, 56.
19. Psalm 139:14.

CHAPTER 3

1. "Man to Man," Focus on the Family Radio Series, Feb. 22–23, 1991. This tape can be ordered for $5.00 from Focus on the Family, 102 North Cascade, Colorado Springs, CO 80903.
2. Clarence Tucker Craig, "Introduction to 1 Corinthians," *Interpreter's Bible,* vol. X (New York: Abingdon Press, 1952), 34.
3. Arthur Crudup, "All Shook Up," RCA Records, 1958.

4. Michael Martin Murphey, "You're Talkin' to the Wrong Man," Timberwolf Music, Inc., 1988.
5. John Bradshaw develops this notion in his *Healing the Shame That Binds You* (Deerfield Beach: Health Communications, Inc., 1988), viii, stating that shame as a healthy human emotion can be transformed into shame as a state of being —that is, to believe that one's being is flawed, that one is defective as a human being.
6. John Sandford and Paula Sandford, *The Transformation of the Inner Man* (Tulsa, OK: Victory House, 1982), 278.

CHAPTER 5
1. Kay Ray, "In Houston, Women Lead," *USA Today*, July 2, 1990, 2.
2. Jan Halper, "Male Mystique," *American Way Magazine*, August 1, 1989, 42–48.

CHAPTER 6
1. Mike Mason, *The Mystery of Marriage* (Portland, Oreg.: Multnomah, 1985), 47.
2. William J. Peterson, *C. S. Lewis Had a Wife* (Wheaton, Ill.: Tyndale, 1987), 174–75.
3. R. Paul Stevens, *Getting Ready for a Great Marriage* (Colorado Springs: NavPress, 1990), 20.

CHAPTER 13
1. Ed Wheat, M.D., *Secret Choices* (Grand Rapids, Mich.: Zondervan, 1989), 11.
2. Paul Lee Tan, *Encyclopedia of 7700 Illustrations* (Rockville, Md.: Assurance Publishers, 1979), 284.

CHAPTER 15
1. Deuteronomy 34:7 KJV.
2. See Genesis 5:3 and 21:1.
3. See Solomon's Song of Songs.
4. Two excellent critiques of Darwin's evolutionary hypotheses are Robert E. D. Clark, *Darwin, Before and After* (London: Paternoster Press, 1950), and Gertrude Himmelfarb, *Darwin and the Darwinian Revolution* (New York: Norton, 1968).
5. See Mark 12:24–25.

CHAPTER 16
1. Joseph C. Dillow, *Solomon on Sex* (Nashville: Thomas Nelson, 1977), 112.

CHAPTER 21
1. Jerry Hardin and Dianne Sloan, *Getting Ready for Marriage Workbook* (Nashville: Thomas Nelson, 1991).
2. *Ibid.*
3. Frank Minirth, Ike Minirth, Georgia Minirth Beach and Mary Alice Minirth, *Beating the Odds* (Grand Rapids: Baker Books, 1987), 67.
4. Genesis 29:20.

CHAPTER 25

1. Nick Stinnett and John DeFrain, *The Secrets of Strong Families* (NY: Berkley, 1986), 137.
2. Ron Blue, *Master Your Money: A Step-by-Step Plan for Financial Freedom* (Nashville: Thomas Nelson, 1986), 19.

CHAPTER 26

1. The American Cancer Society, *Facts and Figures 1991.*
2. Elizabeth Berg, "Moments of Ease," *Special Report on Health,* Jan. 1991, 9.
3. Dr. James Dobson, interviewing Philip Yancey for *Where Is God When It Hurts?* "Focus on the Family," 1982, 1986.
4. Ibid.
5. Libba Bray, "Putting On Make-up," *Special Report on Health,* Jan. 1991, 10.
6. Tim Hansel, *You Gotta Keep Dancin'* (Elgin, Ill.: David C. Cook, 1985), as quoted in "Through the Pain," *World Challenge,* Jan–Feb 1991, 22.
7. Beth Leuder, "Through the Pain" *World Challenge,* Jan–Feb 1991, 22–23.
8. Ibid., 23.
9. Berg, "Moments of Ease," 9.
10. Elisabeth Elliot, *A Path Through Suffering* (Ann Arbor, Mich.: Servant, 1990), 81, 82.
11. Paul West, "After a Stroke," *Special Report on Health,* Jan. 1991, 10.

CHAPTER 27

1. Hebrews 4:15, J. B. Phillips.
2. Paul Tillich, *The Eternal Now* (New York: Scribner, 1963), p. 17.
3. Ruth Sanford, *Do You Feel Alone in the Spirit?* (Ann Arbor, Mich.: Servant Publications, 1978).
4. I am indebted to C. S. Lewis or George MacDonald, perhaps both, for the idea of these last two sentences.
5. Quoted in Walker Percy's Foreword to *The New Catholics,* ed. Dan O'Neill (New York: Crossroad, 1987).
6. Romans 8:18–21, J. B. Phillips.
7. Psalm 147:3–4, 6, 8–9, 11, New English Bible.

CHAPTER 29

1. David Mace and Vera Mace, *The Sacred Fire* (Nashville: Abingdon, 1986), 67.

CHAPTER 30

1. C. S. Lewis, *The Screwtape Letters* (New York: Macmillan, 1982), 52.
2. Sandra Simpson LeSourd, *The Compulsive Woman* (Old Tappan, N.J.: Revell, Chosen Books, 1987), 1–2.
3. M. Scott Peck, *The Road Less Traveled* (NY: Simon & Schuster, 1988), 99.
4. Ibid., 108.
5. Maggie Scarf, *Unfinished Business* (NY: Ballantine, 1986), 568–69.
6. Cathy Guisewite, "Cathy," *The Equal Rights Monitor,* May-June 1977, 5.
7. Dietrich Bonhoeffer, *Life Together* (New York: Harper & Row, 1976), 36.

8. John Powell, *The Secret of Staying in Love* (Valencia, Calif.: Tabor Publishing, 1974), 54.
9. Ibid., 22.

CHAPTER 33

1. Tim Hansel, *When I Relax I Feel Guilty* (Elgin, Ill.: David C. Cook, 1979), 11–12.
2. H. L. Mencken as quoted by Dolores Curran, *Traits of a Healthy Marriage* (Minneapolis: Winston Press, 1983), 129.
3. Lyn Balster Liontos and Demetri Liontos, "Couple Life," *Denver Post*, Jan. 18, 1981.
4. Philip Blumstein and Pepper Schwarz, *American Couples* (New York: William Morrow, 1983), 174.
5. Liontos and Liontos, "Couple Life."
6. Roger Ricklefs, "Single Mindedness: Firms become willing—or eager—to hire divorced executives," *The Wall Street Journal*, May 18, 1978.
7. Lewis T. Grant in *Harpers*, Oct. 1979.
8. Blumstein and Schwarz, *American Couples*, 312.
9. Hansel, *When I Relax I Feel Guilty*, 12.
10. Norman Cousins, *Anatomy of an Illness* (New York: Norton, 1979).
11. Marilyn Elia, "The Human Angle," Crown Syndicate Inc., 1980.